LUKE

Luke
A LIFE APPLICATION® BIBLE STUDY

Part 1:
Complete text of Luke with study notes
from the *Life Application Bible*

Part 2:
Thirteen lessons for individual or group study

Study questions written and edited by
LINDA CHAFFEE TAYLOR
REV. DAVID R. VEERMAN
DR. JAMES C. GALVIN
DR. BRUCE B. BARTON
DARYL J. LUCAS

Tyndale House Publishers, Inc.
Wheaton, Illinois

Life Application Bible Studies

Genesis TLB	**Matthew** NIV	**Philippians & Colossians** NIV
Joshua TLB	**Mark** TLB & NIV	**1 & 2 Thessalonians &**
Judges NIV	**Luke** NIV	**Philemon** NIV
Ruth & Esther TLB	**John** NIV	**1 & 2 Timothy & Titus** NIV
1 Samuel NIV	**Acts** TLB & NIV	**Hebrews** NIV
Ezra & Nehemiah NIV	**Romans** NIV	**James** NIV
Proverbs NIV	**1 Corinthians** NIV	**1 & 2 Peter & Jude** NIV
Daniel NIV	**2 Corinthians** NIV	**1 & 2 & 3 John** NIV
Hosea & Jonah TLB	**Galatians & Ephesians** NIV	**Revelation** NIV

Life Application Bible Studies: Luke. Copyright © 1991 by Tyndale House Publishers, Inc., Wheaton, Illinois 60189. All rights reserved.

Life Application is a registered trademark of Tyndale House Publishers, Inc.

The "NIV" and "New International Version" trademarks are registered in the United States Patent and Trademark Office by International Bible Society. Use of either trademark requires permission of International Bible Society.

The text of Luke is from the *Holy Bible*, New International Version®. Copyright © 1973, 1978, 1984 by International Bible Society. Used by permission of Zondervan Publishing House. All rights reserved.

Life Application Notes and Bible Helps © 1986 owned by assignment by Tyndale House Publishers, Inc., Wheaton, IL 60189. Maps © 1986 by Tyndale House Publishers, Inc. All rights reserved.

Front cover photo copyright © 1991 by Dennis Frates

ISBN 0-8423-2877-7

Printed in the United States of America

04 03 02 01
   10 9 8 7

This book of Luke is part of the *New International Version* of the Holy Bible, a completely new translation made by over a hundred scholars working directly from the best available Hebrew, Aramaic and Greek texts. It had its beginning in 1965 when, after several years of exploratory study by committees from the Christian Reformed Church and the National Association of Evangelicals, a group of scholars met at Palos Heights, Illinois, and concurred in the need for a new translation of the Bible in contemporary English. This group, though not made up of official church representatives, was transdenominational. Its conclusion was endorsed by a large number of leaders from many denominations who met in Chicago in 1966.

Responsibility for the new version was delegated by the Palos Heights group to a self-governing body of fifteen, the Committee on Bible Translation, composed for the most part of biblical scholars from colleges, universities, and seminaries. In 1967 the New York Bible Society (now the International Bible Society) generously undertook the financial sponsorship of the project—a sponsorship that made it possible to enlist the help of many distinguished scholars. The fact that participants from the United States, Great Britain, Canada, Australia, and New Zealand worked together gave the project its international scope. That they were from many denominations—including Anglican, Assemblies of God, Baptist, Brethren, Christian Reformed, Church of Christ, Evangelical Free, Lutheran, Mennonite, Methodist, Nazarene, Presbyterian, Wesleyan, and other churches—helped to safeguard the translation from sectarian bias.

How it was made helps to give the New International Version its distinctiveness. The translation of each book was assigned to a team of scholars. Next, one of the Intermediate Editorial Committees revised the initial translation, with constant reference to the Hebrew, Aramaic, or Greek. Their work then went to one of the General Editorial Committees, which checked it in detail and made another thorough revision. This revision in turn was carefully reviewed by the Committee on Bible Translation, which made further changes and then released the final version for publication. In this way the entire Bible underwent three revisions, during each of which the translation was examined for its faithfulness to the original languages and for its English style.

All this involved many thousands of hours of research and discussion regarding the meaning of the texts and the precise way of putting them into English. It may well be that no other translation has been made by a more thorough process of review and revision from committee to committee than this one.

From the beginning of the project, the Committee on Bible Translation held to certain goals for the New International Version: that it would be an accurate translation and one that would have clarity and literary quality and so prove suitable for public and private reading, teaching, preaching, memorizing, and liturgical use. The Committee also sought to preserve some measure of continuity with the long tradition of translating the Scriptures into English.

In working toward these goals, the translators were united in their commitment to the authority and infallibility of the Bible as God's Word in written form. They believe that it contains the divine answer to the deepest needs of humanity, that it sheds unique light on our path in a dark world, and that it sets forth the way to our eternal well-being.

The first concern of the translators has been the accuracy of the translation and its fidelity to the thought of the biblical writers. They have striven for more than a word-for-word translation. Because thought patterns and syntax differ from language to language, faithful communication of the meaning of the writers of the Bible demands frequent modifications in sentence structure and constant regard for the contextual meanings of words.

The Committee on Bible Translation submitted the developing version to a number of stylistic consultants. Samples of the translation were tested for clarity and ease of reading by various kinds of people—young and old, highly educated and less well educated, ministers and laymen. Concern for clear and natural English motivated the translators and consultants. In view of the international use of English, the translators sought to avoid obvious Americanisms on the one hand and obvious Anglicisms on the other. A British edition reflects the comparatively few differences of significant idiom and of spelling.

As for the traditional pronouns "thou," "thee," and "thine" in reference to the Deity, the translators judged that to use these archaisms (along with the old verb forms such as "doest," "wouldest," and "hadst") would violate accuracy in translation. Greek does not use special pronouns for the persons of the Godhead. A present-day translation is not enhanced by forms that in the time of the King James Version were used in everyday speech, whether referring to God or man.

The Greek text used in translating the New Testament was an eclectic one. No other piece of ancient literature has such an abundance of manuscript witnesses as does the New Testament. When existing manuscripts differ, the translators made their choice of readings according to accepted principles of New Testament textual criticism. Footnotes call attention to places where there was uncertainty about what the original text was. The best current printed texts of the Greek New Testament were used.

There is a sense in which the work of translation is never wholly finished. This applies to all great literature and uniquely so to the Bible. In 1973 the New Testament in the New International Version was published. Since then, suggestions for corrections and revisions have been received from various sources. The Committee on Bible Translation carefully considered the suggestions and adopted a number of them. These were incorporated in the first printing of the entire Bible in 1978. Additional revisions were made by the Committee on Bible Translation in 1983 and appear in printings after that date.

To achieve clarity the translators sometimes supplied words not in the original texts but required by the context. If there was uncertainty about such material, it is enclosed in brackets. Also for the sake of clarity or style, nouns, including some proper nouns, are sometimes substituted for pronouns, and vice versa. As an aid to the reader, italicized sectional headings are inserted in most of the books. They are not to be regarded as part of the NIV text, are not for oral reading, and are not intended to dictate the interpretation of the sections they head.

The footnotes in this version are of several kinds, most of which need no explanation. Those giving alternative translations begin with "Or" and generally introduce the alternative with the last word preceding it in the text, except when it is a single-word alternative; in poetry quoted in a footnote a slant mark indicates a line division. Footnotes introduced by "Or" do not have uniform significance. In some cases two possible translations were considered to have about equal validity. In other cases, though the translators were convinced that the translation in the text was correct, they judged that another interpretation was possible and of sufficient importance to be represented in a footnote. In the New Testament, footnotes that refer to uncertainty regarding the original text are introduced by "Some manuscripts" or similar expressions.

It should be noted that minerals, flora and fauna, architectural details, articles of clothing and jewelry, musical instruments and other articles cannot always be identified with precision. Also, measures of capacity in the biblical period are particularly uncertain.

Like all translations of the Bible, made as they are by imperfect man, this one undoubtedly falls short of its goals. Yet we are grateful to God for the extent to which he has enabled us to realize these goals and for the strength he has given us and our colleagues to complete our task. We offer this version of the Bible to him in whose name and for whose glory it has been made. We pray that it will lead many into a better understanding of the Holy Scriptures and a fuller knowledge of Jesus Christ the incarnate Word, of whom the Scriptures so faithfully testify.

The Committee on Bible Translation

June 1978
(Revised August 1983)

Names of the translators and editors may be secured
from the International Bible Society,
translation sponsors of the New International Version,
P.O. Box 62970, Colorado Springs, Colorado, 80962-2970 U.S.A.

The New International Version has one of the most accurate and best-organized cross-reference systems available.

The cross-references link words or phrases in the NIV text with counterpart Biblical references listed in a side column on every page. The raised letters containing these cross-references are set in a light italic typeface to distinguish them from the NIV text note letters, which use a bold typeface.

The lists of references are in Biblical order with one exception: If reference is made to a verse within the same chapter, that verse (indicated by "ver") is listed first.

Following is a list of abbreviations used in the cross-references:

ABBREVIATIONS FOR THE BOOKS OF THE BIBLE

Genesis . . . . Ge	Isaiah . . . . Isa	Romans . . . . Ro
Exodus . . . . Ex	Jeremiah . . . . Jer	1 Corinthians 1Co
Leviticus . . . . Lev	Lamentations . . . . La	2 Corinthians 2Co
Numbers . . . . Nu	Ezekiel . . . . Eze	Galatians . . . . Gal
Deuteronomy . . . . Dt	Daniel . . . . Da	Ephesians . . . . Eph
Joshua . . . . Jos	Hosea . . . . Hos	Philippians . . . . Php
Judges . . . . Jdg	Joel . . . . Joel	Colossians . . . . Col
Ruth . . . . Ru	Amos . . . . Am	1 Thessalonians 1Th
1 Samuel 1Sa	Obadiah . . . . Ob	2 Thessalonians 2Th
2 Samuel 2Sa	Jonah . . . . Jnh	1 Timothy 1Ti
1 Kings 1Ki	Micah . . . . Mic	2 Timothy 2Ti
2 Kings 2Ki	Nahum . . . . Na	Titus . . . . Tit
1 Chronicles 1Ch	Habakkuk . . . . Hab	Philemon . . . . Phm
2 Chronicles 2Ch	Zephaniah . . . . Zep	Hebrews . . . . Heb
Ezra . . . . Ezr	Haggai . . . . Hag	James . . . . Jas
Nehemiah . . . . Ne	Zechariah . . . . Zec	1 Peter 1Pe
Esther . . . . Est	Malachi . . . . Mal	2 Peter 2Pe
Job . . . . Job	Matthew . . . . Mt	1 John 1Jn
Psalms . . . . Ps	Mark . . . . Mk	2 John 2Jn
Proverbs . . . . Pr	Luke . . . . Lk	3 John 3Jn
Ecclesiastes . . . . Ecc	John . . . . Jn	Jude . . . . Jude
Song of Songs . . . . SS	Acts . . . . Ac	Revelation . . . . Rev

Have you ever opened your Bible and asked the following:

• What does this passage really mean?
• How does it apply to my life?
• Why does some of the Bible seem irrelevant?
• What do these ancient cultures have to do with today?
• I love God; why can't I understand what he is saying to me through his Word?
• What's going on in the lives of these Bible people?

Many Christians do not read the Bible regularly. Why? Because in the pressures of daily living they cannot find a connection between the timeless principles of Scripture and the ever-present problems of day-by-day living.

God urges us to apply his Word (Isaiah 42:23; 1 Corinthians 10:11; 2 Thessalonians 3:4), but too often we stop at accumulating Bible knowledge. This is why the *Life Application Bible* was developed—to show how to put into practice what we have learned.

Applying God's Word is a vital part of one's relationship with God; it is the evidence that we are obeying him. The difficulty in applying the Bible is not with the Bible itself, but with the reader's inability to bridge the gap between the past and present, the conceptual and practical. When we don't or can't do this, spiritual dryness, shallowness, and indifference result.

The words of Scripture itself cry out to us, "Do not merely listen to the word, and so deceive yourselves. Do what it says" (James 1:22). The *Life Application Bible* helps us do just that. Developed by an interdenominational team of pastors, scholars, family counselors, and a national organization dedicated to promoting God's Word and spreading the gospel, the *Life Application Bible* took many years to complete, and all the work was reviewed by several renowned theologians under the directorship of Dr. Kenneth Kantzer.

The *Life Application Bible* does what a good resource Bible should—it helps you understand the context of a passage, gives important background and historical information, explains difficult words and phrases, and helps you see the interrelationship of Scripture. But it does much more. The *Life Application Bible* goes deeper into God's Word, helping you discover the timeless truth being communicated, see the relevance for your life, and make a personal application. While some study Bibles attempt application, over 75 percent of this Bible is application oriented. The notes answer the questions, "So what?" and "What does this passage mean to me, my family, my friends, my job, my neighborhood, my church, my country?"

Imagine reading a familiar passage of Scripture and gaining fresh insight, as if you were reading it for the first time. How much richer your life would be if you left each Bible reading with a new perspective and a small change for the better. A small change every day adds up to a changed life—and that is the very purpose of Scripture.

The best way to define application is to first determine what it is *not*. Application is *not* just accumulating knowledge. This helps us discover and understand facts and concepts, but it stops there. History is filled with philosophers who knew what the Bible said but failed to apply it to their lives, keeping them from believing and changing. Many think that understanding is the end goal of Bible study, but it is really only the beginning.

Application is *not* just illustration. Illustration only tells us how someone else handled a similar situation. While we may empathize with that person, we still have little direction for our personal situation.

Application is *not* just making a passage "relevant." Making the Bible relevant only helps us to see that the same lessons that were true in Bible times are true today; it does not show us how to apply them to the problems and pressures of our individual lives.

What, then, is application? Application begins by knowing and understanding God's Word and its timeless truths. *But we cannot stop there.* If we do, God's Word may not change our life, and it may become dull, difficult, tedious, and tiring. A good application focuses the truth of God's Word, shows the reader what to do about what is being read, and motivates the reader to respond to what God is teaching. All three are essential to application.

Application is putting into practice what we already know (see Mark 4:24 and Hebrews 5:14) and answering the question "So what?" by confronting us with the right questions and motivating us to take action (see 1 John 2:5, 6 and James 2:26). Application is deeply personal—unique for each individual. It is making a relevant truth a personal truth and involves developing a strategy and action plan to live your life in harmony with the Bible. It is the Biblical "how to" of life.

You may ask, "How can your application notes be relevant to *my* life?" Each application note has three parts: (1) an *explanation* ties the note directly to the Scripture passage and sets up the truth that is being taught, (2) the *bridge* explains the timeless truth and makes it relevant for today, (3) the *application* shows you how to take the timeless truth and apply it to your personal situation. No note, by itself, can apply Scripture directly to your life. It can only teach, direct, lead, guide, inspire, recommend, and urge. It can give you the resources and direction you need to apply the Bible; but only you can take these resources and put them into practice.

A good note, therefore, should not only give you knowledge and understanding but point you to application. Before you buy any kind of resource study Bible, you should evaluate the notes and ask the following questions: (1) Does the note contain enough information to help me understand the point of the Scripture passage? (2) Does the note assume I know too much? (3) Does the note avoid denominational bias? (4) Do the notes touch most of life's experiences? (5) Does the note help me *apply* God's Word?

NOTES

In addition to providing the reader with many application notes, the *Life Application Bible* offers several explanatory notes that help the reader understand culture, history, context, difficult-to-understand passages, background, places, theological concepts, and the relationship of various passages in Scripture to other passages.

BOOK INTRODUCTION

The Book Introduction is divided into several easy-to-find parts:

Timeline. A guide that puts the Bible book into its historical setting. It lists the key events and the dates when they occurred.

Vital Statistics. A list of straight facts about the book—those pieces of information you need to know at a glance.

Overview. A summary of the book with general lessons and applications that can be learned from the book as a whole.

Blueprint. The outline of the book. It is printed in easy-to-understand language and is designed for easy memorization. To the right of each main heading is a key lesson that is taught in that particular section.

Megathemes. A section that gives the main themes of the Bible book, explains their significance, and then tells why they are still important for us today.

Map. If included, this shows the key places found in that book and retells the story of the book from a geographical perspective.

OUTLINE

The *Life Application Bible* has a new, custom-made outline that was designed specifically from an application point of view. Several unique features should be noted:

1. To avoid confusion and to aid memory work, the book outline has only three levels for headings. Main outline heads are marked with a capital letter. Subheads are marked by a number. Minor explanatory heads have no letter or number.

2. Each main outline head marked by a letter also has a brief paragraph below it summarizing the Bible text and offering a general application.

3. Parallel passages are listed where they apply.

PERSONALITY PROFILES

Another unique feature of this Bible is the profiles of key Bible people, including their strengths and weaknesses, greatest accomplishments and mistakes, and key lessons from their lives.

MAPS

The *Life Application Bible* has a thorough and comprehensive Bible atlas built right into the book. There are two kinds of maps: A book introduction map, telling the story of the book, and thumbnail maps in the notes, plotting most geographic movements.

CHARTS AND DIAGRAMS

Many charts and diagrams are included to help the reader better visualize difficult concepts or relationships. Most charts not only present the needed information but show the significance of the information as well.

CROSS-REFERENCES

A carefully organized cross-reference system in the margins of the Bible text helps the reader find related passages quickly.

TEXTUAL NOTES

Directly related to the text of the New International Version, the textual notes provide explanations on certain wording in the translation, alternate translations, and information about readings in the ancient manuscripts.

HIGHLIGHTED NOTES

In each Bible study lesson you will be asked to read specific notes as part of your preparation. These notes have been highlighted by a bullet (•) so that you can find them easily.

Luke begins his account in the temple in Jerusalem, giving us the background for the birth of John the Baptist, then moves on to the town of Nazareth and the story of Mary, chosen to be Jesus' mother (1:26ff). As a result of Caesar's call for a census, Mary and Joseph had to travel to Bethlehem, where Jesus was born in fulfillment of prophecy (2:1ff). Jesus grew up in Nazareth and began his earthly ministry by being baptized by John (3:21, 22) and tempted by Satan (4:1ff). Much of his ministry focused on Galilee—he set up his "home" in Capernaum (4:31ff) and from there he taught throughout the region (8:1ff). Later he visited the Gerasene region, where he healed a demon-possessed man (8:36ff). He fed more than 5,000 people with one lunch on the shores of the Sea of Galilee near Bethsaida (9:10ff). Jesus always traveled to Jerusalem for the major festivals, and he enjoyed visiting friends in nearby Bethany (10:38ff). He healed ten men with leprosy on the border between Galilee and Samaria (17:11), and helped a dishonest tax collector in Jericho turn his life around (19:1ff). The little villages of Bethphage and Bethany on the Mount of Olives were Jesus' resting places during his last days on earth. He was crucified outside Jerusalem's walls, but he would rise again. Two men on the road leading to Emmaus were among the first to see the resurrected Christ (24:13ff).

Modern names and boundaries are shown in gray.

LUKE

VITAL STATISTICS

PURPOSE:
To present an accurate account of the life of Christ and to present Christ as the perfect human and Savior

AUTHOR:
Luke—a doctor (Colossians 4:14), a Greek and Gentile Christian. He is the only known Gentile author in the New Testament. Luke was a close friend and companion of Paul. He also wrote Acts, and the two books go together.

TO WHOM WRITTEN:
Theophilus ("one who loves God"), Gentiles, and people everywhere

DATE WRITTEN:
About A.D. 60

SETTING:
Luke wrote from Rome or possibly from Caesarea.

KEY VERSES:
"Jesus said to him, 'Today salvation has come to this house, because this man, too, is a son of Abraham. For the Son of Man came to seek and to save what was lost'" (19:9, 10).

KEY PEOPLE:
Jesus, Elizabeth, Zechariah, John the Baptist, Mary, the disciples, Herod the Great, Pilate, Mary Magdalene

KEY PLACES:
Bethlehem, Galilee, Judea, Jerusalem

SPECIAL FEATURES:
This is the most comprehensive Gospel. The general vocabulary and diction show that the author was educated. He makes frequent references to illnesses and diagnoses. Luke stresses Jesus' relationships with people; emphasizes prayer, miracles, and angels; records inspired hymns of praise; and gives a prominent place to women. Most of 9:51—18:35 is not found in any other Gospel.

EVERY birth is a miracle, and every child is a gift from God. But nearly 20 centuries ago, there was the miracle of miracles. A baby was born, but he was the Son of God. The Gospels tell of this birth, but Dr. Luke, as though he were the attending physician, provides most of the details surrounding this awesome occasion. With divine Father and human mother, Jesus entered history—God in the flesh.

Luke affirms Jesus' divinity, but the real emphasis of his book is to show Jesus' humanity—Jesus, the Son of God, is also the Son of Man. As a doctor, Luke was a man of science, and as a Greek, he was a man of detail. It is not surprising, then, that he begins by outlining his extensive research and explaining that he is reporting the facts (1:1–4). Luke also was a close friend and traveling companion of Paul, so he could interview the other disciples, had access to other historical accounts, and was an eyewitness to the birth and growth of the early church. His Gospel and book of Acts are reliable, historical documents.

Luke's story begins with angels appearing to Zechariah and then to Mary, telling them of the upcoming births of their sons. From Zechariah and Elizabeth would come John the Baptist, who would prepare the way for Christ. And Mary would conceive by the Holy Spirit and bear Jesus, the Son of God. Soon after John's birth, Caesar Augustus declared a census, and so Mary and Joseph traveled to Bethlehem, the town of David, their ancient ancestor. There the child was born. Angels announced the joyous event to shepherds, who rushed to the manger. When the shepherds left, they were praising God and spreading the news. Eight days later, Jesus was circumcised and then dedicated to God in the temple, where Simeon and Anna confirmed Jesus' identity as the Savior, their Messiah.

Luke gives us a glimpse of Jesus at age 12—discussing theology with the teachers of the law at the temple (2:41–52). The next event occurred 18 years later, when we read of John the Baptist preaching in the desert. Jesus came to John to be baptized before beginning his public ministry (3:1–38). At this point, Luke traces Jesus' genealogy on his stepfather Joseph's side, through David and Abraham back to Adam, underscoring Jesus' identity as the Son of Man.

After the temptation (4:1–13), Jesus returned to Galilee to preach, teach, and heal (4:14—21:38). During this time, he began gathering his group of 12 disciples (5:1–10, 27–29). Later Jesus commissioned the disciples and sent them out to proclaim the kingdom of God. When they returned, Jesus revealed to them his mission, his true identity, and what it means to be his disciple (9:18–62). His mission would take him to Jerusalem (9:51–53), where he would be rejected, tried, and crucified.

While Jesus carried his own cross to Golgotha, some women in Jerusalem wept for him, but Jesus told them to weep for themselves and for their children (23:28). But Luke's Gospel does not end in sadness. It concludes with the thrilling account of Jesus' resurrection from the dead, his appearances to the disciples, and his promise to send the Holy Spirit (24:1–53). Read Luke's beautifully written and accurate account of the life of Jesus, Son of Man and Son of God. Then praise God for sending the Savior for all people—our risen and triumphant Lord.

THE BLUEPRINT

A. BIRTH AND PREPARATION OF JESUS, THE SAVIOR (1:1—4:13)

From an infant who could do nothing on his own, Jesus grew to become completely able to fulfill his mission on earth. He was fully human, developing in all ways like us. Yet he remained fully God. He took no shortcuts and was not isolated from the pressures and temptations of life. There are no shortcuts for us either as we prepare for a life of service to God.

B. MESSAGE AND MINISTRY OF JESUS, THE SAVIOR (4:14—21:38)
1. Jesus' ministry in Galilee
2. Jesus' ministry on the way to Jerusalem
3. Jesus' ministry in Jerusalem

Jesus taught great crowds of people, especially through parables, which are stories with great truths. But only those with ears to hear will understand. We should pray that God's Spirit would help us understand the implications of these truths for our lives so we can become more and more like Jesus.

C. DEATH AND RESURRECTION OF JESUS, THE SAVIOR (22:1—24:53)

The Savior of the world was arrested and executed. But death could not destroy him, and Jesus came back to life and ascended to heaven. In Luke's careful, historical account, we receive the facts about Jesus' resurrection. We must not only believe that these facts are true, but we must also trust Christ as our Savior. It is shortsighted to neglect the facts, but how sad it is to accept the facts and neglect the forgiveness that Jesus offers to each of us.

MEGATHEMES

THEME	EXPLANATION	IMPORTANCE
Jesus Christ, the Savior	Luke describes how God's Son entered human history. Jesus lived as the perfect example of a human. After a perfect ministry, he provided a perfect sacrifice for our sin so we could be saved.	Jesus is our perfect leader and Savior. He offers forgiveness to all who will accept him as Lord of their lives and believe that what he says is true.
History	Luke was a medical doctor and historian. He put great emphasis on dates and details, connecting Jesus to events and people in history.	Luke gives details so we can believe in the reliability of the history of Jesus' life. Even more important, we can believe with certainty that Jesus is God.
People	Jesus was deeply interested in people and relationships. He showed warm concern for his followers and friends—men, women, and children.	Jesus' love for people is good news for everyone. His message is for all people in every nation. Each one of us has an opportunity to respond to him in faith.
Compassion	As a perfect human, Jesus showed tender sympathy to the poor, the despised, the hurt, and the sinful. No one was rejected or ignored by him.	Jesus is more than an idea or teacher—he cares for you. Only this kind of deep love can satisfy your need.
Holy Spirit	The Holy Spirit was present at Jesus' birth, baptism, ministry, and resurrection. As a perfect example for us, Jesus lived in dependence on the Holy Spirit.	The Holy Spirit was sent by God as confirmation of Jesus' authority. The Holy Spirit is given to enable people to live for Christ. By faith we can have the Holy Spirit's presence and power to witness and to serve.

A. BIRTH AND PREPARATION OF JESUS, THE SAVIOR (1:1 — 4:13)

Luke gives us the most detailed account of Jesus' birth. In describing Jesus' birth, childhood, and development, Luke lifts up the humanity of Jesus. Our Savior was the ideal human. Fully prepared, the ideal human was now ready to live the perfect life.

Luke's Purpose in Writing
(1)

1 Many have undertaken to draw up an account of the things that have been fulfilled[a] among us, 2just as they were handed down to us by those who from the first[a] were eyewitnesses[b] and servants of the word. 3Therefore, since I myself have carefully investigated everything from the beginning, it seemed good also to me to write an orderly account[c] for you, most excellent Theophilus,[d] 4so that you may know the certainty of the things you have been taught.

1:2
[a] Jn 15:27
[b] Heb 2:3;
2Pe 1:16

1:3
[c] Ac 11:4
[d] Ac 1:1

An Angel Promises the Birth of John to Zechariah
(4)

5In the time of Herod king of Judea[e] there was a priest named Zechariah, who belonged to the priestly division of Abijah;[f] his wife Elizabeth was also a descendant of Aaron. 6Both of them were upright in the sight of God, observing all the Lord's commandments and regulations blamelessly. 7But they had no children, because Elizabeth was barren; and they were both well along in years.

1:5
[e] Mt 2:1
[f] 1Ch 24:10

8Once when Zechariah's division was on duty and he was serving as priest before God,[g] 9he was chosen by lot, according to the custom of the priesthood, to go into the temple of the Lord and burn incense.[h] 10And when the time for the burning of incense came, all the assembled worshipers were praying outside.[i]

11Then an angel of the Lord appeared to him, standing at the right side of the altar of incense. 12When Zechariah saw him, he was startled and was gripped with fear.

1:8
[g] 1Ch 24:19;
2Ch 8:14

1:9
[h] Ex 30:7, 8

1:10
[i] Lev 16:17

[a] 1 Or *been surely believed*

● **1:1, 2** Luke tells Jesus' story from Luke's unique perspective of a Gentile, a physician, and the first historian of the early church. Though not an eyewitness of Jesus' ministry, Luke nevertheless is concerned that eyewitness accounts be preserved accurately and that the foundations of Christian belief be transmitted intact to the next generation. In Luke's Gospel are many of Jesus' parables. In addition, more than any other Gospel, it gives specific instances of Jesus' concern for women.

● **1:1-4** There was a lot of interest in Jesus, and many people had written firsthand accounts about him. Luke may have used these accounts and all other available resources as material for an accurate and complete account of Jesus' life, teachings, and ministry. Because truth was important to Luke, he relied heavily on eyewitness accounts. Christianity doesn't say, "Close your eyes and believe," but rather, "Check it out for yourself." The Bible encourages you to investigate its claims thoroughly (John 1:46; 21:24; Acts 17:11, 12), because your conclusion about Jesus is a life-and-death matter.

● **1:3** *Theophilus* means "one who loves God." The book of Acts, also written by Luke, is likewise addressed to Theophilus. This preface may be a general dedication to all Christian readers. Theophilus may have been Luke's patron who helped to finance the book's writing. More likely, Theophilus was a Roman acquaintance of Luke's with a strong interest in the new Christian religion.

● **1:3, 4** As a medical doctor, Luke knew the importance of being thorough. He used his skills in observation and analysis to thoroughly investigate the stories about Jesus. His diagnosis? The gospel of Jesus Christ is true! You can read Luke's account of Jesus' life with confidence that it was written by a clear thinker and a thoughtful researcher. Because the gospel is founded on historical truth, our spiritual growth must involve careful, disciplined, and thorough investigation of God's Word so that we can understand how God has acted in history. If this kind of study is not part of your life, find a pastor, teacher, or even a book to help you get started and to guide you in this important part of Christian growth.

1:5 This was Herod the Great, confirmed by the Roman Senate as king of the Jews. Only half Jewish himself and eager to please his Roman superiors, Herod expanded and beautified the Jerusalem temple — but he placed a Roman eagle over the entrance. When he helped the Jews, it was for political purposes and not because he cared about their God. Herod the Great later ordered a massacre of infants in a futile attempt to kill the infant Jesus, whom some were calling the new "king of the Jews" (Matthew 2:16–18).

1:5 A Jewish priest was a minister of God who worked at the temple managing its upkeep, teaching the people the Scriptures, and directing the worship services. At this time there were about 20,000 priests throughout the country — far too many to minister in the temple at one time. Therefore the priests were divided into 24 separate groups of about 1,000 each, according to David's directions (1 Chronicles 24:3–19).

Zechariah was a member of the Abijah division, on duty this particular week. Each morning a priest was to enter the Holy Place in the temple and burn incense. Lots were cast to decide who would enter the sacred room, and one day the lot fell to Zechariah. But it was not by chance that Zechariah was on duty and that he was chosen that day to enter the Holy Place — perhaps a once-in-a-lifetime opportunity. God was guiding the events of history to prepare the way for Jesus to come to earth.

1:6 Zechariah and Elizabeth didn't merely go through the motions in following God's laws; they backed up their outward compliance with inward obedience. Unlike the religious leaders whom Jesus called hypocrites, Zechariah and Elizabeth did not stop with the letter of the law. Their obedience was from the heart, and that is why they are called "upright in the sight of God."

1:9 Incense was burned in the temple twice daily. When the people saw the smoke from the burning incense, they prayed. The smoke drifting heavenward symbolized their prayers ascending to God's throne.

1:11, 12 Angels are spirit beings who live in God's presence and do his will. Only two angels are mentioned by name in Scripture —

1:13
j ver 60, 63
1:15
k Nu 6:3;
Jdg 13:4;
Lk 7:33
l Jer 1:5

¹³But the angel said to him: "Do not be afraid, Zechariah; your prayer has been heard. Your wife Elizabeth will bear you a son, and you are to give him the name John.*ʲ* ¹⁴He will be a joy and delight to you, and many will rejoice because of his birth, ¹⁵for he will be great in the sight of the Lord. He is never to take wine or other fermented drink,*ᵏ* and he will be filled with the Holy Spirit even from birth.*ᵇˡ*

ᵇ 15 Or from his mother's womb

Zechariah was told before anyone else that God was setting in motion his own visit to earth. Zechariah and his wife, Elizabeth, were known for their personal holiness. They were well suited to doing a special work for God. But they shared the pain of not having children, and in Jewish culture this was considered not having God's blessing. Zechariah and Elizabeth were old, and they had stopped even asking for children.

This trip to the temple in Jerusalem for Zechariah's turn at duty had included an unexpected blessing. Zechariah was chosen to be the priest who would enter the Holy Place to offer incense to God for the people. Suddenly, much to his surprise and terror, he found himself face to face with an angel. The angel's message was too good to be true! But Zechariah did not respond to the news of the coming Savior as much as he expressed doubts about his own ability to father the child the angel promised him. His age spoke more loudly than God's promise. As a result, God prevented Zechariah from speaking until the promise became reality.

The record of the prayer in Luke 1 is our last glimpse of Zechariah. Like so many of God's most faithful servants, he passed quietly from the scene once his part was done. He becomes our hero for those times when we doubt God and yet are willing to obey. We gain hope from Zechariah's story that God can do great things through anyone who is available to him.

Strengths and accomplishments:
• Known as a righteous man
• Was a priest before God
• One of the few people to be directly addressed by an angel
• Fathered John the Baptist

Weakness and mistake:
• Momentarily doubted the angel's promise of a son because of his own old age

Lessons from his life:
• Physical limitations do not limit God
• God accomplishes his will, sometimes in unexpected ways

Vital statistics:
• Occupation: Priest
• Relatives: Wife: Elizabeth. Son: John the Baptist

Key verses:
"Both of them were upright in the sight of God, observing all the Lord's commandments and regulations blamelessly. But they had no children, because Elizabeth was barren; and they were both well along in years" (Luke 1:6, 7).

Zechariah's story is told in Luke 1.

Michael and Gabriel – but there are many who act as God's messengers. Here, Gabriel (1:19) delivered a special message to Zechariah. This was not a dream or a vision. The angel appeared in visible form and spoke audible words to the priest.

• **1:13** Zechariah, while burning incense on the altar, was also praying, perhaps for a son or for the coming of the Messiah. In either case, his prayer was answered. He would soon have a son, who would prepare the way for the Messiah. God answers prayer in his own way and in his own time. He worked in an "impossible" situation – Zechariah's wife was barren – to bring about the fulfillment of all the prophecies concerning the Messiah. If we want to have our prayers answered, we must be open to what God can do in impossible situations. And we must wait for God to work in his way, in his time.

1:13 *John* means "the LORD is gracious," and *Jesus* means "the LORD saves." Both names were prescribed by God, not chosen by human parents. Throughout the Gospels, God acts graciously and

saves his people. He will not withhold salvation from anyone who sincerely comes to him.

1:15 John was set apart for special service to God. He may have been forbidden to drink wine as part of the Nazirite vow, an ancient vow of consecration to God (see Numbers 6:1–8). Samson (Judges 13) was under the Nazirite vow, and Samuel may have been also (1 Samuel 1:11).

1:15 This is Luke's first mention of the Holy Spirit, the third person of the Trinity; Luke refers to the Holy Spirit more than any other Gospel writer. Because Luke also wrote the book of Acts, we know he was thoroughly informed about the work of the Holy Spirit. Luke recognized and emphasized the Holy Spirit's work in directing the founding of Christianity and in guiding the early church. The presence of the Spirit is God's gift given to the entire church at Pentecost. Prior to that, God's Spirit was given to the faithful for special tasks. We need the Holy Spirit's help to do God's work effectively.

16Many of the people of Israel will he bring back to the Lord their God. 17And he will go on before the Lord, in the spirit and power of Elijah,*m* to turn the hearts of the fathers to their children and the disobedient to the wisdom of the righteous — to make ready a people prepared for the Lord."

18Zechariah asked the angel, "How can I be sure of this? I am an old man and my wife is well along in years."*n*

19The angel answered, "I am Gabriel.*o* I stand in the presence of God, and I have been sent to speak to you and to tell you this good news. 20And now you will be silent and not able to speak until the day this happens, because you did not believe my words, which will come true at their proper time."

21Meanwhile, the people were waiting for Zechariah and wondering why he stayed so long in the temple. 22When he came out, he could not speak to them. They realized he had seen a vision in the temple, for he kept making signs*p* to them but remained unable to speak.

23When his time of service was completed, he returned home. 24After this his wife Elizabeth became pregnant and for five months remained in seclusion. 25"The Lord has done this for me," she said. "In these days he has shown his favor and taken away my disgrace*q* among the people."

An Angel Promises the Birth of Jesus to Mary
(5)

26In the sixth month, God sent the angel Gabriel to Nazareth, a town in Galilee, 27to a virgin pledged to be married to a man named Joseph,*r* a descendant of David. The virgin's name was Mary. 28The angel went to her and said, "Greetings, you who are highly favored! The Lord is with you."

29Mary was greatly troubled at his words and wondered what kind of greeting this might be. 30But the angel said to her, "Do not be afraid, Mary, you have found

1:17
*m*Mt 11:14

1:18
*n*Ge 17:17

1:19
*o*Da 8:16; 9:21

1:22
*p*ver 62

1:25
*q*Ge 30:23;
Isa 4:1

1:27
*r*Mt 1:16, 18, 20

● **1:17** John's role was to be almost identical to that of an Old Testament prophet — to encourage people to turn away from sin and back to God. John is often compared to the great prophet Elijah, who was known for standing up to evil rulers (Malachi 4:5; Matthew 11:14; 17:10–13). See Elijah's Profile in 1 Kings 18.

● **1:17** In preparing people for the Messiah's arrival, John would do "heart transplants." He would take stony hearts and exchange them for hearts that were soft, pliable, trusting, and open to change. (See Ezekiel 11:19, 20 and 36:25–29 for more on "heart transplants.") Are you as open to God as you should be? Or do you need a change of heart?

● **1:18** When told he would have a son, Zechariah doubted the angel's word. From Zechariah's human perspective, his doubts were understandable — but with God, anything is possible. Although Zechariah and Elizabeth were past the age of childbearing, God gave them a child. It is easy to doubt or misunderstand what God wants to do in our lives. Even God's people sometimes make the mistake of trusting their intellect or experience rather than God. When tempted to think that one of God's promises is impossible, remember his work throughout history. God's power is not confined by narrow perspective or bound by human limitations. Trust him completely.

1:20 Zechariah thought it incredible that he and his wife, at their old age, could conceive a child. But what God promises, he delivers. And God delivers *on time!* You can have complete confidence that God will keep his promises. Their fulfillment may not be the next day, but they will be "at their proper time." If you are waiting for God to answer some request or to fill some need, remain patient. No matter how impossible God's promises may seem, what he has said in his Word will come true at the right time.

1:21 The people were waiting outside for Zechariah to come out and pronounce the customary blessing upon them as found in Numbers 6:24–26.

1:25 Zechariah and Elizabeth were both faithful people, and yet

they were suffering. Some Jews at that time did not believe in a bodily resurrection, so their hope of immortality was in their children. In addition, children cared for their parents in their old age and added to the family's financial security and social status. Children were considered a blessing, and childlessness was seen as a curse. Zechariah and Elizabeth had been childless for many years, and at this time they were too old to expect any change in their situation. They felt humiliated and hopeless. But God was waiting for the right time to encourage them and take away their disgrace.

1:26 Gabriel appeared not only to Zechariah and to Mary but also to the prophet Daniel more than 500 years earlier (Daniel 8:15–17; 9:21). Each time Gabriel appeared, he brought important messages from God.

1:26 Nazareth, Joseph's and Mary's hometown, was a long way from Jerusalem, the center of Jewish life and worship. Located on a major trade route, Nazareth was frequently visited by Gentile merchants and Roman soldiers. It was known for its independent and aloof attitude. Jesus was born in Bethlehem but grew up in Nazareth. Nevertheless, the people of Nazareth would reject him as the Messiah (4:22–30).

1:27, 28 Mary was young, poor, female — all characteristics that, to the people of her day, would make her seem unusable by God for any major task. But God chose Mary for one of the most important acts of obedience he has ever demanded of anyone. You may feel that your ability, experience, or education makes you an unlikely candidate for God's service. Don't limit God's choices. He can use you if you trust him.

1:30, 31 God's favor does not automatically bring instant success or fame. His blessing on Mary, the honor of being the mother of the Messiah, would lead to much pain: her peers would ridicule her; her fiancé would come close to leaving her; her son would be rejected and murdered. But through her son would come the world's only hope, and this is why Mary has been praised by countless generations as the young girl who "found favor with

favor with God. 31You will be with child and give birth to a son, and you are to give him the name Jesus. s 32He will be great and will be called the Son of the Most High. t The Lord God will give him the throne of his father David, 33and he will reign over the house of Jacob forever; his kingdom will never end."u

34"How will this be," Mary asked the angel, "since I am a virgin?"

35The angel answered, "The Holy Spirit will come upon you, and the power of the Most Highv will overshadow you. So the holy one to be born will be calledc the Son of God. w 36Even Elizabeth your relative is going to have a child in her old age, and she who was said to be barren is in her sixth month. 37For nothing is impossible with God."x

38"I am the Lord's servant," Mary answered. "May it be to me as you have said." Then the angel left her.

c 35 Or So the child to be born will be called holy,

1:31
sLk 2:21

1:32
tMk 5:7

1:33
uDa 2:44; 7:14, 27

1:35
vver 32, 76
wMt 4:3

1:37
xMt 19:26

GOD'S UNUSUAL METHODS
One of the best ways to understand God's willingness to communicate to people is to note the various methods, some of them quite unexpected, that he has used to give his message. Following is a sample of his methods and the people he contacted.

Person/Group	Method	Reference
Jacob, Zechariah, Mary, Shepherds	Angels	Genesis 32:22–32; Luke 1:13, 30; 2:10
Jacob, Joseph, a baker, a cupbearer, Pharaoh, Isaiah, Joseph, the Magi	Dreams	Genesis 28:10–22; 37:5–10; 40:5; 41:7, 8; Isaiah 1:1; Matthew 1:20; 2:12, 13
Belshazzar	Writing on the wall	Daniel 5:5–9
Balaam	Talking donkey	Numbers 22:21–35
People of Israel	Pillar of cloud and fire	Exodus 13:21, 22
Jonah	Being swallowed by a fish	Jonah 2
Abraham, Moses, Jesus at his baptism, Paul	Verbally	Genesis 12:1–4; Exodus 7:8; Matthew 3:13–17; Acts 18:9
Moses	Fire	Exodus 3:2
Us	God's Son	Hebrews 1:1, 2

God." Her submission was part of God's plan to bring about our salvation. If sorrow weighs you down and dims your hope, think of Mary and wait patiently for God to finish working out his plan.

1:31–33 *Jesus*, a Greek form of the Hebrew name *Joshua*, was a common name meaning "the LORD saves." Just as Joshua had led Israel into the promised land (see Joshua 1:1, 2), so Jesus would lead his people into eternal life. The symbolism of his name was not lost on the people of his day, who took names seriously and saw them as a source of power. In Jesus' name people were healed, demons were banished, and sins were forgiven.

1:32, 33 Centuries earlier, God had promised David that David's kingdom would last forever (2 Samuel 7:16). This promise was fulfilled in the coming of Jesus, a direct descendant of David, whose reign will continue throughout eternity.

1:34 The birth of Jesus to a virgin is a miracle that many people find hard to believe. These three facts can aid our faith: (1) Luke was a medical doctor, and he knew perfectly well how babies are made. It would have been just as hard for him to believe in a virgin birth as it is for us, and yet he reports it as fact. (2) Luke was a painstaking researcher who based his Gospel on eyewitness accounts. Tradition holds that he talked with Mary about the events he recorded in the first two chapters. This is Mary's story, not a fictional invention. (3) Christians and Jews, who worship God as the Creator of the universe, should believe that God has the power to create a child in a virgin's womb.

1:35 Jesus was born without the sin that entered the world through Adam. He was born holy, just as Adam was created sinless. In contrast to Adam, who disobeyed God, Jesus obeyed God and was thus able to face sin's consequences in our place and make us acceptable to God (Romans 5:14–19).

1:38 A young unmarried girl who became pregnant risked disaster. Unless the father of the child agreed to marry her, she would probably remain unmarried for life. If her own father rejected her, she could be forced into begging or prostitution in order to earn her living. And Mary, with her story about being made pregnant by the Holy Spirit, risked being considered crazy as well. Still Mary said, despite the possible risks, "May it be to me as you have said." When Mary said that, she didn't know about the tremendous opportunity she would have. She only knew that God was asking her to serve him, and she willingly obeyed. Don't wait to see the bottom line before offering your life to God. Offer yourself willingly, even when the outcome seems disastrous.

● **1:38** God's announcement of a child to be born was met with various responses throughout Scripture. Sarah, Abraham's wife, laughed (Genesis 18:9–15). Zechariah doubted (Luke 1:18). By contrast, Mary submitted. She believed the angel's words and agreed to bear the child, even under humanly impossible circumstances. God is able to do the impossible. Our response to his demands should not be laughter or doubt, but willing acceptance.

Mary Visits Elizabeth

(6)

³⁹At that time Mary got ready and hurried to a town in the hill country of Judea,^y
⁴⁰where she entered Zechariah's home and greeted Elizabeth. ⁴¹When Elizabeth
heard Mary's greeting, the baby leaped in her womb, and Elizabeth was filled with
the Holy Spirit. ⁴²In a loud voice she exclaimed: "Blessed are you among
women,^z and blessed is the child you will bear! ⁴³But why am I so favored, that
the mother of my Lord should come to me? ⁴⁴As soon as the sound of your greeting
reached my ears, the baby in my womb leaped for joy. ⁴⁵Blessed is she who has
believed that what the Lord has said to her will be accomplished!"

⁴⁶And Mary said:

> "My soul glorifies the Lord^a
> ⁴⁷   and my spirit rejoices in God my Savior,
> ⁴⁸for he has been mindful
>   of the humble state of his servant.^b
>   From now on all generations will call me blessed,^c
> ⁴⁹   for the Mighty One has done great things^d for me —
>   holy is his name.
> ⁵⁰His mercy extends to those who fear him,
>   from generation to generation.^e
> ⁵¹He has performed mighty deeds with his arm;^f
>   he has scattered those who are proud in their inmost thoughts.
> ⁵²He has brought down rulers from their thrones
>   but has lifted up the humble.
> ⁵³He has filled the hungry with good things
>   but has sent the rich away empty.
> ⁵⁴He has helped his servant Israel,
>   remembering to be merciful^g
> ⁵⁵to Abraham and his descendants^h forever,
>   even as he said to our fathers."

⁵⁶Mary stayed with Elizabeth for about three months and then returned home.

John the Baptist Is Born

(7)

⁵⁷When it was time for Elizabeth to have her baby, she gave birth to a son. ⁵⁸Her
neighbors and relatives heard that the Lord had shown her great mercy, and they
shared her joy.

⁵⁹On the eighth day they came to circumciseⁱ the child, and they were going to

1:39
^yver 65

1:42
^zJdg 5:24

1:46
^aPs 34:2, 3

1:48
^bPs 138:6
^cLk 11:27

1:49
^dPs 71:19

1:50
^ePs 103:17

1:51
^fPs 98:1

1:54
^gPs 98:3

1:55
^hGal 3:16

1:59
ⁱGe 17:12;
Lev 12:3

1:41-43 Apparently the Holy Spirit told Elizabeth that Mary's child was the Messiah because Elizabeth called her young relative "the mother of my Lord" as she greeted her. As Mary rushed off to visit her relative, she must have been wondering if the events of the last few days were real. Elizabeth's greeting must have strengthened her faith. Mary's pregnancy may have seemed impossible, but her wise relative believed in the Lord's faithfulness and rejoiced in Mary's blessed condition.

1:42, 43 Even though she herself was pregnant with a long-awaited son, Elizabeth could have envied Mary, whose son would be even greater than her own. Instead she was filled with joy that the mother of her Lord would visit her. Have you ever envied people whom God has apparently singled out for special blessing? A cure for jealousy is to rejoice with those people, realizing that God uses his people in ways best suited to his purpose.

1:46-55 This song is often called the *Magnificat*, the first word in the Latin translation of this passage. Mary's song has often been used as the basis for choral music and hymns. Like Hannah, the mother of Samuel (1 Samuel 2:1-10), Mary glorified God in song for what he was going to do for the world through her. Notice that

in both songs, God is pictured as a champion of the poor, the oppressed, and the despised.

1:48 When Mary said, "From now on all generations will call me blessed," was she being proud? No, she was recognizing and accepting the gift God had given her. If Mary had denied her incredible position, she would have been throwing God's blessing back at him. Pride is refusing to accept God's gifts or taking credit for what God has done; humility is accepting the gifts and using them to praise and serve God. Don't deny, belittle, or ignore your gifts. Thank God for them and use them to his glory.

1:54, 55 God kept his promise to Abraham to be merciful to God's people forever (Genesis 22:16-18). Christ's birth fulfilled the promise, and Mary understood this. She was not surprised when her special son eventually announced that he was the Messiah. She had known Jesus' mission from before his birth. Some of God's promises to Israel are found in 2 Samuel 22:50, 51; Psalms 89:2-4; 103:17, 18; Micah 7:18-20.

1:56 Because travel was not easy, long visits were customary. Mary must have been a great help to Elizabeth, who was experiencing the discomforts of a first pregnancy in old age.

name him after his father Zechariah, 60but his mother spoke up and said, "No! He is to be called John."

61They said to her, "There is no one among your relatives who has that name."

1:62
*i*ver 22

62Then they made signs*i* to his father, to find out what he would like to name the child. 63He asked for a writing tablet, and to everyone's astonishment he wrote, "His name is John." 64Immediately his mouth was opened and his tongue was loosed, and he began to speak, praising God. 65The neighbors were all filled with awe, and throughout the hill country of Judea people were talking about all these things. 66Everyone who heard this wondered about it, asking, "What then is this child going to be?" For the Lord's hand was with him.*k*

1:66
*k*Ge 39:2;
Ac 11:21

67His father Zechariah was filled with the Holy Spirit and prophesied:*l*

1:67
*l*Joel 2:28

68"Praise be to the Lord, the God of Israel,
  because he has come and has redeemed his people.*m*

1:68
*m*Ps 111:9;
Lk 7:16

69He has raised up a horn**d***n* of salvation for us
  in the house of his servant David

1:69
*n*Ps 18:2; 132:17

70(as he said through his holy prophets of long ago),*o*

1:70
*o*Jer 23:5

71salvation from our enemies
  and from the hand of all who hate us —
72to show mercy to our fathers
  and to remember his holy covenant,
73   the oath he swore to our father Abraham:
74to rescue us from the hand of our enemies,

1:74
*p*Heb 9:14

  and to enable us to serve him*p* without fear
75   in holiness and righteousness*q* before him all our days.

1:75
*q*Eph 4:24

d *69 Horn* here symbolizes strength.

DOUBTERS IN THE BIBLE	*Doubter*	*Doubtful Moment*	*Reference*
	Abraham	When God told him he would be a father in old age	Genesis 17:17
	Sarah	When she heard she would be a mother in old age	Genesis 18:12
	Moses	When God told him to return to Egypt to lead the people	Exodus 3:10–15
	Israelites	Whenever they faced difficulties in the desert	Exodus 16:1–3
	Gideon	When told he would be a judge and leader	Judges 6:14–23
	Zechariah	When told he would be a father in old age	Luke 1:18
	Thomas	When told Jesus had risen from the dead	John 20:24, 25

Many of the people God used to accomplish great things started out as real doubters. With all of them, God showed great patience. Honest doubt was not a bad starting point as long as they didn't stay there. How great a part does doubt have in your willingness to trust God?

1:59 The circumcision ceremony was an important event to the family of a Jewish baby boy. God commanded circumcision when he was beginning to form his holy nation (Genesis 17:4–14), and he reaffirmed it through Moses (Leviticus 12:1–3). This ceremony was a time of joy when friends and family members celebrated the baby's becoming part of God's covenant nation.

1:59 Family lines and family names were important to the Jews. The people naturally assumed the child would receive Zechariah's name or at least a family name. Thus they were surprised that both Elizabeth and Zechariah wanted to name the boy John, as the angel had told them to do (see 1:13).

1:62 Zechariah's relatives talked to him by gestures, because he was apparently deaf as well as speechless and had not heard what his wife had said.

1:67–79 Zechariah praised God with his first words after months of silence. In a song that is often called the *Benedictus* after the first words in the Latin translation of this passage, Zechariah prophesied the coming of a Savior who would redeem his people, and he predicted that his son John would prepare the Messiah's way. All the Old Testament prophecies were coming true — no wonder Zechariah praised God! The Messiah would come in Zechariah's lifetime, and his son had been chosen to pave the way.

1:71 The Jews were eagerly awaiting the Messiah, but they thought he would come to save them from the powerful Roman empire. They were ready for a military Savior, but not for a peaceful Messiah who would conquer sin.

1:72, 73 This was God's promise to Abraham to bless all peoples through him (see Genesis 12:3). It would be fulfilled through the Messiah, Abraham's descendant.

76And you, my child, will be called a prophet*r* of the Most High;
for you will go on before the Lord to prepare the way for him,
77to give his people the knowledge of salvation
through the forgiveness of their sins,*s*
78because of the tender mercy of our God,
by which the rising sun will come to us from heaven
79to shine on those living in darkness
and in the shadow of death,*t*
to guide our feet into the path of peace."

1:76
*r*Mt 11:9

1:77
*s*Mk 1:4

1:79
*t*Isa 9:2;
Mt 4:16

80And the child grew and became strong in spirit;*u* and he lived in the desert until he appeared publicly to Israel.

1:80
*u*Lk 2:40, 52

Jesus Is Born in Bethlehem
(9)

2 In those days Caesar Augustus*v* issued a decree that a census should be taken of the entire Roman world. 2(This was the first census that took place while Quirinius was governor of Syria.) 3And everyone went to his own town to register.

2:1
*v*Lk 3:1

4So Joseph also went up from the town of Nazareth in Galilee to Judea, to Bethlehem the town of David, because he belonged to the house and line of David. 5He went there to register with Mary, who was pledged to be married to him and was expecting a child. 6While they were there, the time came for the baby to be born, 7and she gave birth to her firstborn, a son. She wrapped him in cloths and placed him in a manger, because there was no room for them in the inn.

1:76 Zechariah had just recalled hundreds of years of God's sovereign work in history, beginning with Abraham and going on into eternity. Then, in tender contrast, he personalized the story. His son had been chosen for a key role in the drama of the ages. Although God has unlimited power, he chooses to work through frail humans who begin as helpless babies. Don't minimize what God can do through those who are faithful to him.

1:80 Why did John live out in the desert? Prophets used the isolation of the uninhabited desert to enhance their spiritual growth and to focus their message on God. By being in the desert, John remained separate from the economic and political powers so that he could aim his message against them. He also remained separate from the hypocritical religious leaders of his day. His message was different from theirs, and his life proved it.

2:1 Luke is the only Gospel writer who related the events he recorded to world history. His account was addressed to a predominantly Greek audience that would have been interested in and familiar with the political situation. Palestine was under the rule of the Roman empire; Emperor Caesar Augustus, the first Roman emperor, was in charge. The Roman rulers, considered to be like gods, stood in contrast to the tiny baby in a manger who was truly God in the flesh.

2:1 A Roman census (registration) was taken to aid military conscription or tax collection. The Jews didn't have to serve in the Roman army, but they could not avoid paying taxes. Augustus's decree went out in God's perfect timing and according to God's perfect plan to bring his Son into the world.

2:3–6 The government forced Joseph to make a long trip just to pay his taxes. His fiancée, who had to go with him, was going to have a baby any moment. But when they arrived in Bethlehem, they couldn't even find a place to stay. When we do God's will, we are not guaranteed a comfortable life. But we are promised that everything, even our discomfort, has meaning in God's plan.

2:4 God controls all history. By the decree of Emperor Augustus, Jesus was born in the very town prophesied for his birth (Micah 5:2), even though his parents did not live there.

2:4 Joseph and Mary were both descendants of David. The Old

Testament is filled with prophecies that the Messiah would be born in David's royal line (see, for example, Isaiah 11:1; Jeremiah 33:15; Ezekiel 37:24; Hosea 3:5).

THE JOURNEY TO BETHLEHEM
Caesar's decree for a census of the entire Roman empire made it necessary for Joseph and Mary to leave their hometown, Nazareth, and journey the 70 miles to the Judean village of Bethlehem.

2:7 Bands of cloth were used to keep a baby warm and give it a sense of security. These cloths were believed to protect its internal organs. The custom of wrapping infants this way is still practiced in many Mideastern countries.

2:7 This mention of the manger is the basis for the traditional belief that Jesus was born in a stable. Stables were often caves with feeding troughs (mangers) carved into the rock walls. Despite popular Christmas card pictures, the surroundings were dark and dirty. This was not the atmosphere the Jews expected as the birthplace of the Messiah King. They thought their promised Messiah would be born in royal surroundings. We should not limit God by our expectations. He is at work wherever he is needed in our sin-darkened and dirty world.

Shepherds Visit Jesus
(10)

8And there were shepherds living out in the fields nearby, keeping watch over their flocks at night. 9An angel*w* of the Lord appeared to them, and the glory of the Lord shone around them, and they were terrified. 10But the angel said to them, "Do not be afraid.*x* I bring you good news of great joy that will be for all the people. 11Today in the town of David a Savior has been born to you; he is Christ*e**y* the Lord. 12This will be a sign*z* to you: You will find a baby wrapped in cloths and lying in a manger."

13Suddenly a great company of the heavenly host appeared with the angel, praising God and saying,

14"Glory to God in the highest,
  and on earth peace*a* to men on whom his favor rests."

15When the angels had left them and gone into heaven, the shepherds said to one another, "Let's go to Bethlehem and see this thing that has happened, which the Lord has told us about."

e 11 Or *Messiah.* "The Christ" (Greek) and "the Messiah" (Hebrew) both mean "the Anointed One"; also in verse 26.

2:9
w Ac 5:19

2:10
x Mt 14:27

2:11
y Mt 1:16; 16:16, 20; Ac 2:36

2:12
z 1Sa 2:34

2:14
a Ro 5:1

TO FEAR OR NOT TO FEAR	Person	Reference
	Abraham	Genesis 15:1
	Moses	Numbers 21:34
		Deuteronomy 3:2
	Joshua	Joshua 8:1
	Jeremiah	Lamentations 3:57
	Daniel	Daniel 10:12, 19
	Zechariah	Luke 1:13
	Mary	Luke 1:30
	Shepherds	Luke 2:10
	Peter	Luke 5:10
	Paul	Acts 27:23, 24
	John	Revelation 1:17, 18

People in the Bible who were confronted by God or his angels all had one consistent response—fear. To each of them, God's response was always the same—don't be afraid. As soon as they sensed that God accepted them and wanted to communicate with them, their fear subsided. He had given them freedom to be his friends. Has he given you the same freedom?

2:7 Although our first picture of Jesus is as a baby in a manger, it must not be our last. The Christ-child in the manger has been made into a beautiful Christmas scene, but we cannot leave him there. This tiny, helpless baby lived an amazing life, died for us, ascended to heaven, and will come back to this earth as King of kings. Christ will rule the world and judge all people according to their decisions about him. Do you still picture Jesus as a baby in a manger—or is he your Lord? Make sure you don't underestimate Jesus. Let him grow up in your life.

● **2:8** God continued to reveal his Son, but not to those we might expect. Luke records that Jesus' birth was announced to shepherds in the fields. These may have been the shepherds who supplied the lambs for the temple sacrifices that were performed for the forgiveness of sin. Here the angels invited these shepherds to greet the Lamb of God (John 1:36), who would take away the sins of the whole world forever.

● **2:8–15** What a birth announcement! The shepherds were terrified, but their fear turned to joy as the angels announced the Messiah's birth. First the shepherds ran to see the baby; then they spread the word. Jesus is *your* Messiah, *your* Savior. Do you look forward to meeting him in prayer and in his Word each day? Have you discovered a Lord so wonderful that you can't help

sharing your joy with your friends?

2:9, 10 The greatest event in history had just happened! The Messiah had been born! For ages the Jews had waited for this, and when it finally occurred, the announcement came to humble shepherds. The good news about Jesus is that he comes to all, including the plain and the ordinary. He comes to anyone with a heart humble enough to accept him. Whoever you are, whatever you do, you can have Jesus in your life. Don't think you need extraordinary qualifications—he accepts you as you are.

2:11–14 Some of the Jews were waiting for a savior to deliver them from Roman rule; others hoped the Christ (Messiah) would deliver them from physical ailments. But Jesus, while healing their illnesses and establishing a spiritual kingdom, delivered them from sin. His work is more far-reaching than anyone could imagine. Christ paid the price for sin and opened the way to peace with God. He offers us more than temporary political or physical changes—he offers us new hearts that will last for eternity.

2:14 The story of Jesus' birth resounds with music that has inspired composers for 2,000 years. The angels' song is an all-time favorite. Often called the *Gloria* after its first word in the Latin translation, it is the basis of modern choral works, traditional Christmas carols, and ancient liturgical chants.

16So they hurried off and found Mary and Joseph, and the baby, who was lying in the manger. 17When they had seen him, they spread the word concerning what had been told them about this child, 18and all who heard it were amazed at what the shepherds said to them. 19But Mary treasured up all these things and pondered them in her heart. b 20The shepherds returned, glorifying and praising God for all the things they had heard and seen, which were just as they had been told.

2:19
bver 51

Mary and Joseph Bring Jesus to the Temple
(11)

21On the eighth day, when it was time to circumcise him, c he was named Jesus, the name the angel had given him before he had been conceived. d

2:21
cLk 1:59
dLk 1:31

22When the time of their purification according to the Law of Moses had been completed, Joseph and Mary took him to Jerusalem to present him to the Lord 23(as it is written in the Law of the Lord, "Every firstborn male is to be consecrated to the Lord"f), e 24and to offer a sacrifice in keeping with what is said in the Law of the Lord: "a pair of doves or two young pigeons."g

2:23
eEx 13:2, 12, 15

25Now there was a man in Jerusalem called Simeon, who was righteous and devout. He was waiting for the consolation of Israel, f and the Holy Spirit was upon him. 26It had been revealed to him by the Holy Spirit that he would not die before he had seen the Lord's Christ. 27Moved by the Spirit, he went into the temple courts. When the parents brought in the child Jesus to do for him what the custom of the Law required, 28Simeon took him in his arms and praised God, saying:

2:25
fver 38

> 29"Sovereign Lord, as you have promised, g
> you now dismiss h your servant in peace.
> 30For my eyes have seen your salvation, h
> 31 which you have prepared in the sight of all people,
> 32a light for revelation to the Gentiles
>   and for glory to your people Israel."i

2:29
gver 26

2:30
hIsa 52:10

2:32
iIsa 42:6; 49:6;
Ac 13:47

33The child's father and mother marveled at what was said about him. 34Then Simeon blessed them and said to Mary, his mother: "This child is destined to cause the fallingj and rising of many in Israel, and to be a sign that will be spoken against, 35so that the thoughts of many hearts will be revealed. And a sword will pierce your own soul too."

2:34
jMt 21:44;
1Co 1:23;
2Co 2:16;
1Pe 2:7, 8

36There was also a prophetess, Anna, the daughter of Phanuel, of the tribe of

f 23 Exodus 13:2,12 g 24 Lev. 12:8 h 29 Or promised, / now dismiss

---

2:21-24 Jewish families went through several ceremonies soon after a baby's birth: (1) *Circumcision.* Every boy was circumcised and named on the eighth day after birth (Leviticus 12:3; Luke 1:59, 60). Circumcision symbolized the Jews' separation from Gentiles and their unique relationship with God (see the second note on 1:59). (2) *Redemption of the firstborn.* A firstborn son was presented to God one month after birth (Exodus 13:2, 11–16; Numbers 18:15, 16). The ceremony included buying back — "redeeming" — the child from God through an offering. Thus the parents acknowledged that the child belonged to God, who alone has the power to give life. (3) *Purification of the mother.* For 40 days after the birth of a son and 80 days after the birth of a daughter, the mother was ceremonially unclean and could not enter the temple. At the end of her time of separation, the parents were to bring a lamb for a burnt offering and a dove or pigeon for a sin offering. The priest would sacrifice these animals and declare her to be clean. If a lamb was too expensive, the parents could bring a second dove or pigeon instead. This is what Mary and Joseph did.

Jesus was God's Son, but his family carried out these ceremonies according to God's law. Jesus was not born above the law; instead, he fulfilled it perfectly.

2:28-32 When Mary and Joseph brought Jesus to the temple to be consecrated to God, they met an old man who told them what their child would become. Simeon's song is often called the *Nunc Dimittis,* because these are the first words of its Latin translation. Simeon could die in peace because he had seen the Messiah.

2:32 The Jews were well acquainted with the Old Testament prophecies that spoke of the Messiah's blessings to their nation. They did not always give equal attention to the prophecies saying that he would bring salvation to the entire world, not just the Jews (see, for example, Isaiah 49:6). Many thought that Christ had come to save only his own people. Luke made sure his Greek audience understood that Christ had come to save *all* who believe, Gentiles as well as Jews.

2:33 Joseph and Mary "marveled" (were amazed) for three reasons: Simeon said that Jesus was a gift from God; Simeon recognized Jesus as the Messiah; and Simeon said Jesus would be a light to the entire world. This was at least the second time that Mary had been greeted with a prophecy about her son; the first time was when Elizabeth welcomed her as the mother of her Lord (1:42–45).

2:34, 35 Simeon prophesied that Jesus would have a paradoxical effect on Israel. Some would fall because of him (see Isaiah 8:14, 15), while others would rise (see Malachi 4:2). With Jesus, there would be no neutral ground: people would either joyfully accept him or totally reject him. As Jesus' mother, Mary would be grieved by the widespread rejection he would face. This is the first note of sorrow in Luke's Gospel.

Asher. She was very old; she had lived with her husband seven years after her marriage, 37and then was a widow until she was eighty-four.¹ She never left the temple but worshiped night and day, fasting and praying. ᵏ 38Coming up to them at that very moment, she gave thanks to God and spoke about the child to all who were looking forward to the redemption of Jerusalem. ˡ

39When Joseph and Mary had done everything required by the Law of the Lord, they returned to Galilee to their own town of Nazareth. 40And the child grew and became strong; he was filled with wisdom, and the grace of God was upon him. ᵐ

2:37
ᵏ1Ti 5:5

2:38
ˡver 25

2:40
ᵐver 52;
Lk 1:80

ˡ37 Or *widow for eighty-four years*

ELIZABETH

In societies like Israel, in which a woman's value was largely measured by her ability to bear children, to be aging and without children often led to personal hardship and public shame. For Elizabeth, a childless old age was a painful and lonely time during which she remained faithful to God.

Both Elizabeth and Zechariah came from priestly families. For two weeks each year, Zechariah had to go to the temple in Jerusalem to attend to his priestly duties. After one of those trips, Zechariah returned home excited, but speechless. He had to write down his good news, because he couldn't give it any other way. And what a wonderful surprise he had for his wife—their faded dream would become an exciting reality! Soon Elizabeth became pregnant, and she knew her child was a long-hoped-for gift from God.

News traveled fast among the family. Seventy miles to the north, in Nazareth, Elizabeth's relative, Mary, also unexpectedly became pregnant. Within days after the angel's message that she would bear the Messiah, Mary went to visit Elizabeth. They were instantly bound together by the unique gifts God had given them. Elizabeth knew that Mary's son would be even greater than her own, for John would be the messenger for Mary's son.

When the baby was born, Elizabeth insisted on his God-given name: John. Zechariah's written agreement freed his tongue, and everyone in town wondered what would become of this obviously special child.

Elizabeth whispered her praise as she cared for God's gift. Knowing about Mary must have made her marvel at God's timing. Things had worked out even better than she could have planned. We too need to remember that God is in control of every situation. When did you last pause to recognize God's timing in the events of your life?

Strengths and accomplishments:
• Known as a deeply spiritual woman
• Showed no doubts about God's ability to fulfill his promise
• Mother of John the Baptist
• The first woman besides Mary to hear of the coming Savior

Lessons from her life:
• God does not forget those who have been faithful to him
• God's timetable and methods do not have to conform to what we expect

Vital statistics:
• Occupation: Homemaker
• Relatives: Husband: Zechariah. Son: John the Baptist. Relative: Mary
• Contemporaries: Joseph, Herod the Great

Key verses:
"But why am I so favored, that the mother of my Lord should come to me? As soon as the sound of your greeting reached my ears, the baby in my womb leaped for joy. Blessed is she who has believed that what the Lord has said to her will be accomplished!" (Luke 1:43–45).

Elizabeth's story is told in Luke 1:5–80.

2:36 Although Simeon and Anna were very old, they had never lost their hope that they would see the Messiah. Led by the Holy Spirit, they were among the first to bear witness to Jesus. In the Jewish culture, elders were respected, so because of Simeon's and Anna's age, their prophecies carried extra weight. Our society, however, values youthfulness over wisdom, and potential contributions by the elderly are often ignored. As Christians, we should reverse those values wherever we can. Encourage older people to share their wisdom and experience. Listen carefully when they speak. Offer them your friendship and help them find ways to continue to serve God.

2:36, 37 Anna was called a prophetess, indicating that she was unusually close to God. Prophets did not necessarily predict the future. Their main role was to speak for God, proclaiming his truth.

2:39 Did Mary and Joseph return immediately to Nazareth, or did they remain in Bethlehem for a time (as implied in Matthew 2)? Apparently there is a gap of several years between verses 38 and 39—ample time for them to find a place to live in Bethlehem, flee to Egypt to escape Herod's wrath, and return to Nazareth when it was safe to do so.

2:40 Jesus was filled with wisdom, which is not surprising since he stayed in close contact with his heavenly Father. James 1:5 says God gives wisdom generously to all who ask. Like Jesus, we can grow in wisdom by walking with God.

Jesus Speaks with the Religious Teachers
(15)

41Every year his parents went to Jerusalem for the Feast of the Passover.[n] 2:41
42When he was twelve years old, they went up to the Feast, according to the cus- [n]Ex 23:15;
tom. 43After the Feast was over, while his parents were returning home, the boy Dt 16:1-8
Jesus stayed behind in Jerusalem, but they were unaware of it. 44Thinking he was
in their company, they traveled on for a day. Then they began looking for him
among their relatives and friends. 45When they did not find him, they went back to
Jerusalem to look for him. 46After three days they found him in the temple courts,
sitting among the teachers, listening to them and asking them questions. 47Every-
one who heard him was amazed at his understanding and his answers. 48When his
parents saw him, they were astonished. His mother said to him, "Son, why have
you treated us like this? Your father and I have been anxiously searching for you."
49"Why were you searching for me?" he asked. "Didn't you know I had to be in
my Father's house?"[o] 50But they did not understand what he was saying to them. 2:49
51Then he went down to Nazareth with them and was obedient to them. But his [o]Jn 2:16
mother treasured all these things in her heart.[p] 52And Jesus grew in wisdom and 2:51
stature, and in favor with God and men.[q] [p]ver 19

2:52
[q]ver 40

John the Baptist Prepares the Way for Jesus
(16/Matthew 3:1–12; Mark 1:1–8)

3 In the fifteenth year of the reign of Tiberius Caesar—when Pontius Pilate was
governor of Judea, Herod tetrarch of Galilee, his brother Philip tetrarch of Itu-
rea and Traconitis, and Lysanias tetrarch of Abilene— 2during the high priesthood

---

2:41, 42 According to God's law, every male was required to go to Jerusalem three times a year for the great festivals (Deuteronomy 16:16). In the spring, the Passover was celebrated, followed immediately by the week-long Feast of Unleavened Bread. Passover commemorated the night of the Jews' escape from Egypt when God had killed the Egyptian firstborn but had passed over Israelite homes (see Exodus 12:21–36). Passover was the most important of the three annual festivals.

2:43–45 At age 12, Jesus was considered almost an adult, and so he didn't spend a lot of time with his parents during the feast. Those who attended these feasts often traveled in caravans for protection from robbers along the Palestine roads. It was customary for the women and children to travel at the front of the caravan, with the men bringing up the rear. A 12-year-old boy conceivably could have been in either group, and both Mary and Joseph assumed Jesus was with the other one. But when the caravan left Jerusalem, Jesus stayed behind, absorbed in his discussion with the religious leaders.

2:46, 47 The temple courts were famous throughout Judea as a place of learning. The apostle Paul studied in Jerusalem, perhaps in the temple courts, under Gamaliel, one of its foremost teachers (Acts 22:3). At the time of the Passover, the greatest rabbis of the land would assemble to teach and to discuss great truths among themselves. The coming Messiah would no doubt have been a popular discussion topic, for everyone was expecting him soon. Jesus would have been eager to listen and to ask probing questions. It was not his youth, but the depth of his wisdom, that astounded these teachers.

2:48 Mary had to let go of her child and let him become a man, God's Son, the Messiah. Fearful that she hadn't been careful enough with this God-given child, she searched frantically for him. But she was looking for a boy, not the young man who was in the temple astounding the religious leaders with his questions. It is hard to let go of people or projects we have nurtured. It is both sweet and painful to see our children as adults, our students as teachers, our subordinates as managers, our inspirations as institutions. But when the time comes to step back and let go, we must do so in spite of the hurt. Then our protégés can exercise their wings, take flight, and soar to the heights God intended for them.

• **2:49, 50** This is the first mention of Jesus' awareness that he was God's Son. But even though he knew his real Father, he did not reject his earthly parents. He went back to Nazareth with them and lived under their authority for another 18 years. God's people do not despise human relationships or family responsibilities. If the Son of God obeyed his human parents, how much more should we honor our family members! Don't use commitment to God's work to justify neglecting your family.

2:50 Jesus' parents didn't understand what he meant about his Father's house. They didn't realize he was making a distinction between his earthly father and his heavenly Father. Jesus knew that he had a unique relationship with God. Although Mary and Joseph knew he was God's Son, they didn't understand what his mission would involve. Besides, they had to raise him, along with his brothers and sisters (Matthew 13:55, 56), as a normal child. They knew he was unique, but they did not know what was going on in his mind.

• **2:52** The Bible does not record any events of the next 18 years of Jesus' life, but Jesus undoubtedly was learning and maturing. As the oldest in a large family, he assisted Joseph in his carpentry work. Joseph may have died during this time, leaving Jesus to provide for the family. The normal routines of daily life gave Jesus a solid understanding of the Judean people.

• **2:52** The second chapter of Luke shows us that although Jesus was unique, he had a normal childhood and adolescence. In terms of development, he went through the same progression we do. He grew physically and mentally, he related to other people, and he was loved by God. A full human life is not unbalanced. It was important to Jesus—and it should be important to all believers—to develop fully and harmoniously in each of these key areas: physical, mental, social, and spiritual.

3:1 Tiberius, the Roman emperor, ruled from A.D. 14 to 37. Pilate was the Roman governor responsible for the province of Judea; Herod (Antipas) and Philip were half brothers and sons of the cruel Herod the Great, who had been dead more than 20 years. Antipas, Philip, Pilate, and Lysanias apparently had equal powers in governing their separate territories. All were subject to Rome and

of Annas and Caiaphas, the word of God came to John son of Zechariah in the desert. ³He went into all the country around the Jordan, preaching a baptism of

Motherhood is a painful privilege. Young Mary of Nazareth had the unique privilege of being mother to the very Son of God. Yet the pains and pleasures of her motherhood can be understood by mothers everywhere. Mary was the only human present at Jesus' birth who also witnessed his death. She saw him arrive as her baby son, and she watched him die as her Savior.

Until Gabriel's unexpected visit, Mary's life was quite satisfactory. She had recently become engaged to a carpenter, Joseph, and was anticipating married life. But her life was about to change forever.

Angels don't usually make appointments before visiting. As if she were being congratulated for winning the grand prize in a contest she had never entered, Mary found the angel's greeting puzzling and his presence frightening. What she heard next was the news almost every woman in Israel hoped to hear—that her child would be the Messiah, God's promised Savior. Mary did not doubt the message, but rather asked how pregnancy would be possible. Gabriel told her the baby would be God's Son. Her answer was the one God waits in vain to hear from so many other people: "I am the Lord's servant. . . . May it be to me as you have said" (Luke 1:38). Later, her song of joy shows us how well she knew God, for her thoughts were filled with his words from the Old Testament.

Within a few weeks of his birth, Jesus was taken to the temple to be dedicated to God. There Joseph and Mary were met by two devout people, Simeon and Anna, who recognized the child as the Messiah and praised God. Simeon directed some words to Mary that must have come to her mind many times in the years that followed: "A sword will pierce your own soul" (Luke 2:35). A big part of her painful privilege of motherhood would be to see her son rejected and crucified by the people he came to save.

We can imagine that even if she had known all she would suffer as Jesus' mother, Mary would still have given the same response. Are you, like Mary, available to be used by God?

Strengths and accomplishments:
• The mother of Jesus, the Messiah
• The one human who was with Jesus from birth to death
• Willing to be available to God
• Knew and applied Old Testament Scriptures

Lessons from her life:
• God's best servants are often ordinary people available to him
• God's plans involve extraordinary events in ordinary people's lives
• A person's character is revealed by his or her response to the unexpected

Vital statistics:
• Where: Nazareth, Bethlehem
• Occupation: Homemaker
• Relatives: Husband: Joseph. Relatives: Zechariah and Elizabeth. Children: Jesus, James, Joseph, Judas, Simon, and daughters

Key verse:
" 'I am the Lord's servant,' Mary answered. 'May it be to me as you have said.' Then the angel left her" (Luke 1:38).

Mary's story is told throughout the Gospels. She is also mentioned in Acts 1:14.

responsible for keeping peace in their respective lands.

3:2 Under Jewish law there was only one high priest. He was appointed from Aaron's line, and he held his position for life. By this time, however, the religious system had been corrupted, and the Roman government was appointing its own religious leaders to maintain greater control over the Jews. Apparently the Roman authorities had deposed the Jewish-appointed Annas and had replaced him with Annas's son-in-law, Caiaphas. Nevertheless, Annas retained his title (see Acts 4:6) and probably also much of the power it carried. Because the Jews believed the high priest's position to be for life, they would have continued to call Annas their high priest.

3:2 This is John the Baptist, whose birth story is told in chapter 1. See his Profile in John 1.

3:2 Pilate, Herod, and Caiaphas were the most powerful leaders in Palestine, but they were upstaged by a desert prophet from rural Judea. God chose to speak through the loner John the Baptist, who has gone down in history as greater than any of the rulers of his day. How often we judge people by our culture's standards—power, wealth, beauty—and miss the truly great people through whom God works! Greatness is not measured by what you have, but by your faith in God. Like John, give yourself entirely to God so God's power can work through you.

3:3 Repentance has two sides—turning away from sins and turning toward God. To be truly repentant, we must do both. We can't just say we believe and then live any way we choose (see 3:7, 8), and neither can we simply live a morally correct life without a personal relationship with God, because that cannot bring forgiveness from sin. Determine to rid your life of any sins God points out, and put your trust in him alone to guide you.

repentance for the forgiveness of sins. ⁴As is written in the book of the words of Isaiah the prophet:

> "A voice of one calling in the desert,
> 'Prepare the way for the Lord,
>   make straight paths for him.
> ⁵Every valley shall be filled in,
>   every mountain and hill made low.
> The crooked roads shall become straight,
>   the rough ways smooth.
> ⁶And all mankind will see God's salvation.' "ʲʳ

⁷John said to the crowds coming out to be baptized by him, "You brood of vipers! Who warned you to flee from the coming wrath? ⁸Produce fruit in keeping with repentance. And do not begin to say to yourselves, 'We have Abraham as our father.'ˢ For I tell you that out of these stones God can raise up children for Abraham. ⁹The ax is already at the root of the trees, and every tree that does not produce good fruit will be cut down and thrown into the fire."

¹⁰"What should we do then?"ᵗ the crowd asked.

¹¹John answered, "The man with two tunics should share with him who has none, and the one who has food should do the same."

¹²Tax collectors also came to be baptized.ᵘ "Teacher," they asked, "what should we do?"

¹³"Don't collect any more than you are required to,"ᵛ he told them.

¹⁴Then some soldiers asked him, "And what should we do?"

He replied, "Don't extort money and don't accuse people falselyʷ—be content with your pay."

16 Isaiah 40:3-5

3:6 ʳPs 98:2; Isa 52:10; Lk 2:30
3:8 ˢJn 8:33, 39
3:10 ᵗAc 2:37
3:12 ᵘLk 7:29
3:13 ᵛLk 19:8
3:14 ʷEx 23:1; Lev 19:11

3:4, 5 In John's day, before a king took a trip, messengers would tell those he was planning to visit to prepare the roads for him. Similarly John told his listeners to make their lives ready so the Lord could come to them. To prepare for Jesus' coming to us, we must focus on him, listen to his words, and respond obediently to his directions.

3:6 This book was written to a non-Jewish audience. Luke quoted from Isaiah to show that salvation is for all people, not just the Jews (Isaiah 40:3-5; 52:10). John the Baptist called all mankind to prepare to meet Jesus. That includes you, no matter what your standing is with religious organizations and authorities. Don't let feelings of being an outsider cause you to hold back. No one who wants to follow Jesus is an outsider in God's kingdom.

3:7 What motivates your faith—fear of the future, or a desire to be a better person in a better world? Some people wanted to be baptized by John so they could escape eternal punishment, but they didn't turn to God for salvation. John had harsh words for such people. He knew that God values reformation above ritual. Is your faith motivated by a desire for a new, changed life, or is it only like a vaccination or insurance policy against possible disaster?

3:8 Many of John's hearers were shocked when he said that being Abraham's descendants was not enough for God. The religious leaders relied more on their family lines than on their faith for their standing with God. For them, religion was inherited. But a personal relationship with God is not handed down from parents to children. Everyone has to commit to it on his or her own. Don't rely on someone else's faith for your salvation. Put your own faith in Jesus, and then exercise it every day.

3:8, 9 Confession of sins and a changed life are inseparable. Faith without deeds is dead (James 2:14-26). Jesus' harshest words were to the respectable religious leaders who lacked the desire for real change. They wanted to be known as religious authorities, but they didn't want to change their hearts and minds.

Thus their lives were unproductive. Repentance must be tied to action, or it isn't real. Following Jesus means more than saying the right words; it means acting on what he says.

3:11-14 John's message demanded at least three specific responses: (1) share what you have with those who need it, (2) whatever your job is, do it well and with fairness, and (3) be content with what you're earning. John had no time to address comforting messages to those who lived careless or selfish lives—he was calling the people to right living. What changes can you make in sharing what you have, doing your work honestly and well, and being content?

3:12 Tax collectors were notorious for their dishonesty. Romans gathered funds for their government by farming out the collection privilege. Tax collectors earned their own living by adding a sizable sum—whatever they could get away with—to the total and keeping this money for themselves. Unless the people revolted and risked Roman retaliation, they had to pay whatever was demanded. Obviously they hated the tax collectors, who were generally dishonest, greedy, and ready to betray their own countrymen for cold cash. Yet, said John, God would accept even these men; God desires to pour out mercy on those who confess, and then to give strength to live changed lives.

3:12-14 John's message took root in unexpected places—among the poor, the dishonest, and even the hated occupation army. These people were painfully aware of their needs. Too often we confuse respectability with right living. They are not the same. Respectability can even hinder right living if it keeps us from seeing our need for God. If you had to choose, would you protect your character or your reputation?

3:14 These soldiers were the Roman troops sent to keep peace in this distant province. Many of them oppressed the poor and used their power to take advantage of all the people. John called them to repent and change their ways.

15The people were waiting expectantly and were all wondering in their hearts if John might possibly be the Christ.k 16John answered them all, "I baptize you withl water. But one more powerful than I will come, the thongs of whose sandals I am not worthy to untie. He will baptize you with the Holy Spirit and with fire. 17His winnowing forkx is in his hand to clear his threshing floor and to gather the wheat into his barn, but he will burn up the chaff with unquenchable fire."y 18And with many other words John exhorted the people and preached the good news to them.

3:17
xIsa 30:24
yMt 13:30

Herod Puts John in Prison
(26)

19But when John rebuked Herod the tetrarch because of Herodias, his brother's wife, and all the other evil things he had done, 20Herod added this to them all: He locked John up in prison.z

3:20
zMt 14:3, 4

John Baptizes Jesus
(17/Matthew 3:13–17; Mark 1:9–11)

21When all the people were being baptized, Jesus was baptized too. And as he was praying,a heaven was opened 22and the Holy Spirit descended on himb in bodily form like a dove. And a voice came from heaven: "You are my Son, whom I love; with you I am well pleased."

3:21
aMt 14:23;
Lk 5:16; 9:18, 28
3:22
bAc 10:38

k 15 Or *Messiah* l 16 Or *in*

● **3:15** There had not been a prophet in Israel for more than 400 years. It was widely believed that when the Messiah came, prophecy would reappear (Joel 2:28, 29; Malachi 3:1; 4:5). When John burst onto the scene, the people were excited. He was obviously a great prophet, and they were sure that the eagerly awaited age of the Messiah had come. Some, in fact, thought John himself was the Messiah. John spoke like the prophets of old, saying that the people must turn from their sin to avoid punishment and turn to God to experience his mercy and approval. This is a message for all times and places, but John spoke it with particular urgency — he was preparing the people for the coming Messiah.

● **3:16** John's baptism with water symbolized the washing away of sins. His baptism coordinated with his message of repentance and reformation. Jesus' baptism with fire includes the power needed to do God's will. The baptism with the Holy Spirit was fulfilled at Pentecost (Acts 2) when the Holy Spirit came upon believers in the form of tongues of fire, empowering them to proclaim Jesus' resurrection in many languages. The baptism with fire also symbolizes the work of the Holy Spirit in bringing God's judgment on those who refuse to repent.

3:17 John warned of impending judgment by comparing those who refuse to live for God to chaff, the useless outer husk of the grain. By contrast, he compared those who repent and reform their lives to the nourishing wheat itself. The winnowing fork was a pitchfork used to toss wheat so that the kernels would separate from the blades. Those who refuse to be used by God will be discarded because they have no value in furthering God's work. Those who repent and believe, however, hold great value in God's eyes because they are beginning a new life of productive service for him.

3:19, 20 In these two verses Luke flashes forward to continue his explanation about John the Baptist. See the Harmony of the Gospels for the chronological order of events.

3:19, 20 This is Herod Antipas (see Mark 6 for his Profile). Herodias was Herod's niece and also his brother's wife. She treacherously plotted John the Baptist's death (Matthew 14:1–12). The Herods were a murderous and deceitful family. Rebuking a tyrannical Roman official who could imprison and execute him was ex-tremely dangerous, yet that is what John did. Herod seemingly had the last word, but the story is not finished. At the last judgment, Herod, not John, will be the one in danger.

3:21 Luke emphasizes Jesus' human nature. Jesus was born to humble parents, a birth unannounced except to shepherds and foreigners. This baptism recorded here was the first public declaration of Jesus' ministry. Instead of going to Jerusalem and identifying with the established religious leaders, Jesus went to a river and identified himself with those who were repenting of sin. When Jesus, at age 12, visited the temple, he understood his mission (2:49). Eighteen years later, at his baptism, he began carrying it out. And as Jesus prayed, God spoke and confirmed his decision to act. God was breaking into human history through Jesus the Christ.

3:21, 22 If baptism was a sign of repentance from sin, why did Jesus ask to be baptized? Several explanations are often given: (1) Jesus' baptism was one step in fulfilling his earthly mission of identifying with our humanity and sin; (2) by endorsing the rite of baptism, Jesus was giving us an example to follow; (3) Jesus was announcing the beginning of his public ministry; (4) Jesus was being baptized for the sins of the nation. The Holy Spirit's appearance in the form of a dove showed that God's plan for salvation was centered in Jesus. Jesus was the perfect human who didn't need baptism for repentance, but he was baptized anyway on our behalf.

3:21, 22 This is one of several places in Scripture where all the members of the Trinity are mentioned — Father, Son, and Holy Spirit. In the traditional words of the church, the one God exists in three persons but one substance, coeternal and coequal. No amount of explanation can adequately portray the power and intricacy of this unique relationship. There are no perfect analogies in nature because there is no other relationship like the Trinity.

The Ancestors of Jesus
(3/Matthew 1:1–17)

23Now Jesus himself was about thirty years old when he began his ministry. *c* He was the son, so it was thought, of Joseph,

3:23
*c*Mt 4:17;
Ac 1:1

the son of Heli, 24the son of Matthat,
the son of Levi, the son of Melki,
the son of Jannai, the son of Joseph,
25the son of Mattathias, the son of Amos,
the son of Nahum, the son of Esli,
the son of Naggai, 26the son of Maath,
the son of Mattathias, the son of Semein,
the son of Josech, the son of Joda,
27the son of Joanan, the son of Rhesa,
the son of Zerubbabel, *d* the son of Shealtiel,
the son of Neri, 28the son of Melki,
the son of Addi, the son of Cosam,
the son of Elmadam, the son of Er,
29the son of Joshua, the son of Eliezer,
the son of Jorim, the son of Matthat,
the son of Levi, 30the son of Simeon,
the son of Judah, the son of Joseph,
the son of Jonam, the son of Eliakim,
31the son of Melea, the son of Menna,
the son of Mattatha, the son of Nathan, *e*
the son of David, 32the son of Jesse,
the son of Obed, the son of Boaz,
the son of Salmon, *m* the son of Nahshon,
33the son of Amminadab, the son of Ram, *n*
the son of Hezron, the son of Perez, *f*
the son of Judah, 34the son of Jacob,
the son of Isaac, the son of Abraham,
the son of Terah, the son of Nahor, *g*
35the son of Serug, the son of Reu,
the son of Peleg, the son of Eber,
the son of Shelah, 36the son of Cainan,
the son of Arphaxad, *h* the son of Shem,
the son of Noah, the son of Lamech,
37the son of Methuselah, the son of Enoch,
the son of Jared, the son of Mahalalel,
the son of Kenan, 38the son of Enosh,
the son of Seth, the son of Adam,
the son of God.

3:27
*d*Mt 1:12

3:31
*e*2Sa 5:14;
1Ch 3:5

3:33
*f*Ru 4:18-22;
1Ch 2:10-12

3:34
*g*Ge 11:24, 26

3:36
*h*Ge 11:12

m 32 Some early manuscripts *Sala*   *n 33* Some manuscripts *Amminadab, the son of Admin, the son of Arni*; other manuscripts vary widely.

● **3:23** Imagine the Savior of the world working in a small-town carpenter's shop until he was 30 years old! It seems incredible that Jesus would have been content to remain in Nazareth all that time, but he patiently trusted the Father's timing for his life and ministry. Thirty was the prescribed age for priests to begin their ministry (Numbers 4:3). Joseph was 30 years old when he began serving the king of Egypt (Genesis 41:46), and David was 30 years old when he began to reign over Judah (2 Samuel 5:4). Age 30, then, was a good time to begin an important task in the Jewish culture. Like Jesus, we need to resist the temptation to jump ahead before receiving the Spirit's direction. Are you waiting and wondering what your next step should be? Don't jump ahead — trust God's timing.

3:23 Heli may have been Joseph's father-in-law. If that were the case, this would be Mary's genealogy that Luke may have received personally from her. It is fitting that Luke would show Mary's genealogy because of the prominence he gives women in his Gospel.

3:23–38 Matthew's genealogy goes back to Abraham and shows that Jesus was related to all Jews (Matthew 1). Luke's genealogy goes back to Adam, showing that Jesus is related to all human beings. This is consistent with Luke's picture of Jesus as the Savior of the whole world.

Satan Tempts Jesus in the Desert
(18/Matthew 4:1–11; Mark 1:12, 13)

4:1
*i*ver 14, 18
*j*Lk 2:27
4:2
*k*Ex 34:28

4 Jesus, full of the Holy Spirit,*i* returned from the Jordan and was led by the Spirit*j* in the desert, ²where for forty days*k* he was tempted by the devil. He ate nothing during those days, and at the end of them he was hungry.

³The devil said to him, "If you are the Son of God, tell this stone to become bread."

4:4
*l*Dt 8:3

⁴Jesus answered, "It is written: 'Man does not live on bread alone.'**o**"*l*

⁵The devil led him up to a high place and showed him in an instant all the kingdoms of the world. ⁶And he said to him, "I will give you all their authority and splendor, for it has been given to me,*m* and I can give it to anyone I want to. ⁷So if you worship me, it will all be yours."

4:6
*m*Jn 12:31

o *4* Deut. 8:3

4:1 Sometimes we feel that if the Holy Spirit leads us, it will always be "beside quiet waters" (Psalm 23:2). But that is not necessarily true. He led Jesus into the desert for a long and difficult time of testing, and he may also lead us into difficult situations. When facing trials, first make sure you haven't brought them on yourself through sin or unwise choices. If you find no sin to confess or unwise behavior to change, then ask God to strengthen you for your test. Finally, be careful to follow faithfully wherever the Holy Spirit leads.

4:1 Temptation will often come after a high point in our spiritual lives or ministries (see 1 Kings 18; 19 for Elijah's story of great victory followed by despair). Remember that Satan chooses the times for his attacks. We need to be on our guard in times of victory just as much as in times of discouragement. See the third note on Matthew 4:1ff for a comment on how Satan tempts us when we're vulnerable.

4:1, 2 The devil, who tempted Adam and Eve in the garden, also tempted Jesus in the desert. Satan is a real being, a created but rebellious fallen angel, and not a symbol or an idea. He constantly fights against God and those who follow and obey God. Jesus was a prime target for the devil's temptations. Satan succeeded with Adam and Eve, and he hoped to succeed with Jesus too.

4:1–13 Knowing and obeying God's Word is an effective weapon against temptation, the only *offensive* weapon provided in the Christian's "armor" (Ephesians 6:17). Jesus used Scripture to counter Satan's attacks, and you can too. But to use it effectively you must have faith in God's promises, because Satan also knows Scripture and is adept at twisting it to suit his purpose. Obeying the Scriptures is more important than simply having a verse to quote, so read them daily and apply them to your life. Then your "sword" will always be sharp.

● **4:2** Why was it necessary for Jesus to be tempted? First, temptation is part of the human experience. For Jesus to be fully human, for him to understand us completely, he had to face temptation (see Hebrews 4:15). Second, Jesus had to undo Adam's work. Adam, though created perfect, gave in to temptation and passed sin on to the whole human race. Jesus, by contrast, resisted Satan. His victory offers salvation to all of Adam's descendants (see Romans 5:12–19).

4:3 Satan may tempt us to doubt Christ's true identity. He knows that once we begin to question whether or not Jesus is God, it's far easier to get us to do what he wants. Times of questioning can help us sort out our beliefs and strengthen our faith, but those times can also be dangerous. If you are dealing with doubt, realize that you are especially vulnerable to temptation. Even as you search for answers, protect yourself by meditating on the unshakable truths of God's Word.

4:3 Sometimes what we are tempted to do isn't wrong in itself. Turning stones into bread wasn't necessarily bad. The sin was not in the act but in the reason behind it. The devil was trying to get Je-

sus to take a shortcut, to solve Jesus' immediate problem at the expense of his long-range goals, to seek comfort at the sacrifice of his discipline. Satan often works that way — persuading us to take action, even right action, for the wrong reason or at the wrong time. The fact that something is not wrong in itself does not mean that it is good for you at a given time. Many people sin by attempting to fulfill legitimate desires outside of God's will or ahead of his timetable. First ask, "Is the Holy Spirit leading me to do this? Or is Satan trying to get me off the track?"

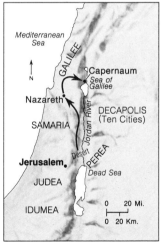

JESUS' TEMPTATION AND RETURN TO GALILEE
Jesus was tempted by Satan in the rough Desert of Judea before returning to his boyhood home, Nazareth. John's Gospel tells of Jesus' journeys in Galilee, Samaria, and Judea (see John 1–4) before he moved to Capernaum to set up his base of operations (see Matthew 4:12, 13).

4:3ff Often we are tempted not through our weaknesses, but through our strengths. The devil tempted Jesus where he was strong. Jesus had power over stones, the kingdoms of the world, and even angels, and Satan wanted him to use that power without regard to his mission. When we give in to the devil and wrongly use our strengths, we become proud and self-reliant. Trusting in our own powers, we feel little need of God. To avoid this trap, we must realize that all our strengths are God's gifts to us, and we must dedicate those strengths to his service.

4:6, 7 The devil arrogantly hoped to succeed in his rebellion against God by diverting Jesus from his mission and winning his worship. "This world is mine, not God's," he was saying, "and if you hope to do anything worthwhile here, you'd better recognize that fact." Jesus didn't argue with Satan about who owns the world, but Jesus refused to validate Satan's claim by worshiping him. Jesus knew that he would redeem the world through giving up his life on the cross, not through making an alliance with a corrupt angel.

8Jesus answered, "It is written: 'Worship the Lord your God and serve him only.'ᵖ"ⁿ

9The devil led him to Jerusalem and had him stand on the highest point of the temple. "If you are the Son of God," he said, "throw yourself down from here. 10For it is written:

> " 'He will command his angels concerning you
>   to guard you carefully;
> 11they will lift you up in their hands,
>   so that you will not strike your foot against a stone.'q"o

12Jesus answered, "It says: 'Do not put the Lord your God to the test.'r"p

13When the devil had finished all this tempting,q he left him until an opportune time.

4:8
ⁿDt 6:13

4:11
oPs 91:11, 12

4:12
pDt 6:16

4:13
qHeb 4:15

B. MESSAGE AND MINISTRY OF JESUS, THE SAVIOR (4:14—21:38)

Luke accurately records the actions and teachings of Christ, helping us understand the way of salvation. There is much unique material in Luke, especially the parables of Jesus. Jesus came to teach us how to live and how to find salvation. How carefully, then, we should study the words and life of our Savior.

1. Jesus' ministry in Galilee

Jesus Preaches in Galilee
(30/Matthew 4:12–17; Mark 1:14, 15; John 4:43–45)

14Jesus returned to Galileeʳ in the power of the Spirit, and news about him spread through the whole countryside. 15He taught in their synagogues, and everyone praised him.

4:14
ʳMt 4:12

Jesus Is Rejected at Nazareth
(32)

16He went to Nazareth, where he had been brought up, and on the Sabbath day he went into the synagogue,ˢ as was his custom. And he stood up to read. 17The scroll of the prophet Isaiah was handed to him. Unrolling it, he found the place where it is written:

4:16
ˢMt 13:54

> 18"The Spirit of the Lord is on me,
>   because he has anointed me
>   to preach good news to the poor.
> He has sent me to proclaim freedom for the prisoners
>   and recovery of sight for the blind,
>   to release the oppressed,
> 19   to proclaim the year of the Lord's favor."ˢᵗ

4:19
ᵗIsa 61:1, 2

p 8 Deut. 6:13   q 11 Psalm 91:11,12   r 12 Deut. 6:16   s 19 Isaiah 61:1,2

4:9-11 Here the devil misinterpreted Scripture. The intention of Psalm 91 is to show God's protection of his people, not to incite them to use God's power for sensational or foolish displays.

4:13 Christ's defeat of the devil in the desert was decisive but not final. Throughout his ministry, Jesus would confront Satan in many forms. Too often we see temptation as once and for all. In reality, we need to be constantly on guard against the devil's ongoing attacks. Where are you most susceptible to temptation right now? How are you preparing to withstand it?

4:16 Synagogues were very important in Jewish religious life. During the exile when the Jews no longer had their temple, synagogues were established as places of worship on the Sabbath and as schools for young boys during the week. Synagogues continued to exist even after the temple was rebuilt. A synagogue could be set up in any town where there were at least ten Jewish families. It was administered by one leader and an assistant. At the synagogue, the leader often would invite a visiting rabbi to read

from the Scriptures and to teach.

4:16 Jesus went to the synagogue "as was his custom." Even though he was the perfect Son of God, and his local synagogue undoubtedly left much to be desired, Jesus attended services every week. His example makes our excuses for not attending church sound weak and self-serving. Make regular worship a part of your life.

4:17-21 Jesus was quoting from Isaiah 61:1, 2. Isaiah pictures the deliverance of Israel from exile in Babylon as a Year of Jubilee when all debts are cancelled, all slaves are freed, and all property is returned to original owners (Leviticus 25). But the release from Babylonian exile had not brought the fulfillment the people had expected; they were still a conquered and oppressed people. So Isaiah must have been referring to a future Messianic age. Jesus boldly announced, "Today this scripture is fulfilled in your hearing." Jesus was proclaiming himself as the One who would bring this good news to pass, but in a way that the people would not yet be able to grasp.

4:20
u ver 17

4:22
v Mt 13:54, 55;
Jn 6:42

4:24
w Mt 13:57;
Jn 4:44

4:25
x 1Ki 18:1;
Jas 5:17, 18

4:26
y 1Ki 17:8-16

4:27
z 2Ki 5:1-14

4:29
a Nu 15:35;
Ac 7:58

4:30
b Jn 8:59; 10:39

4:31
c Mt 4:13

4:32
d Mt 7:28

4:34
e ver 41

4:35
f ver 39, 41;
Mt 8:26

4:36
g ver 32

4:37
h ver 14

20Then he rolled up the scroll, gave it back to the attendant and sat down. u The eyes of everyone in the synagogue were fastened on him, 21and he began by saying to them, "Today this scripture is fulfilled in your hearing."

22All spoke well of him and were amazed at the gracious words that came from his lips. "Isn't this Joseph's son?" they asked. v

23Jesus said to them, "Surely you will quote this proverb to me: 'Physician, heal yourself! Do here in your hometown what we have heard that you did in Capernaum.' "

24"I tell you the truth," he continued, "no prophet is accepted in his hometown. w 25I assure you that there were many widows in Israel in Elijah's time, when the sky was shut for three and a half years and there was a severe famine throughout the land. x 26Yet Elijah was not sent to any of them, but to a widow in Zarephath in the region of Sidon. y 27And there were many in Israel with leprosyt in the time of Elisha the prophet, yet not one of them was cleansed — only Naaman the Syrian."z

28All the people in the synagogue were furious when they heard this. 29They got up, drove him out of the town, a and took him to the brow of the hill on which the town was built, in order to throw him down the cliff. 30But he walked right through the crowd and went on his way. b

Jesus Teaches with Great Authority
(34/Mark 1:21–28)

31Then he went down to Capernaum, c a town in Galilee, and on the Sabbath began to teach the people. 32They were amazed at his teaching, d because his message had authority.

33In the synagogue there was a man possessed by a demon, an evilu spirit. He cried out at the top of his voice, 34"Ha! What do you want with us, Jesus of Nazareth? Have you come to destroy us? I know who you are — the Holy One of God!"e

35"Be quiet!" Jesus said sternly. f "Come out of him!" Then the demon threw the man down before them all and came out without injuring him.

36All the people were amazed and said to each other, "What is this teaching? With authorityg and power he gives orders to evil spirits and they come out!" 37And the news about him spread throughout the surrounding area. h

Jesus Heals Peter's Mother-in-Law and Many Others
(35/Matthew 8:14–17; Mark 1:29–34)

38Jesus left the synagogue and went to the home of Simon. Now Simon's mother-in-law was suffering from a high fever, and they asked Jesus to help her.

t 27 The Greek word was used for various diseases affecting the skin—not necessarily leprosy. u 33 Greek unclean; also in verse 36

● **4:24** Even Jesus himself was not accepted as a prophet in his hometown. Many people have a similar attitude — an expert is anyone who carries a briefcase and comes from more than 200 miles away. Don't be surprised when your Christian life and faith are not easily understood or accepted by those who know you well.

4:28 Jesus' remarks filled the people of Nazareth with rage because he was saying that God sometimes chose to reach Gentiles rather than Jews. Jesus implied that his hearers were as unbelieving as the citizens of the northern kingdom of Israel in the days of Elijah and Elisha, a time notorious for its great wickedness.

4:31 Jesus had recently moved to Capernaum from Nazareth (Matthew 4:13). Capernaum was a thriving city with great wealth as well as great decadence. Because it was the headquarters for many Roman troops, word about Jesus could spread all over the Roman empire.

4:31 Why was Jesus allowed to teach in the synagogues? Jesus was taking advantage of the policy of allowing visitors to teach. Itinerant rabbis were always welcome to speak to those gathered each Sabbath in the synagogues. The apostle Paul also profited from this practice (see Acts 13:5; 14:1).

4:33 A man possessed by a demon was in the synagogue where Jesus was teaching. This man made his way into the place of worship and verbally abused Jesus. It is naive to think that we will be sheltered from evil in the church. Satan is happy to invade our presence wherever and whenever he can. But Jesus' authority is much greater than Satan's; and where Jesus is present, demons cannot stay for long.

4:34–36 The people were amazed at Jesus' authority to drive out demons — evil spirits ruled by Satan and sent to harass people and tempt them to sin. Demons are fallen angels who have joined Satan in rebellion against God. Demons can cause a person to become mute, deaf, blind, or insane. Jesus faced many demons during his time on earth, and he always exerted authority over them. Not only did the evil spirit leave this man; Luke records that the man was not even injured.

4:36 Evil permeates our world, and it is no wonder that people are often fearful. But Jesus' power is far greater than Satan's. The first step toward conquering fear of evil is to recognize Jesus' authority and power. He has overcome all evil, including Satan himself.

³⁹So he bent over her and rebuked*ⁱ* the fever, and it left her. She got up at once and began to wait on them.

⁴⁰When the sun was setting, the people brought to Jesus all who had various kinds of sickness, and laying his hands on each one,*ʲ* he healed them.*ᵏ* ⁴¹Moreover, demons came out of many people, shouting, "You are the Son of God!"*ˡ* But he rebuked them and would not allow them to speak,*ᵐ* because they knew he was the Christ.*ᵛ*

4:39
*ⁱ*ver 35, 41

4:40
*ʲ*Mk 5:23
*ᵏ*Mt 4:23

4:41
*ˡ*Mt 4:3
*ᵐ*Mt 8:4

Jesus Preaches throughout Galilee
(36/Matthew 4:23–25; Mark 1:35–39)

⁴²At daybreak Jesus went out to a solitary place. The people were looking for him and when they came to where he was, they tried to keep him from leaving them. ⁴³But he said, "I must preach the good news of the kingdom of God to the other towns also, because that is why I was sent." ⁴⁴And he kept on preaching in the synagogues of Judea.*ʷ*

Jesus Provides a Miraculous Catch of Fish
(37)

5 One day as Jesus was standing by the Lake of Gennesaret,*ˣ* with the people crowding around him and listening to the word of God, ²he saw at the water's edge two boats, left there by the fishermen, who were washing their nets. ³He got into one of the boats, the one belonging to Simon, and asked him to put out a little from shore. Then he sat down and taught the people from the boat.*ⁿ*

⁴When he had finished speaking, he said to Simon, "Put out into deep water, and let down*ʸ* the nets for a catch."*ᵒ*

⁵Simon answered, "Master,*ᵖ* we've worked hard all night and haven't caught anything. But because you say so, I will let down the nets."

⁶When they had done so, they caught such a large number of fish that their nets began to break. ⁷So they signaled their partners in the other boat to come and help them, and they came and filled both boats so full that they began to sink.

⁸When Simon Peter saw this, he fell at Jesus' knees and said, "Go away from me, Lord; I am a sinful man!" ⁹For he and all his companions were astonished at the

5:3
*ⁿ*Mt 13:2

5:4
*ᵒ*Jn 21:6

5:5
*ᵖ*Lk 8:24, 45; 9:33, 49; 17:13

v 41 Or *Messiah*   **w** 44 Or *the land of the Jews*; some manuscripts *Galilee*   **x** 1 That is, Sea of Galilee   **y** 4 The Greek verb is plural.

● **4:39** Jesus healed Simon's (Peter's) mother-in-law so completely that not only did the fever leave, but her strength was restored, and immediately she got up and took care of others' needs. What a beautiful attitude of service she showed! God gives us health so that we may serve others.

● **4:40** The people came to Jesus when the sun was setting because this was the Sabbath (4:31), their day of rest. Sabbath lasted from sunset on Friday to sunset on Saturday. The people didn't want to break the law that prohibited travel on the Sabbath, so they waited until the Sabbath hours were over before coming to Jesus. Then, as Luke the physician notes, they came with all kinds of diseases, and Jesus healed each one.

4:41 Why didn't Jesus want the demons to reveal who he was? (1) Jesus commanded them to remain silent to show his authority over them. (2) Jesus wanted his listeners to believe he was the Messiah because of his words, not because of the demons' words. (3) Jesus was going to reveal his identity according to God's timetable, and he would not be pushed by Satan's evil plans. The demons called Jesus "Son of God" or "the Holy One of God" (4:35) because they knew he was the Christ. But Jesus was going to show himself to be the suffering servant before he became the great King. To reveal his identity as King too soon would stir up the crowds with the wrong expectations of what he had come to do.

4:42 Jesus had to get up very early just to get some time alone. If Jesus needed solitude for prayer and refreshment, how much

more is this true for us? Don't become so busy that life turns into a flurry of activity leaving no room for quiet fellowship alone with God. No matter how much you have to do, you should always have time for prayer.

4:43 The kingdom of God was good news! It was good news to the Jews because they had been awaiting the coming of the promised Messiah ever since the Babylonian captivity. It is good news for us also because it means freedom from slavery to sin and selfishness. The kingdom of God is here and now because the Holy Spirit lives in the hearts of believers. Yet it is also in the future because Jesus will return to reign over a perfect kingdom where sin and evil no longer exist.

5:1 The Lake of Gennesaret was also known as the Sea of Galilee or the Sea of Tiberias.

5:2 Fishermen on the Sea of Galilee used nets, often bell-shaped nets with lead weights around the edges. A net would be thrown flat onto the water, and the lead weights would cause it to sink around the fish. Then the fishermen would pull on a cord, drawing the net around the fish. Nets had to be kept in good condition, so they were washed to remove weeds and then mended.

● **5:8** Simon (Peter) was awestruck at this miracle, and his first response was to feel his own insignificance in comparison to this man's greatness. Peter knew that Jesus had healed the sick and driven out demons, but he was amazed that Jesus cared about his day-to-day routine and understood his needs. God is interested not only in saving us, but also in helping us in our daily activities.

catch of fish they had taken, ¹⁰and so were James and John, the sons of Zebedee, Simon's partners.

Then Jesus said to Simon, "Don't be afraid;ᵠ from now on you will catch men." ¹¹So they pulled their boats up on shore, left everything and followed him.ʳ

5:10
ᵠMt 14:27

5:11
ʳver 28

Jesus Heals a Man with Leprosy
(38/Matthew 8:1–4; Mark 1:40–45)

¹²While Jesus was in one of the towns, a man came along who was covered with leprosy.ᶻˢ When he saw Jesus, he fell with his face to the ground and begged him, "Lord, if you are willing, you can make me clean."

¹³Jesus reached out his hand and touched the man. "I am willing," he said. "Be clean!" And immediately the leprosy left him.

¹⁴Then Jesus ordered him, "Don't tell anyone, but go, show yourself to the priest and offer the sacrifices that Moses commandedᵗ for your cleansing, as a testimony to them."

¹⁵Yet the news about him spread all the more,ᵘ so that crowds of people came to hear him and to be healed of their sicknesses. ¹⁶But Jesus often withdrew to lonely places and prayed.ᵛ

5:12
ˢMt 8:2

5:14
ᵗLev 14:2-32

5:15
ᵘMt 9:26

5:16
ᵛLk 3:21

Jesus Heals a Paralyzed Man
(39/Matthew 9:1–8; Mark 2:1–12)

¹⁷One day as he was teaching, Pharisees and teachers of the law,ʷ who had come from every village of Galilee and from Judea and Jerusalem, were sitting there. And the power of the Lord was present for him to heal the sick.ˣ ¹⁸Some men came carrying a paralytic on a mat and tried to take him into the house to lay him before Jesus. ¹⁹When they could not find a way to do this because of the crowd, they went up on the roof and lowered him on his mat through the tiles into the middle of the crowd, right in front of Jesus.

²⁰When Jesus saw their faith, he said, "Friend, your sins are forgiven."ʸ

5:17
ʷMt 15:1;
Lk 2:46
ˣMk 5:30;
Lk 6:19

5:20
ʸLk 7:48, 49

z 12 The Greek word was used for various diseases affecting the skin—not necessarily leprosy.

● **5:11** There are two requirements for coming to God. Like Peter, we must recognize our own sinfulness. Then, like these fishermen, we must realize that we can't save ourselves. If we know that we need help, and if we know that Jesus is the only one who can help us, we will be ready to leave everything and follow him.

● **5:11** This was the disciples' second call. After the first call (Matthew 4:18–22; Mark 1:16–20), Peter, Andrew, James, and John had gone back to fishing. They continued to watch Jesus, however, as he established his authority in the synagogue, healed the sick, and drove out demons. Here he also established his authority in their lives — he met them on their level and helped them in their work. From this point on, they left their nets and remained with Jesus. For us, following Jesus means more than just acknowledging him as Savior. We must leave our past behind and commit our future to him.

5:12 Leprosy was a feared disease because there was no known cure for it, and some forms of it were highly contagious. Leprosy had a similar emotional impact and terror associated with it as AIDS does today. (Sometimes called Hansen's disease, leprosy still exists today in a less contagious form that can be treated.) The priests monitored the disease, banishing lepers who were in a contagious stage to prevent the spread of infection and readmitting lepers whose disease was in remission. Because leprosy destroys the nerve endings, lepers often would unknowingly damage their fingers, toes, and noses. This man with leprosy had an advanced case, so he undoubtedly had lost much bodily tissue. Still, he believed that Jesus could heal every trace of the disease.

5:13 Lepers were considered untouchable because people feared contracting their disease. Yet Jesus reached out and touched the leper to heal him. We may consider certain people who are diseased or disabled to be untouchable or repulsive. We must not be afraid to reach out and touch them with God's love. Whom do you know that needs God's touch of love?

5:16 People were flocking to hear Jesus preach and to have their diseases healed, but Jesus made sure he often withdrew to quiet, solitary places to pray. Many things clamor for our attention, and we often run ourselves ragged attending to them. Like Jesus, however, we should take time to withdraw to a quiet and deserted place to pray. Strength comes from God, and we can only be strengthened by spending time with him.

5:17 The religious leaders spent much time defining and discussing the huge body of religious tradition that had been accumulating for more than 400 years since the Jews' return from exile. They were so concerned with these man-made traditions, in fact, that they often lost sight of Scripture. Here these leaders felt threatened because Jesus challenged their sincerity and because the people were flocking to him.

● **5:18, 19** In Bible times, houses were built of stone and had flat roofs made of mud mixed with straw. Outside stairways led to the roof. These men carried their friend up the stairs to the roof where they took apart as much of the mud and straw mixture as was necessary to lower him in front of Jesus.

5:18–20 It wasn't the paralytic's faith that impressed Jesus, but the faith of his friends. Jesus responded to their faith and healed the man. For better or worse, our faith affects others. We cannot make another person a Christian, but we can do much through our words, actions, and love to give him or her a chance to respond. Look for opportunities to bring your friends to the living Christ.

21The Pharisees and the teachers of the law began thinking to themselves, "Who is this fellow who speaks blasphemy? Who can forgive sins but God alone?"*z* 22Jesus knew what they were thinking and asked, "Why are you thinking these things in your hearts? 23Which is easier: to say, 'Your sins are forgiven,' or to say, 'Get up and walk'? 24But that you may know that the Son of Man has authority on earth to forgive sins. . . ." He said to the paralyzed man, "I tell you, get up, take your mat and go home." 25Immediately he stood up in front of them, took what he had been lying on and went home praising God. 26Everyone was amazed and gave praise to God. They were filled with awe and said, "We have seen remarkable things today."

5:21
z Isa 43:25

Jesus Eats with Sinners at Matthew's House
(40/Matthew 9:9–13; Mark 2:13–17)

27After this, Jesus went out and saw a tax collector by the name of Levi sitting at his tax booth. "Follow me," Jesus said to him, 28and Levi got up, left everything and followed him. *a*

5:28
a ver 11

29Then Levi held a great banquet for Jesus at his house, and a large crowd of tax collectors*b* and others were eating with them. 30But the Pharisees and the teachers of the law who belonged to their sect*c* complained to his disciples, "Why do you eat and drink with tax collectors and 'sinners'?"

5:29
b Lk 15:1
5:30
c Ac 23:9

31Jesus answered them, "It is not the healthy who need a doctor, but the sick. 32I have not come to call the righteous, but sinners to repentance."

Religious Leaders Ask Jesus about Fasting
(41/Matthew 9:14–17; Mark 2:18–22)

5:33
d Lk 7:18

33They said to him, "John's disciples*d* often fast and pray, and so do the disciples of the Pharisees, but yours go on eating and drinking." 34Jesus answered, "Can you make the guests of the bridegroom fast while he is with them? 35But the time will come when the bridegroom will be taken from them;*e* in those days they will fast."

5:35
e Lk 17:22

36He told them this parable: "No one tears a patch from a new garment and sews it on an old one. If he does, he will have torn the new garment, and the patch from the new will not match the old. 37And no one pours new wine into old wineskins. If he does, the new wine will burst the skins, the wine will run out and the wineskins will be ruined. 38No, new wine must be poured into new wineskins.

● **5:21** When Jesus told the paralytic his sins were forgiven, the Jewish leaders accused Jesus of blasphemy — claiming to be God or to do what only God can do. In Jewish law, blasphemy was punishable by death (Leviticus 24:16). In labeling Jesus' claim to forgive sins blasphemous, the religious leaders showed they did not understand that Jesus *is* God, and he has God's power to heal both the body and the soul. Forgiveness of sins was a sign that the Messianic age had come (Isaiah 40:2; Joel 2:32; Micah 7:18, 19; Zechariah 13:1).

5:27 For more about Levi (who was also named Matthew), the disciple and author of the Gospel of Matthew, see his Profile in Matthew 9.

● **5:28, 29** Levi responded as Jesus would want all his followers to do — he followed his Lord immediately, and he called his friends together to meet him too. Levi left a lucrative, though probably dishonest, tax-collecting business to follow Jesus. Then he held a reception for his fellow tax collectors and other notorious "sinners" so they could meet Jesus too. Levi, who left behind a material for-

tune in order to gain a spiritual fortune, was proud to be associated with Jesus.

5:30-32 The Pharisees wrapped their sin in respectability. They made themselves appear good by publicly doing good deeds and pointing at the sins of others. Jesus chose to spend time not with these proud, self-righteous religious leaders, but with people who sensed their own sin and knew that they were not good enough for God. In order to come to God, we must repent; and in order to renounce our sin, we must recognize it for what it is.

5:35 Jesus knew his death was coming. After that time, fasting would be in order. Although he was fully human, Jesus knew he was God and knew why he had come — to die for the sins of the world.

5:36-39 "Wineskins" were goatskins sewed together at the edges to form watertight bags. Because new wine expands as it ages, it had to be put in new, pliable wineskins. A used skin, having become more rigid, would burst and spill the wine. Like old wineskins, the Pharisees were too rigid to accept Jesus, who could not be contained in their traditions or rules. Christianity required

39And no one after drinking old wine wants the new, for he says, 'The old is better.' "

The Disciples Pick Wheat on the Sabbath
(45/Matthew 12:1–8; Mark 2:23–28)

6:1
f Dt 23:25

6 One Sabbath Jesus was going through the grainfields, and his disciples began to pick some heads of grain, rub them in their hands and eat the kernels.*f* 2Some of the Pharisees asked, "Why are you doing what is unlawful on the Sabbath?"

6:3
g 1Sa 21:6

6:4
h Lev 24:5, 9

3Jesus answered them, "Have you never read what David did when he and his companions were hungry?*g* 4He entered the house of God, and taking the consecrated bread, he ate what is lawful only for priests to eat.*h* And he also gave some to his companions." 5Then Jesus said to them, "The Son of Man is Lord of the Sabbath."

Jesus Heals a Man's Hand on the Sabbath
(46/Matthew 12:9–14; Mark 3:1–6)

6:6
i ver 1

6On another Sabbath*i* he went into the synagogue and was teaching, and a man was there whose right hand was shriveled. 7The Pharisees and the teachers of the law were looking for a reason to accuse Jesus, so they watched him closely to see if he would heal on the Sabbath. 8But Jesus knew what they were thinking*j* and said to the man with the shriveled hand, "Get up and stand in front of everyone." So he got up and stood there.

6:8
j Mt 9:4

9Then Jesus said to them, "I ask you, which is lawful on the Sabbath: to do good or to do evil, to save life or to destroy it?"

10He looked around at them all, and then said to the man, "Stretch out your hand." He did so, and his hand was completely restored. 11But they were furious and began to discuss with one another what they might do to Jesus.

---

new approaches, new traditions, new structures. Our church programs and ministries should not be so structured that they have no room for a fresh touch of the Spirit, a new method, or a new idea. We, too, must be careful that our hearts do not become so rigid that they prevent us from accepting the new way of thinking that Christ brings. We need to keep our hearts pliable so we can accept Jesus' life-changing message.

6:1, 2 In Jewish legal tradition, there were 39 categories of activities forbidden on the Sabbath — and harvesting was one of them. The teachers of the law even went so far as to describe different methods of harvesting. One method was to rub the heads of grain between the hands, as the disciples were doing here. God's law said farmers were to leave the edges of their fields unplowed so travelers and the poor could eat from this bounty (Deuteronomy 23:25), so the disciples were not guilty of stealing grain. Neither were they breaking the Sabbath by doing their daily work on it. In fact, though they may have been violating the Pharisees' rules, they were not breaking any divine law.

● **6:2** The Pharisees thought their religious system had all the answers. They could not accept Jesus because he did not fit into their system. We could miss Christ for the same reason. Beware of thinking that you or your church has all the answers. No religious system is big enough to contain Christ completely or to fulfill perfectly all his desires for the world.

6:3–5 Each week 12 consecrated loaves of bread, representing the 12 tribes of Israel, were placed on a table in the temple. This bread was called the bread of the Presence. After its use in the temple, it was to be eaten only by priests. Jesus, accused of Sabbath-breaking, referred to a well-known story about David

(1 Samuel 21:1–6). On one occasion, when fleeing from Saul, David and his men ate this consecrated bread. Their need was more important than ceremonial regulations. Jesus was appealing to the same principle: human need is more important than human regulations and rules. By comparing himself and his disciples with David and his men, Jesus was saying, "If you condemn me, you must also condemn David."

6:5 When Jesus said he was "Lord of the Sabbath," he meant that he had the authority to overrule the Pharisees' traditions and regulations because he had created the Sabbath. The Creator is always greater than the creation.

6:6, 7 According to the tradition of the religious leaders, no healing could be done on the Sabbath. Healing, they argued, was practicing medicine, and a person could not practice his or her profession on the Sabbath. It was more important for the religious leaders to protect their laws than to free a person from painful suffering.

6:11 Jesus' enemies were furious. Not only had he read their minds; he also flouted their laws and exposed the hatred in their hearts. It is ironic that it was their hatred, combined with their zeal for the law, that drove them to plot murder — an act that was clearly against the law.

Jesus Selects the Twelve Disciples
(48/Mark 3:13–19)

12One of those days Jesus went out to a mountainside to pray, and spent the night praying to God. 13When morning came, he called his disciples to him and chose twelve of them, whom he also designated apostles:*k* 14Simon (whom he named Peter), his brother Andrew, James, John, Philip, Bartholomew, 15Matthew, Thomas, James son of Alphaeus, Simon who was called the Zealot, 16Judas son of James, and Judas Iscariot, who became a traitor.

6:13
*k*Mk 6:30

Jesus Gives the Beatitudes
(49/Matthew 5:1–12)

17He went down with them and stood on a level place. A large crowd of his disciples was there and a great number of people from all over Judea, from Jerusalem, and from the coast of Tyre and Sidon,*l* 18who had come to hear him and to be healed of their diseases. Those troubled by evil**a** spirits were cured, 19and the people all tried to touch him, because power was coming from him and healing them all.*m*

6:17
*l*Mt 4:25;
Mk 3:7, 8

6:19
*m*Lk 5:17

20Looking at his disciples, he said:

> "Blessed are you who are poor,
>   for yours is the kingdom of God.
> 21Blessed are you who hunger now,
>   for you will be satisfied.
> Blessed are you who weep now,
>   for you will laugh.*n*
> 22Blessed are you when men hate you,
>   when they exclude you*o* and insult you
>   and reject your name as evil,
>   because of the Son of Man.

6:21
*n*Isa 61:2, 3

6:22
*o*Jn 9:22; 16:2

23"Rejoice in that day and leap for joy, because great is your reward in heaven. For that is how their fathers treated the prophets.

a 18 Greek *unclean*

6:12 The Gospel writers note that before every important event in Jesus' life, he took time to go off by himself and pray. This time Jesus was preparing to choose his inner circle, the 12 disciples. Make sure that all your important decisions are grounded in prayer.

6:13 Jesus had many *disciples* (learners), but he chose only 12 *apostles* (messengers). The apostles were his inner circle, to whom he gave special training and whom he sent out with his own authority. These were the men who started the Christian church. In the Gospels these 12 men are usually called the disciples, but in the book of Acts they are called apostles.

6:13-16 Jesus selected "ordinary" men with a mixture of backgrounds and personalities to be his disciples. Today, God calls "ordinary" people together to build his church, teach salvation's message, and serve others out of love. Alone we may feel unqualified to serve Christ effectively, but together we make up a group strong enough to serve God in any way. Ask for patience to accept the diversity of people in your church, and build on the variety of strengths represented in your group.

6:14-16 The disciples are not always listed by the same names. For example, Peter is sometimes called Simon or Cephas. Matthew is also known as Levi. Bartholomew is thought to be the same person as Nathanael (John 1:45). Judas the son of James is also called Thaddaeus.

6:19 Once word of Jesus' healing power spread, crowds gathered just to touch him. For many, he had become a symbol of

good fortune, a lucky charm, or a magician. Instead of desiring God's pardon and love, they only wanted physical healing or a chance to see spectacular events. Some people still see God as a cosmic magician and consider prayer as a way to get God to do his tricks. But God is not a magician — he is the Master. Prayer is not a way for us to control God; it is a way for us to put ourselves under his control.

6:20ff This may be Luke's account of the sermon that Matthew records in Matthew 5 – 7, or it may be that Jesus gave similar sermons on several different occasions. Some believe that this was not one sermon, but a composite based on Jesus' customary teachings.

● **6:20–23** These verses are called the *Beatitudes,* from the Latin word meaning "blessing." They describe what it means to be Christ's follower; they are standards of conduct; they contrast kingdom values with worldly values, showing what Christ's followers can expect from the world and what God will give them; they contrast fake piety with true humility; and finally, they show how Old Testament expectations are fulfilled in God's kingdom.

● **6:21** Some believe that the hunger about which Jesus spoke is a hunger for righteousness (Matthew 5:6). Others say this is physical hunger. In any case, in a nation where riches were seen as a sign of God's favor, Jesus startled his hearers by pronouncing blessings on the hungry. In doing so, however, he was in line with an ancient tradition. The Old Testament is filled with texts proclaiming God's concern for the poor and needy. See, for example, 1 Samuel 2:5; Psalm 146:7; Isaiah 58:6, 7; and Jesus' own mother's prayer in Luke 1:53.

6:24
p Jas 5:1
q Lk 16:25

6:25
r Isa 65:13
s Pr 14:13

24"But woe to you who are rich, p

for you have already received your comfort. q

25Woe to you who are well fed now,

for you will go hungry. r

Woe to you who laugh now,

for you will mourn and weep. s

26Woe to you when all men speak well of you,

for that is how their fathers treated the false prophets.

Jesus Teaches about Loving Enemies
(57/Matthew 5:43–48)

6:27
t ver 35;
Mt 5:44;
Ro 12:20

6:30
u Dt 15:7, 8, 10;
Pr 21:26

6:31
v Mt 7:12

6:32
w Mt 5:46

6:34
x Mt 5:42

27"But I tell you who hear me: Love your enemies, do good to those who hate you, t 28bless those who curse you, pray for those who mistreat you. 29If someone strikes you on one cheek, turn to him the other also. If someone takes your cloak, do not stop him from taking your tunic. 30Give to everyone who asks you, and if anyone takes what belongs to you, do not demand it back. u 31Do to others as you would have them do to you. v

32"If you love those who love you, what credit is that to you? w Even 'sinners' love those who love them. 33And if you do good to those who are good to you, what credit is that to you? Even 'sinners' do that. 34And if you lend to those from whom you expect repayment, what credit is that to you? x Even 'sinners' lend to 'sinners,' expecting to be repaid in full. 35But love your enemies, do good to them, and lend to them without expecting to get anything back. Then your reward will be great, and you will be sons of the Most High, because he is kind to the ungrateful and wicked. 36Be merciful, just as your Father is merciful.

Jesus Teaches about Criticizing Others
(63/Matthew 7:1–6)

6:37
y Mt 7:1

6:39
z Mt 15:14

6:40
a Jn 13:16

37"Do not judge, and you will not be judged. y Do not condemn, and you will not be condemned. Forgive, and you will be forgiven. 38Give, and it will be given to you. A good measure, pressed down, shaken together and running over, will be poured into your lap. For with the measure you use, it will be measured to you."

39He also told them this parable: "Can a blind man lead a blind man? Will they not both fall into a pit? z 40A student is not above his teacher, but everyone who is fully trained will be like his teacher. a

41"Why do you look at the speck of sawdust in your brother's eye and pay no

---

● **6:24**   If you are trying to find fulfillment only through riches, wealth may be the only reward you will ever get — and it does not last. We should not seek comfort now at the expense of eternal life.

● **6:26**   There were many false prophets in Old Testament times. They were praised by kings and crowds because their predictions — prosperity and victory in war — were exactly what the people wanted to hear. But popularity is no guarantee of truth, and human flattery does not bring God's approval. Sadness lies ahead for those who chase after the crowd's praise rather than God's truth.

● **6:27**   The Jews despised the Romans because they oppressed God's people, but Jesus told the people to love these enemies. Such words turned many away from Christ. But Jesus wasn't talking about having affection for enemies; he was talking about an act of the will. You can't "fall into" this kind of love — it takes conscious effort. Loving our enemies means acting in their best interests. We can pray for them, and we can think of ways to help them. Jesus loved the whole world, even though the world was in rebellion against God. Jesus asks us to follow his example by loving our enemies. Grant your enemies the same respect and rights as you desire for yourself.

● **6:35**   Love means action. One way to put love to work is to take the initiative in meeting specific needs. This is easy to do with people who love us, people whom we trust; but love means doing this even to those who dislike us or plan to hurt us. The money we give others should be considered a gift, not a high-interest loan that will help us more than them. Give as though you are giving to God.

● **6:37, 38**   A forgiving spirit demonstrates that a person has received God's forgiveness. Jesus uses the picture of measuring grain in a basket to ensure the full amount. If we are critical rather than compassionate, we will also receive criticism. If we treat others generously, graciously, and compassionately, however, these qualities will come back to us in full measure. We are to love others, not judge them.

6:39, 40   Make sure you're following the right teachers and leaders, because you will go no farther than they do. Look for leaders who will show you more about faith and whose guidance you can trust.

6:41   Jesus doesn't mean we should ignore wrongdoing, but we should not be so worried about others' sins that we overlook our own. We often rationalize our sins by pointing out the same mistakes in others. What kinds of specks in others' eyes are the easiest for you to criticize? Remember your own "planks" when you feel like criticizing, and you may find that you have less to say.

attention to the plank in your own eye? 42How can you say to your brother, 'Brother, let me take the speck out of your eye,' when you yourself fail to see the plank in your own eye? You hypocrite, first take the plank out of your eye, and then you will see clearly to remove the speck from your brother's eye.

Jesus Teaches about Fruit in People's Lives
(66/Matthew 7:15–20)

43"No good tree bears bad fruit, nor does a bad tree bear good fruit. 44Each tree is recognized by its own fruit. b People do not pick figs from thornbushes, or grapes from briers. 45The good man brings good things out of the good stored up in his heart, and the evil man brings evil things out of the evil stored up in his heart. For out of the overflow of his heart his mouth speaks. c

6:44
b Mt 12:33

6:45
c Mt 12:34, 35;
Mk 7:20

Jesus Teaches about Those Who Build Houses on Rock and Sand
(67/Matthew 7:21–29)

46"Why do you call me, 'Lord, Lord,' and do not do what I say? d 47I will show you what he is like who comes to me and hears my words and puts them into practice. e 48He is like a man building a house, who dug down deep and laid the foundation on rock. When a flood came, the torrent struck that house but could not shake it, because it was well built. 49But the one who hears my words and does not put them into practice is like a man who built a house on the ground without a foundation. The moment the torrent struck that house, it collapsed and its destruction was complete."

6:46
d Mal 1:6;
Mt 7:21

6:47
e Jas 1:22-25

A Roman Centurion Demonstrates Faith
(68/Matthew 8:5–13)

7 When Jesus had finished saying all this f in the hearing of the people, he entered Capernaum. 2There a centurion's servant, whom his master valued highly, was sick and about to die. 3The centurion heard of Jesus and sent some elders of the Jews to him, asking him to come and heal his servant. 4When they came to Jesus, they pleaded earnestly with him, "This man deserves to have you do this, 5because he loves our nation and has built our synagogue." 6So Jesus went with them.

7:1
f Mt 7:28

6:42 We should not be so afraid of the label hypocrite that we stand still in our Christian life, hiding our faith and making no attempts to grow. A person who tries to do right but often fails is not a hypocrite. Neither are those who fulfill their duty even when they don't feel like doing it — it is often necessary and good to set aside our desires in order to do what needs doing. It is not hypocrisy to be weak in faith. A hypocrite is a person who puts on religious behavior in order to gain attention, approval, acceptance, or admiration from others.

● **6:45** Jesus reminds us that our speech and actions reveal the true underlying beliefs, attitudes, and motivations. The good impressions we try to make cannot last if our hearts are deceptive. What is in your heart will come out in your speech and behavior.

6:46–49 Obeying God is like building a house on a strong, solid foundation that stands firm when storms come. When life is calm, our foundations don't seem to matter. But when crises come, our foundations are tested. Be sure your life is built on the solid foundation of knowing and trusting Jesus Christ.

6:49 Why would people build a house without a foundation? Perhaps to save time and avoid the hard work of preparing a stone foundation. Possibly because the waterfront scenery is more attractive or because beach houses have higher social status than cliff houses. Perhaps because they want to join their friends who have already settled in sandy areas. Maybe because they haven't heard about the violent storms coming, or because they have discounted the reports, or for some reason they think disaster can't happen to them. Whatever their reason, those with no foundation are shortsighted, and they will be sorry. When you find yourself listening but not obeying, what are your reasons?

7:2 A centurion was a Roman army officer in charge of 100 men. This man came to Jesus not as a last resort or magic charm, but because he believed Jesus was sent from God. Apparently the centurion recognized that the Jews possessed God's message for mankind — it is recorded that he loved the nation and built the synagogue. Thus, in his time of need, it was natural for him to turn to Jesus.

7:3 Why did the centurion send Jewish elders to Jesus instead of going himself? Since he was well aware of the Jewish hatred for Roman soldiers, he may not have wanted to interrupt a Jewish gathering. As an army captain, he daily delegated work and sent groups on missions, so this was how he chose to get his message to Jesus.

7:3 Matthew 8:5 says the Roman centurion visited Jesus himself, while Luke 7:3 says he sent Jewish elders to present his request to

He was not far from the house when the centurion sent friends to say to him: "Lord, don't trouble yourself, for I do not deserve to have you come under my roof. 7That is why I did not even consider myself worthy to come to you. But say the word, and my servant will be healed. 8For I myself am a man under authority, with soldiers under me. I tell this one, 'Go,' and he goes; and that one, 'Come,' and he comes. I say to my servant, 'Do this,' and he does it."

9When Jesus heard this, he was amazed at him, and turning to the crowd following him, he said, "I tell you, I have not found such great faith even in Israel." 10Then the men who had been sent returned to the house and found the servant well.

Jesus Raises a Widow's Son from the Dead
(69)

7:13
g ver 19;
Lk 10:1; 13:15; 17:5;
22:61; 24:34;
Jn 11:2

7:14
h Lk 8:54;
Jn 11:43;
Ac 9:40

7:16
i Lk 1:65
j Mt 9:8
k Mt 21:11
l Lk 1:68

7:17
m Mt 9:26

11Soon afterward, Jesus went to a town called Nain, and his disciples and a large crowd went along with him. 12As he approached the town gate, a dead person was being carried out — the only son of his mother, and she was a widow. And a large crowd from the town was with her. 13When the Lord*g* saw her, his heart went out to her and he said, "Don't cry."

14Then he went up and touched the coffin, and those carrying it stood still. He said, "Young man, I say to you, get up!"*h* 15The dead man sat up and began to talk, and Jesus gave him back to his mother.

16They were all filled with awe*i* and praised God.*j* "A great prophet*k* has appeared among us," they said. "God has come to help his people."*l* 17This news about Jesus spread throughout Judea*b* and the surrounding country.*m*

b 17 Or *the land of the Jews*

Jesus. In dealing with the messengers, Jesus was dealing with the centurion. For his Jewish audience, Matthew emphasized the man's faith. For his Gentile audience, Luke highlighted the good relationship between the Jewish elders and the Roman centurion.

7:9 The Roman centurion didn't come to Jesus, and he didn't expect Jesus to come to him. Just as this officer did not need to be present to have his orders carried out, so Jesus didn't need to be present to heal. The centurion's faith was especially amazing because he was a Gentile who had not been brought up to know a loving God.

● **7:11–15** The widow's situation was serious. She had lost her husband, and here her only son was dead — her last means of support. The crowd of mourners would go home, and she would be left penniless and alone. The widow was probably past the age of childbearing and would not marry again. Unless a relative came to her aid, her future was bleak. She would be an easy prey for swindlers, and she would likely be reduced to begging for food. In fact, as Luke repeatedly emphasizes, this woman was just the kind of person Jesus had come to help — and help her he did. Jesus has the power to bring hope out of any tragedy.

7:11–17 This story illustrates salvation. The whole world was dead in sin (Ephesians 2:1), just as the widow's son was dead. Being dead, we could do nothing to help ourselves — we couldn't even ask for help. But God had compassion on us, and he sent Jesus to raise us to life with him (Ephesians 2:4–7). The dead man did not earn his second chance at life, and we cannot earn our new life in Christ. But we can accept God's gift of life, praise God for it, and use our lives to do his will.

7:12 Honoring the dead was important in Jewish tradition. A funeral procession — the relatives of the dead person following the body that was wrapped and carried on a kind of stretcher — would make its way through town, and bystanders would be expected to join the procession. In addition, hired mourners would cry aloud and draw attention to the procession. The family's mourning would continue for 30 days.

JESUS RAISES A WIDOW'S SON
Jesus traveled to Nain and met a funeral procession leaving the village. A widow's only son had died, leaving her virtually helpless, but Jesus brought the young man back to life. This miracle, recorded only in Luke, reveals Jesus' compassion for people's needs.

7:16 The people thought of Jesus as a prophet because, like the Old Testament prophets, he boldly proclaimed God's message and sometimes raised the dead. Both Elijah and Elisha raised children from the dead (1 Kings 17:17–24; 2 Kings 4:18–37). The people were correct in thinking that Jesus was a prophet, but he was much more — he is God himself.

Jesus Eases John's Doubt
(70/Matthew 11:1–19)

18John's disciples told him about all these things. Calling two of them, 19he sent them to the Lord to ask, "Are you the one who was to come, or should we expect someone else?"

20When the men came to Jesus, they said, "John the Baptist sent us to you to ask, 'Are you the one who was to come, or should we expect someone else?' "

21At that very time Jesus cured many who had diseases, sicknesses[n] and evil spirits, and gave sight to many who were blind. 22So he replied to the messengers, "Go back and report to John what you have seen and heard: The blind receive sight, the lame walk, those who have leprosy[c] are cured, the deaf hear, the dead are raised, and the good news is preached to the poor.[o] 23Blessed is the man who does not fall away on account of me."

24After John's messengers left, Jesus began to speak to the crowd about John: "What did you go out into the desert to see? A reed swayed by the wind? 25If not, what did you go out to see? A man dressed in fine clothes? No, those who wear expensive clothes and indulge in luxury are in palaces. 26But what did you go out to see? A prophet? Yes, I tell you, and more than a prophet. 27This is the one about whom it is written:

> " 'I will send my messenger ahead of you,
>   who will prepare your way before you.'[d][p]

28I tell you, among those born of women there is no one greater than John; yet the one who is least in the kingdom of God is greater than he."

29(All the people, even the tax collectors, when they heard Jesus' words, acknowledged that God's way was right, because they had been baptized by John.[q] 30But the Pharisees and experts in the law[r] rejected God's purpose for themselves, because they had not been baptized by John.)

31"To what, then, can I compare the people of this generation? What are they like? 32They are like children sitting in the marketplace and calling out to each other:

> " 'We played the flute for you,
>   and you did not dance;
> we sang a dirge,
>   and you did not cry.'

c 22 The Greek word was used for various diseases affecting the skin—not necessarily leprosy.   d 27 Mal. 3:1

Cross references:
7:21 n Mt 4:23
7:22 o Isa 29:18, 19; 35:5, 6; 61:1, 2; Lk 4:18
7:27 p Mal 3:1; Mt 11:10; Mk 1:2
7:29 q Mt 21:32; Lk 3:12
7:30 r Mt 22:35

7:18-23 John was confused because the reports he received about Jesus were unexpected and incomplete. John's doubts were natural, and Jesus didn't rebuke him for them. Instead, Jesus responded in a way that John would understand: Jesus explained that he had accomplished what the Messiah was supposed to accomplish. God can handle our doubts, and he welcomes our questions. Do you have questions about Jesus—about who he is or what he expects of you? Admit them to yourself and to God, and begin looking for answers. Only as you face your doubts honestly can you begin to resolve them.

7:20-22 The proofs listed here for Jesus' being the Messiah are significant. They consist of observable deeds, not theories—actions that Jesus' contemporaries saw and reported for us to read today. The prophets had said that the Messiah would do these very acts (see Isaiah 35:5, 6; 61:1). These physical proofs helped John—and will help all of us—to recognize who Jesus is.

7:28 Of all people, no one fulfilled his God-given purpose better than John. Yet in God's kingdom, all who come after John have a greater spiritual heritage because they have clearer knowledge of the purpose of Jesus' death and resurrection. John was the last to function like the Old Testament prophets, the last to prepare the people for the coming Messianic age. Jesus was not contrasting the man John with individual Christians; he was contrasting life before Christ with life in the fullness of Christ's kingdom.

7:29, 30 The tax collectors (who embodied evil in most people's minds) and common people heard John's message and repented. In contrast, the Pharisees and experts in the law—religious leaders—rejected his words. Wanting to live their own way, they justified their own point of view and refused to listen to other ideas. Rather than trying to force your plans on God, try to discover his plan for you.

7:31-35 The religious leaders hated anyone who spoke the truth and exposed their own hypocrisy, and they did not bother to be consistent in their faultfinding. They criticized John the Baptist because he fasted and drank no wine; they criticized Jesus because he ate heartily and drank wine with tax collectors and "sinners." Their real objection to both men, of course, had nothing to do with dietary habits. What the Pharisees and experts in the law couldn't stand was being exposed for their hypocrisy.

7:33, 34 The Pharisees weren't troubled by their inconsistency toward John the Baptist and Jesus. They were good at justifying their "wisdom." Most of us can find compelling reasons to do or

7:33
sLk 1:15

7:34
tLk 5:29, 30; 15:1, 2

³³For John the Baptist came neither eating bread nor drinking wine,ˢ and you say, 'He has a demon.' ³⁴The Son of Man came eating and drinking, and you say, 'Here is a glutton and a drunkard, a friend of tax collectors and "sinners." 'ᵗ ³⁵But wisdom is proved right by all her children."

A Sinful Woman Anoints Jesus' Feet
(72)

³⁶Now one of the Pharisees invited Jesus to have dinner with him, so he went to the Pharisee's house and reclined at the table. ³⁷When a woman who had lived a sinful life in that town learned that Jesus was eating at the Pharisee's house, she brought an alabaster jar of perfume, ³⁸and as she stood behind him at his feet weeping, she began to wet his feet with her tears. Then she wiped them with her hair, kissed them and poured perfume on them.

7:39
uver 16

³⁹When the Pharisee who had invited him saw this, he said to himself, "If this man were a prophet,ᵘ he would know who is touching him and what kind of woman she is—that she is a sinner."

⁴⁰Jesus answered him, "Simon, I have something to tell you."

"Tell me, teacher," he said.

⁴¹"Two men owed money to a certain moneylender. One owed him five hundred denarii,ᵉ and the other fifty. ⁴²Neither of them had the money to pay him back, so he canceled the debts of both. Now which of them will love him more?"

⁴³Simon replied, "I suppose the one who had the bigger debt canceled."

"You have judged correctly," Jesus said.

7:44
vGe 18:4; 19:2;
43:24;
Jdg 19:21;
1Ti 5:10

7:46
wPs 23:5;
Ecc 9:8

⁴⁴Then he turned toward the woman and said to Simon, "Do you see this woman? I came into your house. You did not give me any water for my feet,ᵛ but she wet my feet with her tears and wiped them with her hair. ⁴⁵You did not give me a kiss, but this woman, from the time I entered, has not stopped kissing my feet. ⁴⁶You did not put oil on my head,ʷ but she has poured perfume on my feet. ⁴⁷Therefore, I tell you, her many sins have been forgiven—for she loved much. But he who has been forgiven little loves little."

7:48
xMt 9:2

⁴⁸Then Jesus said to her, "Your sins are forgiven."ˣ

⁴⁹The other guests began to say among themselves, "Who is this who even forgives sins?"

7:50
yMt 9:22

⁵⁰Jesus said to the woman, "Your faith has saved you;ʸ go in peace."

e 41 A denarius was a coin worth about a day's wages.

---

believe whatever suits our purposes. If we do not examine our ideas in the light of God's truth, however, we may be just as obviously self-serving as the Pharisees.

7:35 Wisdom's children were the followers of Jesus and John. These followers lived changed lives. Their righteous living demonstrated the wisdom that Jesus and John taught.

7:36 A similar incident occurred later in Jesus' ministry (see Matthew 26:6–13; Mark 14:3–9; John 12:1–11).

7:37 Alabaster jars were carved, expensive, and beautiful.

7:38 Although the woman was not an invited guest, she entered the house anyway and knelt behind Jesus at his feet. In Jesus' day, it was customary to recline while eating. Dinner guests would lie on couches with their heads near the table, propping themselves up on one elbow and stretching their feet out behind them. The woman could easily anoint Jesus' feet without approaching the table.

● **7:44ff** Again Luke contrasts the Pharisees with sinners—and again the sinners come out ahead. Simon had committed several social errors in neglecting to wash Jesus' feet (a courtesy extended to guests because sandaled feet got very dirty), anoint his head with oil, and offer him the kiss of greeting. Did Simon perhaps

feel that he was too good to treat Jesus as an equal? The sinful woman, by contrast, lavished tears, expensive perfume, and kisses on her Savior. In this story it is the grateful prostitute, and not the stingy religious leader, whose sins were forgiven. Although it is God's grace through faith that saves us, and not acts of love or generosity, this woman's act demonstrated her true faith, and Jesus honored her faith.

7:47 Overflowing love is the natural response to forgiveness and the appropriate consequence of faith. But only those who realize the depth of their sin can appreciate the complete forgiveness God offers them. Jesus has rescued all of his followers, whether they were once extremely wicked or conventionally good, from eternal death. Do you appreciate the wideness of God's mercy? Are you grateful for his forgiveness?

7:49, 50 The Pharisees believed that only God could forgive sins, so they wondered why this man Jesus was saying that the woman's sins were forgiven. They did not grasp the fact that Jesus was indeed God.

Women Accompany Jesus and the Disciples
(73)

8 After this, Jesus traveled about from one town and village to another, proclaiming the good news of the kingdom of God. *z* The Twelve were with him, ²and also some women who had been cured of evil spirits and diseases: Mary (called Magdalene)*a* from whom seven demons had come out; ³Joanna the wife of Cuza, the manager of Herod's*b* household; Susanna; and many others. These women were helping to support them out of their own means.

8:1
z Mt 4:23

8:2
a Mt 27:55, 56

8:3
b Mt 14:1

Jesus Tells the Parable of the Four Soils
(77/Matthew 13:1–9; Mark 4:1–9)

⁴While a large crowd was gathering and people were coming to Jesus from town after town, he told this parable: ⁵"A farmer went out to sow his seed. As he was scattering the seed, some fell along the path; it was trampled on, and the birds of the air ate it up. ⁶Some fell on rock, and when it came up, the plants withered because they had no moisture. ⁷Other seed fell among thorns, which grew up with it and choked the plants. ⁸Still other seed fell on good soil. It came up and yielded a crop, a hundred times more than was sown."

When he said this, he called out, "He who has ears to hear, let him hear."*c*

8:8
c Mt 11:15

Jesus Explains the Parable of the Four Soils
(78/Matthew 13:10–23; Mark 4:10–25)

⁹His disciples asked him what this parable meant. ¹⁰He said, "The knowledge of the secrets of the kingdom of God has been given to you, but to others I speak in parables, so that,

" 'though seeing, they may not see;
though hearing, they may not understand.'†*d*

8:10
d Isa 6:9;
Mt 13:13, 14

¹¹"This is the meaning of the parable: The seed is the word of God. ¹²Those along the path are the ones who hear, and then the devil comes and takes away the word from their hearts, so that they may not believe and be saved. ¹³Those on the rock are the ones who receive the word with joy when they hear it, but they have no root. They believe for a while, but in the time of testing they fall away. ¹⁴The seed that fell among thorns stands for those who hear, but as they go on their way they

† *10* Isaiah 6:9

● **8:2, 3** Jesus lifted women up from the agony of degradation and servitude to the joy of fellowship and service. In Jewish culture, women were not supposed to learn from rabbis. By allowing these women to travel with him, Jesus was showing that all people are equal under God. These women supported Jesus' ministry with their own money. They owed a great debt to him because he had driven demons out of some and had healed others.

8:2, 3 Here we catch a glimpse of a few of the people behind the scenes in Jesus' ministry. The ministry of those in the foreground is often supported by those whose work is less visible but just as essential. Offer your resources to God, whether or not you will be on center stage.

8:4 Jesus often communicated spiritual truth through *parables*— short stories or descriptions that take a familiar object or situation and give it a startling new twist. By linking the known with the hidden and forcing listeners to think, parables can point to spiritual truths. A parable compels listeners to discover the truth for themselves, and it conceals the truth from those too lazy or dull to understand it. In reading Jesus' parables, we must be careful not to read too much into them. Most have only one point and one meaning.

8:5 Why would a farmer allow precious seed to land on the path, on rocks, or among thorns? This is not an irresponsible farmer scattering seeds at random. He is using the acceptable method of hand-seeding a large field—tossing it by handfuls as he walks through the field. His goal is to get as much seed as possible to take root in good soil, but there is inevitable waste as some falls or is blown into less productive areas. That some of the seed produced no crop was not the fault of the faithful farmer or of the seed. The yield depended on the condition of the soil where the seed fell. It is our responsibility to spread the seed (God's message), but we should not give up when some of our efforts fail. Remember, not every seed falls on good soil.

8:10 Why didn't the crowds understand Jesus' words? Perhaps they were looking for a military leader or a political Messiah and could not fit his gentle teaching style into their preconceived idea. Perhaps they were afraid of pressure from religious leaders and did not want to look too deeply into Jesus' words. God told Isaiah that people would hear without understanding and see without perceiving (Isaiah 6:9), and that kind of reaction confronted Jesus. The parable of the sower was an accurate picture of the people's reaction to the rest of his parables.

8:11–15 "Path" people, like many of the religious leaders, refused to believe God's message. "Rock" people, like many in the crowds who followed Jesus, believed his message but never got around to doing anything about it. "Thorn patch" people, overcome by worries and the lure of materialism, left no room in their lives for God. "Good soil" people, in contrast to all the other groups, followed Jesus no matter what the cost. Which type of soil are you?

are choked by life's worries, riches and pleasures, and they do not mature. 15But the seed on good soil stands for those with a noble and good heart, who hear the word, retain it, and by persevering produce a crop.

16"No one lights a lamp and hides it in a jar or puts it under a bed. Instead, he puts it on a stand, so that those who come in can see the light. *e* 17For there is nothing hidden that will not be disclosed, and nothing concealed that will not be known or brought out into the open. *f* 18Therefore consider carefully how you listen. Whoever has will be given more; whoever does not have, even what he thinks he has will be taken from him." *g*

8:16
e Mt 5:15

8:17
f Mt 10:26;
Mk 4:22;
Lk 12:2

8:18
g Mt 25:29

Jesus Describes His True Family
(76/Matthew 12:46–50; Mark 3:31–35)

19Now Jesus' mother and brothers came to see him, but they were not able to get near him because of the crowd. 20Someone told him, "Your mother and brothers are standing outside, wanting to see you."

21He replied, "My mother and brothers are those who hear God's word and put it into practice." *h*

8:21
h Lk 11:28

Jesus Calms the Storm
(87/Matthew 8:23–27; Mark 4:35–41)

22One day Jesus said to his disciples, "Let's go over to the other side of the lake." So they got into a boat and set out. 23As they sailed, he fell asleep. A squall came down on the lake, so that the boat was being swamped, and they were in great danger.

24The disciples went and woke him, saying, "Master, Master, *i* we're going to drown!"

8:24
i Lk 5:5

JESUS AND WOMEN		
	Jesus talks to a Samaritan woman at the well	John 4:1–26
	Jesus raises a widow's son from the dead	Luke 7:11–17
	A sinful woman anoints Jesus' feet	Luke 7:36–50
	The adulterous woman	John 8:1–11
	The group of women travels with Jesus	Luke 8:1–3
	Jesus visits Mary and Martha	Luke 10:38–42
	Jesus heals a crippled woman	Luke 13:10–17
	Jesus heals the daughter of a Gentile woman	Mark 7:24–30
	Weeping women follow Jesus on his way to the cross	Luke 23:27–31
	Jesus' mother and other women gather at the cross	John 19:25–27
	Jesus appears to Mary Magdalene	Mark 16:9–11
	Jesus appears to other women after his resurrection	Matthew 28:8–10

As a non-Jew recording the words and works of Jesus' life, Luke demonstrates a special sensitivity to other "outsiders" with whom Jesus came into contact. For instance, Luke records five events involving women that are not mentioned in the other Gospels. In first-century Jewish culture, women were usually treated as second-class citizens with few of the rights men had. But Jesus crossed those barriers, and Luke showed the special care Jesus had for women. Jesus treated all people with equal respect. The above passages tell of his encounters with women.

8:16, 17 When the light of the truth about Jesus illuminates us, it is our duty to shine that light to help others. Our witness for Christ should be public, not hidden. We should not keep the benefits for ourselves alone but pass them on to others. In order to be helpful, we need to be well placed. Seek opportunities to be there when unbelievers need help.

8:18 Applying God's Word helps us grow. This is a principle of growth in physical, mental, and spiritual life. For example, a muscle, when exercised, will grow stronger, but an unused muscle will grow weak and flabby. If you are not growing stronger, you are growing weaker; it is impossible for you to stand still. How are you using what God has taught you?

8:21 Jesus' true family are those who hear and obey his words. Hearing without obeying is not enough. As Jesus loved his mother (see John 19:25–27), so he loves us. Christ offers us an intimate family relationship with him.

● **8:23** The Sea of Galilee (actually a large lake) is even today the scene of fierce storms, sometimes with waves as high as 20 feet. Jesus' disciples were not frightened without cause. Even though several of them were expert fishermen and knew how to handle a boat, their peril was real.

He got up and rebuked/ the wind and the raging waters; the storm subsided, and all was calm. 25"Where is your faith?" he asked his disciples.

8:24
/Lk 4:35, 39, 41

In fear and amazement they asked one another, "Who is this? He commands even the winds and the water, and they obey him."

Jesus Sends the Demons into a Herd of Pigs
(88/Matthew 8:28–34; Mark 5:1–20)

26They sailed to the region of the Gerasenes,9 which is across the lake from Galilee. 27When Jesus stepped ashore, he was met by a demon-possessed man from the town. For a long time this man had not worn clothes or lived in a house, but had lived in the tombs. 28When he saw Jesus, he cried out and fell at his feet, shouting at the top of his voice, "What do you want with me,k Jesus, Son of the Most High God?/ I beg you, don't torture me!" 29For Jesus had commanded the evilh spirit to come out of the man. Many times it had seized him, and though he was chained hand and foot and kept under guard, he had broken his chains and had been driven by the demon into solitary places.

8:28
kMt 8:29
/Mk 5:7

30Jesus asked him, "What is your name?"

"Legion," he replied, because many demons had gone into him. 31And they begged him repeatedly not to order them to go into the Abyss.m

8:31
mRev 9:1, 2, 11;
11:7; 17:8; 20:1, 3

32A large herd of pigs was feeding there on the hillside. The demons begged Jesus to let them go into them, and he gave them permission. 33When the demons came out of the man, they went into the pigs, and the herd rushed down the steep bank into the laken and was drowned.

8:33
nver 22, 23

34When those tending the pigs saw what had happened, they ran off and reported

g 26 Some manuscripts *Gadarenes*; other manuscripts *Gergesenes*; also in verse 37   **h** 29 Greek *unclean*

HEALING A DEMON-POSSESSED MAN
As he traveled through Galilee, Jesus told many parables and met many people, as recorded in Matthew and Mark. Later, from Capernaum, Jesus and the disciples set out in a boat, only to encounter a fierce storm. Jesus calmed the storm and, when they landed, exorcised a "legion" of demons.

could do to them. Demons, Satan's messengers, are powerful and destructive. Still active today, they attempt to distort and destroy people's relationship with God. Demons and demon-possession are real. It is vital that believers recognize the power of Satan and his demons, but we shouldn't let curiosity lead us to get involved with demonic forces (Deuteronomy 18:10–12). Demons are powerless against those who trust in Jesus. If we resist the devil, he will leave us alone (James 4:7).

8:29–31 The demons begged Jesus to spare them from the Abyss, which is also mentioned in Revelation 9:1 and 20:1–3 as the place of confinement for Satan and his messengers. The demons, of course, knew all about this place of confinement, and they didn't want to go there.

● **8:30** The demon's name was Legion. A legion was the largest unit in the Roman army, having between 3,000 and 6,000 soldiers. The man was possessed by not one, but many demons.

● **8:33** Why didn't Jesus just destroy these demons — or send them to the Abyss? Because the time for such work had not yet come. He healed many people of the destructive effects of demon-possession, but he did not yet destroy demons. The same question could be asked today — why doesn't Jesus stop all the evil in the world? His time for that has not yet come. But it will come. The book of Revelation portrays the future victory of Jesus over Satan, his demons, and all evil.

8:33–37 The demons destroyed the pigs, which hurt the finances of those tending the pigs, but can pigs and money compare with a human life? A man had been freed from the devil's power, but the people thought only about their livestock. People have always tended to value financial gain above needy people. Throughout history, most wars have been fought to protect economic interests. Much injustice and oppression, both at home and abroad, is the direct result of some individual's or company's urge to get rich. People are continually being sacrificed to the god of money. Don't think more highly of "pigs" than of people. Think carefully about how your decisions will affect other human beings, and be willing to choose a simpler life-style if it will keep other people from being harmed.

● **8:25** When caught in the storms of life, it is easy to think that God has lost control and that we're at the mercy of the winds of fate. In reality, God is sovereign. He controls the history of the world as well as our personal destinies. Just as Jesus calmed the waves, he can calm whatever storms you may face.

8:26 The region of the Gerasenes was a Gentile region southeast of the Sea of Galilee, home of the Decapolis, or the Ten Cities. These were Greek cities that belonged to no country and were self-governing. Although Jews would not have raised pigs because the Jewish religion labeled them unclean, the Gentiles had no such aversion.

● **8:27, 28** These demons recognized Jesus and his authority immediately. They knew who Jesus was and what his great power

this in the town and countryside, 35and the people went out to see what had happened. When they came to Jesus, they found the man from whom the demons had gone out, sitting at Jesus' feet,º dressed and in his right mind; and they were afraid. 36Those who had seen it told the people how the demon-possessedᵖ man had been cured. 37Then all the people of the region of the Gerasenes asked Jesus to leave them,�q because they were overcome with fear. So he got into the boat and left.

8:35
ºLk 10:39

8:36
ᵖMt 4:24

8:37
qAc 16:39

38The man from whom the demons had gone out begged to go with him, but Jesus sent him away, saying, 39"Return home and tell how much God has done for you." So the man went away and told all over town how much Jesus had done for him.

Jesus Heals a Bleeding Woman and Restores a Girl to Life
(89/Matthew 9:18–26; Mark 5:21–43)

40Now when Jesus returned, a crowd welcomed him, for they were all expecting him. 41Then a man named Jairus, a ruler of the synagogue,ʳ came and fell at Jesus' feet, pleading with him to come to his house 42because his only daughter, a girl of about twelve, was dying.

8:41
ʳver 49;
Mk 5:22

As Jesus was on his way, the crowds almost crushed him. 43And a woman was there who had been subject to bleeding for twelve years,ˡ but no one could heal her. 44She came up behind him and touched the edge of his cloak, and immediately her bleeding stopped.

45"Who touched me?" Jesus asked.

When they all denied it, Peter said, "Master,ˢ the people are crowding and pressing against you."

8:45
ˢLk 5:5

46But Jesus said, "Someone touched me; I know that power has gone out from me."ᵗ

8:46
ᵗLk 5:17; 6:19

47Then the woman, seeing that she could not go unnoticed, came trembling and fell at his feet. In the presence of all the people, she told why she had touched him and how she had been instantly healed. 48Then he said to her, "Daughter, your faith has healed you.ᵘ Go in peace."

8:48
ᵘMt 9:22

49While Jesus was still speaking, someone came from the house of Jairus, the synagogue ruler.ᵛ "Your daughter is dead," he said. "Don't bother the teacher any more."

8:49
ᵛver 41

50Hearing this, Jesus said to Jairus, "Don't be afraid; just believe, and she will be healed."

51When he arrived at the house of Jairus, he did not let anyone go in with him

ˡ43 Many manuscripts *years, and she had spent all she had on doctors*

8:38, 39 Often Jesus asked those he healed to be quiet about the healing, but he urged this man to return to his family and tell them what God had done for him. Why? (1) Jesus knew the man would be an effective witness to those who knew his previous condition and could attest to the miraculous healing. (2) Jesus wanted to expand his ministry by introducing his message into this Gentile area. (3) Jesus knew that the Gentiles, since they were not expecting a Messiah, would not divert his ministry by trying to crown him king. When God touches your life, don't be afraid to share the wonderful events with your family and friends.

8:41 The synagogue was the local center of worship. The synagogue ruler was responsible for administration, building maintenance, and worship supervision. It would have been quite unusual for a respected synagogue ruler to fall at the feet of an itinerant preacher and beg him to heal his daughter. Jesus honored this man's humble faith (8:50, 54–56).

● **8:43–48** Many people surrounded Jesus as he made his way toward Jairus's house. It was virtually impossible to get through the multitude, but one woman fought her way desperately through the crowd in order to touch Jesus. As soon as she did so, she was healed. What a difference there is between the crowds that are curious about Jesus and the few who reach out and touch him! Today, many people are vaguely familiar with Jesus, but nothing in their lives is changed or bettered by this passing acquaintance. It is only faith that releases God's healing power. Are you just curious about God, or do you reach out to him in faith, knowing that his mercy will bring healing to your body, soul, and spirit?

● **8:45** It isn't that Jesus didn't know who had touched him; it's that he wanted the woman to step forward and identify herself. Jesus wanted to teach her that his cloak did not contain magical properties, but that her faith in him had healed her. He may also have wanted to teach the crowds a lesson. According to Jewish law, a man who touched a menstruating woman became ceremonially unclean (Leviticus 15:19–28). This was true whether her bleeding was normal or, as in this woman's case, the result of illness. To protect themselves from such defilement, Jewish men carefully avoided touching, speaking to, or even looking at women. By contrast, Jesus proclaimed to hundreds of people that this "unclean" woman had touched him—and then he healed her. In Jesus' mind, this suffering woman was not to be overlooked. As God's creation, she deserved attention and respect.

except Peter, John and James, and the child's father and mother. 52Meanwhile, all the people were wailing and mourning[w] for her. "Stop wailing," Jesus said. "She is not dead but asleep."

53They laughed at him, knowing that she was dead. 54But he took her by the hand and said, "My child, get up!"[x] 55Her spirit returned, and at once she stood up. Then Jesus told them to give her something to eat. 56Her parents were astonished, but he ordered them not to tell anyone what had happened.[y]

8:52
wLk 23:27

8:54
xLk 7:14

8:56
yMt 8:4

Jesus Sends Out the Twelve Disciples
(93/Matthew 10:1–16; Mark 6:7–13)

9 When Jesus had called the Twelve together, he gave them power and authority to drive out all demons[z] and to cure diseases, 2and he sent them out to preach the kingdom of God and to heal the sick. 3He told them: "Take nothing for the journey — no staff, no bag, no bread, no money, no extra tunic.[a] 4Whatever house you enter, stay there until you leave that town. 5If people do not welcome you, shake the dust off your feet when you leave their town, as a testimony against them."[b] 6So they set out and went from village to village, preaching the gospel and healing people everywhere.

9:1
zMt 10:1

9:3
aLk 10:4; 22:35

9:5
bMt 10:14

Herod Kills John the Baptist
(95/Matthew 14:1–12; Mark 6:14–29)

7Now Herod[c] the tetrarch heard about all that was going on. And he was perplexed, because some were saying that John had been raised from the dead,[d] 8others that Elijah had appeared, and still others that one of the prophets of long ago had come back to life. 9But Herod said, "I beheaded John. Who, then, is this I hear such things about?" And he tried to see him.[e]

9:7
cMt 14:1
dver 19

9:9
eLk 23:8

● **8:56** Jesus told the parents not to talk about their daughter's healing because he knew the facts would speak for themselves. Besides, Jesus was concerned for his ministry. He did not want to be known as just a miracle worker; he wanted people to listen to his words that would heal their broken spiritual lives.

9:1–10 Note Jesus' methods of leadership. He empowered his disciples (9:1), gave them specific instructions so they knew what to do (9:3, 4), told them how to deal with tough times (9:5), and held them accountable (9:10). As you lead others, study the Master Leader's pattern. Which of these elements do you need to incorporate into your leadership?

9:2 Jesus announced his kingdom by both preaching and healing. If he had limited his message to preaching, people might have seen his kingdom as spiritual only. On the other hand, if he had healed without preaching, people might not have realized the spiritual importance of his mission. Most of his listeners expected a Messiah who would bring wealth and power to their nation; they preferred material benefits to spiritual discernment. The truth about Jesus is that he is both God and man, both spiritual and physical; and the salvation that he offers is both for the soul and the body. Any group or teaching that emphasizes soul at the expense of body, or body at the expense of soul, is in danger of distorting Jesus' Good News.

9:3, 4 Why were the disciples instructed to depend on others while they went from town to town preaching the gospel? Their purpose was to blanket Judea with Jesus' message, and by traveling light they could move quickly. Their dependence on others had other good effects as well: (1) it clearly showed that the Messiah had not come to offer wealth to his followers; (2) it forced the disciples to rely on God's power and not on their own provision; (3) it involved the villagers and made them more eager to hear the message. This was an excellent approach for the disciples' short-term mission; it was not intended, however, to be a permanent way of life for them.

9:4 The disciples were told to stay in only one home in each town because they were not to offend their hosts by moving to a home that was more comfortable or socially prominent. To remain in one home was not a burden for the homeowner, because the disciples' stay in each community was short.

9:5 Shaking the dust of unaccepting towns from their feet had deep cultural implications. Pious Jews would do this after passing through Gentile cities to show their separation from Gentile practices. If the disciples shook the dust of a Jewish town from their feet, it would show their separation from Jews who rejected their Messiah. This action also showed that the disciples were not responsible for how the people responded to their message. Neither are we responsible if we have carefully and truthfully presented Christ, but our message is rejected. Like the disciples, we must move on to others whom God desires to reach.

9:7 For more information on Herod, also known as Herod Antipas, see his Profile in Mark 6.

9:7, 8 It was so difficult for the people to accept Jesus as the Son of God that they tried to come up with other solutions — most of which sound quite unbelievable to us. Many thought that he must be someone who had come back to life, perhaps John the Baptist or another prophet. Some suggested that he was Elijah, the great prophet who did not die but was taken to heaven in a chariot of fire (2 Kings 2:1–11). Very few found the correct answer, as Peter did (9:20). For many people today, it is still not easy to accept Jesus as the fully human yet fully divine Son of God. People are still trying to find alternate explanations — a great prophet, a radical political leader, a self-deceived rabble-rouser. None of these explanations can account for Jesus' miracles or, especially, his glorious resurrection — so these realities too have to be explained away. In the end, the attempts to explain away Jesus are far more difficult to believe than the truth.

9:9 For the story of how Herod had John beheaded, see Mark 6:14–29.

Jesus Feeds Five Thousand
(96/Matthew 14:13–21; Mark 6:30–44; John 6:1–15)

9:10
f Mk 6:30
g Mt 11:21

10When the apostles *f* returned, they reported to Jesus what they had done. Then he took them with him and they withdrew by themselves to a town called Bethsaida, *g* 11but the crowds learned about it and followed him. He welcomed them and spoke to them about the kingdom of God, and healed those who needed healing.

12Late in the afternoon the Twelve came to him and said, "Send the crowd away so they can go to the surrounding villages and countryside and find food and lodging, because we are in a remote place here."

13He replied, "You give them something to eat."

They answered, "We have only five loaves of bread and two fish — unless we go and buy food for all this crowd." 14(About five thousand men were there.)

But he said to his disciples, "Have them sit down in groups of about fifty each." 15The disciples did so, and everybody sat down. 16Taking the five loaves and the two fish and looking up to heaven, he gave thanks and broke them. Then he gave them to the disciples to set before the people. 17They all ate and were satisfied, and the disciples picked up twelve basketfuls of broken pieces that were left over.

Peter Says Jesus Is the Messiah
(109/Matthew 16:13–20; Mark 8:27–30)

18Once when Jesus was praying in private and his disciples were with him, he asked them, "Who do the crowds say I am?"

9:19
h ver 7, 8

19They replied, "Some say John the Baptist; others say Elijah; and still others, that one of the prophets of long ago has come back to life." *h*

9:20
i Jn 6:66-69

20"But what about you?" he asked. "Who do you say I am?"

Peter answered, "The Christ*j* of God." *i*

Jesus Predicts His Death the First Time
(110/Matthew 16:21–28; Mark 8:31 – 9:1)

9:21
i Mk 8:30
9:22
k Mt 16:21

21Jesus strictly warned them not to tell this to anyone. *i* 22And he said, "The Son of Man must suffer many things *k* and be rejected by the elders, chief priests and teachers of the law, and he must be killed and on the third day be raised to life."

j 20 Or Messiah

9:10, 11 Jesus had tried to slip quietly away from the crowds, but they found out where he was going and followed him. Instead of showing impatience at this interruption, Jesus welcomed the people and ministered to their needs. How do you see people who interrupt your schedule – as nuisances, or as the reason for your life and ministry?

9:11 The kingdom of God was a focal point of Jesus' teaching. He explained that it was not just a future kingdom; it was among them, embodied in him, the Messiah. Even though the kingdom will not be complete until Jesus comes again in glory, we do not have to wait to taste it. The kingdom of God begins in the hearts of those who believe in Jesus (17:21). It is as present with us today as it was with the Judeans almost 2,000 years ago.

● **9:13, 14** When the disciples expressed concern about where the crowd of thousands would eat, Jesus offered a surprising solution – "You give them something to eat." The disciples protested, focusing their attention on what they didn't have (food and money). Do you think God would ask you to do something that you and he together couldn't handle? Don't let your lack of resources blind you to seeing God's power.

● **9:16, 17** Why did Jesus bother to feed these people? He could just as easily have sent them on their way. But Jesus does not ignore needs. He is concerned with every aspect of our lives – the physical as well as the spiritual. As we work to bring wholeness to people's lives, we must never ignore the fact that all of us have

both physical and spiritual needs. It is impossible to minister effectively to one type of need without considering the other.

9:18–20 The Christian faith goes beyond knowing what others believe. It requires us to hold beliefs for ourselves. When Jesus asks, "Who do you say I am?" he wants us to take a stand. Who do *you* say Jesus is?

9:21 Jesus told his disciples not to tell anyone that he was the Christ because at this point they didn't fully understand the significance of that confession – nor would anyone else. Everyone still expected the Messiah to come as a conquering king. But even though Jesus was the Messiah, he still had to suffer, be rejected by the leaders, be killed, and rise from the dead. When the disciples saw all this happen to Jesus, they would understand what the Messiah had come to do. Only then would they be equipped to share the gospel around the world.

9:22 This was the turning point in Jesus' instruction to his disciples. From then on he began teaching clearly and specifically what they could expect, so that they would not be surprised when it happened. He explained that he would not *now* be the conquering Messiah because he first had to suffer, die, and rise again. But one day he would return in great glory to set up his eternal kingdom.

23Then he said to them all: "If anyone would come after me, he must deny himself and take up his cross daily and follow me.^{l} 24For whoever wants to save his life will lose it, but whoever loses his life for me will save it. 25What good is it for a man to gain the whole world, and yet lose or forfeit his very self? 26If anyone is ashamed of me and my words, the Son of Man will be ashamed of him^m when he comes in his glory and in the glory of the Father and of the holy angels. 27I tell you the truth, some who are standing here will not taste death before they see the kingdom of God."

9:23
^{l}Mt 10:38;
Lk 14:27

9:26
^{m}Mt 10:33;
Lk 12:9;
2Ti 2:12

Jesus Is Transfigured on the Mountain
(111/Matthew 17:1–13; Mark 9:2–13)

28About eight days after Jesus said this, he took Peter, John and James with him and went up onto a mountain to pray.^{n} 29As he was praying, the appearance of his face changed, and his clothes became as bright as a flash of lightning. 30Two men, Moses and Elijah, 31appeared in glorious splendor, talking with Jesus. They spoke about his departure,^{o} which he was about to bring to fulfillment at Jerusalem. 32Peter and his companions were very sleepy,^{p} but when they became fully awake, they saw his glory and the two men standing with him. 33As the men were leaving Jesus, Peter said to him, "Master,^{q} it is good for us to be here. Let us put up three shelters — one for you, one for Moses and one for Elijah." (He did not know what he was saying.)

34While he was speaking, a cloud appeared and enveloped them, and they were afraid as they entered the cloud. 35A voice came from the cloud, saying, "This is

9:28
^{n}Lk 3:21

9:31
^{o}2Pe 1:15

9:32
^{p}Mt 26:43

9:33
^{q}Lk 5:5

9:23 Christians follow their Lord by imitating his life and obeying his commands. To take up the cross meant to carry your own cross to the place where you would be killed. Many Galileans had been killed that way by the Romans. Applied to the disciples, it meant to identify completely with Christ's message, even if it meant death. We must deny our selfish desires to use our time and money our own way and to choose our own direction in life without regard to Christ. Following Christ is costly now, but in the long run, it is well worth the pain and effort.

9:23-26 People are willing to pay a high price for something they value. Is it any surprise that Jesus would demand this much commitment from his followers? There are at least three conditions that must be met by people who want to follow Jesus. We must be willing to deny self, to take up our crosses, and to follow him. Anything less is superficial lip service.

9:24, 25 If this present life is most important to you, you will do everything you can to protect it. You will not want to do anything that might endanger your safety, health, or comfort. By contrast, if following Jesus is most important, you may find yourself in unsafe, unhealthy, and uncomfortable places. You will risk death, but you will not fear it because you know that Jesus will raise you to eternal life. Nothing material can compensate for the loss of eternal life. Jesus' disciples are not to use their lives on earth for their own pleasure — they should spend their lives serving God and people.

9:26 Luke's Greek audience would have found it difficult to understand a God who could die, just as Jesus' Jewish audience would have been perplexed by a Messiah who would let himself be captured. Both would be ashamed of Jesus if they did not look past his death to his glorious resurrection and second coming. Then they would see Jesus not as a loser but as the Lord of the universe, who through his death brought salvation to all people.

● **9:27** When Jesus said some would not die without seeing the kingdom, he was referring to (1) Peter, James, and John, who would witness the transfiguration eight days later, or in a broader sense (2) to all who would witness the resurrection and ascension, or (3) to all who would take part in the spread of the church after Pentecost. Jesus' listeners were not going to have to wait for another, future Messiah — the kingdom was among them, and it would soon come in power.

● **9:29, 30** Jesus took Peter, James, and John to the top of a mountain to show them who he really was — not just a great prophet, but God's own Son. Moses, representing the law, and Elijah, representing the prophets, appeared with Jesus. Then God's voice singled out Jesus as the long-awaited Messiah who possessed divine authority. Jesus would fulfill both the Law and the Prophets (Matthew 5:17).

9:33 When Peter suggested making three shelters, he may have been thinking of the Feast of Tabernacles, where shelters were set up to commemorate the exodus, God's deliverance from slavery in Egypt. Peter wanted to keep Moses and Elijah with them. But this was not what God wanted. Peter's desire to build shelters for Jesus, Moses, and Elijah may also show his understanding that real faith is built on three cornerstones: the law, the prophets, and Jesus. But Peter grew in his understanding, and eventually he would write of Jesus as the "chosen and precious cornerstone" of the church (1 Peter 2:6).

9:33 Peter, James, and John experienced a wonderful moment on the mountain, and they didn't want to leave. Sometimes we too have such an inspiring experience that we want to stay where we are — away from the reality and problems of our daily lives. Knowing that struggles await us in the valley encourages us to linger on the mountaintop. Yet staying on top of a mountain prohibits our ministering to others. Instead of becoming spiritual giants, we would soon become dwarfed by our self-centeredness. We need times of retreat and renewal, but only so we can return to minister to the world. Our faith must make sense off the mountain as well as on it.

9:35 As God's Son, Jesus has God's power and authority; thus his words should be our final authority. If a person's teaching is true, it will agree with Jesus' teachings. Test everything you hear against Jesus' words, and you will not be led astray. Don't be hasty to seek advice and guidance from merely human sources and thereby neglect Christ's message.

9:35 God clearly identified Jesus as his Son before saying that Peter and the others were to listen to Jesus and not to their own ideas and desires. The ability to follow Jesus comes from confidence about who he is. If we believe he is God's Son, then we surely will want to do what he says.

9:35
ʳMt 3:17

9:36
ˢMt 17:9

my Son, whom I have chosen; listen to him."ʳ ³⁶When the voice had spoken, they found that Jesus was alone. The disciples kept this to themselves, and told no one at that time what they had seen.ˢ

Jesus Heals a Demon-Possessed Boy
(112/Matthew 17:14–21; Mark 9:14–29)

³⁷The next day, when they came down from the mountain, a large crowd met him. ³⁸A man in the crowd called out, "Teacher, I beg you to look at my son, for he is my only child. ³⁹A spirit seizes him and he suddenly screams; it throws him into convulsions so that he foams at the mouth. It scarcely ever leaves him and is destroying him. ⁴⁰I begged your disciples to drive it out, but they could not."

⁴¹"O unbelieving and perverse generation," Jesus replied, "how long shall I stay with you and put up with you? Bring your son here."

⁴²Even while the boy was coming, the demon threw him to the ground in a convulsion. But Jesus rebuked the evilᵏ spirit, healed the boy and gave him back to his father. ⁴³And they were all amazed at the greatness of God.

Jesus Predicts His Death the Second Time
(113/Matthew 17:22, 23; Mark 9:30–32)

While everyone was marveling at all that Jesus did, he said to his disciples, ⁴⁴"Listen carefully to what I am about to tell you: The Son of Man is going to be

9:44
ᵗver 22

9:45
ᵘMk 9:32

betrayed into the hands of men."ᵗ ⁴⁵But they did not understand what this meant. It was hidden from them, so that they did not grasp it,ᵘ and they were afraid to ask him about it.

The Disciples Argue about Who Would Be the Greatest
(115/Matthew 18:1–6; Mark 9:33–37)

⁴⁶An argument started among the disciples as to which of them would be the

9:47
ᵛMt 9:4

9:48
ʷMt 10:40

greatest. ⁴⁷Jesus, knowing their thoughts,ᵛ took a little child and had him stand beside him. ⁴⁸Then he said to them, "Whoever welcomes this little child in my name welcomes me; and whoever welcomes me welcomes the one who sent me.ʷ For he who is least among you all — he is the greatest."

The Disciples Forbid Another to Use Jesus' Name
(116/Mark 9:38–41)

⁴⁹"Master," said John, "we saw a man driving out demons in your name and we tried to stop him, because he is not one of us."

9:50
ˣMt 12:30;
Lk 11:23

⁵⁰"Do not stop him," Jesus said, "for whoever is not against you is for you."ˣ

ᵏ *42* Greek *unclean*

9:37–39 As the disciples came down from the mountain with Jesus, they passed from a reassuring experience of God's presence to a frightening experience of evil. The beauty they had just seen must have made the ugliness seem even uglier. As our spiritual vision improves and allows us to see and understand God better, we will also be able to see and understand evil better. We would be overcome by its horror if we did not have Jesus with us to take us through it safely.

9:40 Why couldn't the disciples drive out the evil spirit? For a possible answer, see the note on Mark 9:18.

9:45, 46 The disciples didn't understand Jesus' words about his death. They still thought of Jesus as only an earthly king, and they were concerned about their places in the kingdom he would set up. So they ignored Jesus' words about his death and began arguing about who would be the greatest.

9:48 Our care for others is a measure of our greatness. How much concern do you show to others? This is a vital question that

can accurately measure your greatness in God's eyes. How have you expressed your care for others lately, especially the helpless, the needy, the poor — those who can't return your love and concern? Your honest answer to that question will give you a good idea of your real greatness.

9:49, 50 The disciples were jealous. Nine of them together were unable to drive out a single evil spirit (9:40), but when they saw a man who was not one of their group driving out demons, they told him to stop. Our pride is hurt when someone else succeeds where we have failed, but Jesus says there is no room for such jealousy in the spiritual warfare of his kingdom. Share Jesus' open-arms attitude to Christian workers outside your group.

2. Jesus' ministry on the way to Jerusalem
Jesus Teaches about the Cost of Following Him
(122/Matthew 8:18–22)

[51] As the time approached for him to be taken up to heaven,[y] Jesus resolutely set out for Jerusalem.[z] [52] And he sent messengers on ahead, who went into a Samaritan[a] village to get things ready for him; [53] but the people there did not welcome him, because he was heading for Jerusalem. [54] When the disciples James and John saw this, they asked, "Lord, do you want us to call fire down from heaven to destroy them!?"[b] [55] But Jesus turned and rebuked them, [56] and[m] they went to another village.

[57] As they were walking along the road,[c] a man said to him, "I will follow you wherever you go."

[58] Jesus replied, "Foxes have holes and birds of the air have nests, but the Son of Man[d] has no place to lay his head."

[59] He said to another man, "Follow me."

But the man replied, "Lord, first let me go and bury my father."

[60] Jesus said to him, "Let the dead bury their own dead, but you go and proclaim the kingdom of God."

[61] Still another said, "I will follow you, Lord; but first let me go back and say good-by to my family."[e]

[62] Jesus replied, "No one who puts his hand to the plow and looks back is fit for service in the kingdom of God."

Jesus Sends Out Seventy-two Messengers
(130)

10 After this the Lord[f] appointed seventy-two[n] others[g] and sent them two by two[h] ahead of him to every town and place where he was about to go.[i] [2] He told them, "The harvest is plentiful, but the workers are few. Ask the Lord of the

9:51
[y] Mk 16:19
[z] Lk 13:22; 17:11;
18:31; 19:28
9:52
[a] Mt 10:5
9:54
[b] 2Ki 1:10, 12
9:57
[c] ver 51
9:58
[d] Mt 8:20
9:61
[e] 1Ki 19:20
10:1
[f] Lk 7:13
[g] Lk 9:1, 2, 51, 52
[h] Mk 6:7
[i] Mt 10:1

[i] 54 Some manuscripts *them, even as Elijah did* [m] 55,56 Some manuscripts *them. And he said, "You do not know what kind of spirit you are of, for the Son of Man did not come to destroy men's lives, but to save them."* 56And [n] 1 Some manuscripts *seventy*; also in verse 17

● **9:51** Although Jesus knew he would face persecution and death in Jerusalem, he was determined to go there. That kind of resolve should characterize our lives too. When God gives us a course of action, we must move steadily toward our destination, no matter what potential hazards await us there.

9:53 After Assyria invaded Israel, the northern kingdom, and resettled it with its own people (2 Kings 17:24–41), the mixed race that developed became known as the Samaritans. "Purebred" Jews hated these "half-breeds," and the Samaritans in turn hated the Jews. So many tensions arose between the two peoples that Jewish travelers between Galilee and southern Judea often walked around rather than through Samaritan territory, even though this lengthened their trip considerably. Jesus held no such prejudices, and he sent messengers ahead to get things ready in a Samaritan village. But the village refused to welcome these Jewish travelers.

9:54 When James and John were rejected by the Samaritan village, they didn't want to stop at shaking the dust from their feet (9:5). They wanted to retaliate by calling down fire from heaven on the people, as Elijah did on the servants of a wicked king of Israel (2 Kings 1). When others reject or scorn us, we too may feel like retaliating. We must remember that judgment belongs to God, and we must not expect him to use his power to carry out our personal vendettas.

● **9:59** Luke does not tell us whether the father is already dead or whether he's terminally ill. It seems likely that if the father were dead, the son would have been fulfilling the burial duties. Jesus was proclaiming that true discipleship requires instant action. Jesus did not teach people to forsake responsibilities to family, but he often gave commands to people in light of their real motives.

Perhaps this man wanted to delay following Christ and used his father as an excuse. There is a cost to following Jesus, and each of us must be ready to serve, even when it requires sacrifice.

● **9:62** What does Jesus want from us? Total dedication, not half-hearted commitment. We can't pick and choose among Jesus' ideas and follow him selectively; we have to accept the cross along with the crown, judgment as well as mercy. We must count the cost and be willing to abandon everything else that has given us security. With our focus on Jesus, we should allow nothing to distract us from the manner of living that he calls good and true.

10:1, 2 Far more than 12 people had been following Jesus. Here Jesus designated a group of 72 to prepare a number of towns for Jesus' later visit. These disciples were not unique in their qualifications. They were not better educated, more capable, or of higher status than other followers of Jesus. What equipped them for this mission was their awareness of Jesus' power and their vision to reach all the people. It is important to dedicate our skills to God's kingdom, but we must also be equipped with his power and have a clear vision of what he wants us to do.

10:2 Jesus was sending 36 teams of two to reach the multitudes. These teams were not to try to do the job without help; rather, they were to ask God for more workers. Some people, as soon as they understand the gospel, want to go to work immediately contacting unsaved people. This story suggests a different approach: begin by mobilizing people to pray. And before praying for unsaved people, pray that other concerned disciples will join you in reaching out to them.

10:2 In Christian service, there is no unemployment. God has work enough for everyone. Don't just sit back and watch others work—look for ways to help with the harvest.

10:2
/Mt 9:37, 38;
Jn 4:35

10:3
kMt 10:16

10:7
/1Ti 5:18

harvest, therefore, to send out workers into his harvest field./ 3Go! I am sending you out like lambs among wolves. k 4Do not take a purse or bag or sandals; and do not greet anyone on the road.

5"When you enter a house, first say, 'Peace to this house.' 6If a man of peace is there, your peace will rest on him; if not, it will return to you. 7Stay in that house, eating and drinking whatever they give you, for the worker deserves his wages./ Do not move around from house to house.

JAMES

Jesus singled out three of his 12 disciples for special training. James, his brother John, and Peter made up this inner circle. Each eventually played a key role in the early church. Peter became a great speaker, John became a major writer, and James was the first of the 12 disciples to die for the faith.

The fact that his name is always mentioned before John's indicates that James was the older brother. Zebedee, their father, owned a fishing business where they worked along with Peter and Andrew. When Peter, Andrew, and John left Galilee to see John the Baptist, James stayed back with the boats and fishing nets. Later, when Jesus called them, James was as eager as his partners to follow.

James enjoyed being in the inner circle of Jesus' disciples, but he misunderstood Jesus' purpose. He and his brother even tried to secure their role in Jesus' kingdom by asking Jesus to promise them each a special position. Like the other disciples, James had a limited view of what Jesus was doing on earth, picturing only an earthly kingdom that would overthrow Rome and restore Israel's former glory. But above all, James wanted to be with Jesus. He had found the right leader, even though he was still on the wrong timetable. It took Jesus' death and resurrection to correct his view.

James was the first of the 12 disciples to die for the gospel. He was willing to die because he knew Jesus had conquered death, the doorway to eternal life. Our expectations about life will be limited if this life is all we can see. Jesus promised eternal life to those willing to trust him. If we believe this promise, he will give us the courage to stand for him even during dangerous times.

Strengths and accomplishments:
• One of the 12 disciples
• One of a special inner circle of three with Peter and John
• First of the 12 disciples to be killed for his faith

Weaknesses and mistakes:
• Two outbursts from James indicate struggles with temper (Luke 9:54) and selfishness (Mark 10:37). Both times, he and his brother, John, spoke as one

Lesson from his life:
• Loss of life is not too heavy a price to pay for following Jesus

Vital statistics:
• Where: Galilee
• Occupations: Fisherman, disciple
• Relatives: Father: Zebedee. Mother: Salome. Brother: John
• Contemporaries: Jesus, Pilate, Herod Agrippa

Key verses:
"Then James and John, the sons of Zebedee, came to him. 'Teacher,' they said, 'we want you to do for us whatever we ask.' 'What do you want me to do for you?' he asked. They replied, 'Let one of us sit at your right and the other at your left in your glory' " (Mark 10:35–37).

James's story is told in the Gospels. He is also mentioned in Acts 1:13 and 12:2.

• **10:3** Jesus said he was sending his disciples out "like lambs among wolves." They would have to be careful because they would surely meet with opposition. We too are sent into the world like lambs among wolves. Be alert, and remember to face your enemies not with aggression but with love and gentleness. A dangerous mission requires sincere commitment.

10:7 Jesus' direction to stay in one house avoided certain problems. Shifting from house to house could offend the families who first took them in. Some families might begin to compete for the disciples' presence, and some might think they weren't good enough to hear their message. If the disciples appeared not to appreciate the hospitality offered them, the town might not accept Jesus when he followed them there. In addition, by staying in one place, the disciples did not have to worry continually about getting good accommodations. They could settle down and do their appointed task.

10:7 Jesus told his disciples to accept hospitality graciously because their work entitled them to it. Ministers of the gospel deserve to be supported, and it is our responsibility to make sure they have what they need. There are several ways to encourage those who serve God in his church. First, see that they have an adequate salary. Second, see that they are supported emotionally; plan a time to express appreciation for something they have done. Third, lift their spirits with special surprises from time to time. Our ministers deserve to know we are giving to them cheerfully and generously.

8"When you enter a town and are welcomed, eat what is set before you. 9Heal the sick who are there and tell them, 'The kingdom of God*m* is near you.' 10But when you enter a town and are not welcomed, go into its streets and say, 11'Even the dust of your town that sticks to our feet we wipe off against you.*n* Yet be sure of this: The kingdom of God is near.' 12I tell you, it will be more bearable on that day for Sodom*o* than for that town.

13"Woe to you, Korazin! Woe to you, Bethsaida! For if the miracles that were performed in you had been performed in Tyre and Sidon, they would have repented long ago, sitting in sackcloth and ashes. 14But it will be more bearable for Tyre and Sidon at the judgment than for you. 15And you, Capernaum, will you be lifted up to the skies? No, you will go down to the depths.*o*

16"He who listens to you listens to me; he who rejects you rejects me; but he who rejects me rejects him who sent me."*p*

The Seventy-two Messengers Return
(131)

17The seventy-two returned with joy and said, "Lord, even the demons submit to us in your name."

18He replied, "I saw Satan fall like lightning from heaven.*q* 19I have given you authority to trample on snakes*r* and scorpions and to overcome all the power of the enemy; nothing will harm you. 20However, do not rejoice that the spirits submit to you, but rejoice that your names are written in heaven."

21At that time Jesus, full of joy through the Holy Spirit, said, "I praise you, Father, Lord of heaven and earth, because you have hidden these things from the wise and learned, and revealed them to little children. Yes, Father, for this was your good pleasure.

22"All things have been committed to me by my Father. No one knows who the Son is except the Father, and no one knows who the Father is except the Son and those to whom the Son chooses to reveal him."

23Then he turned to his disciples and said privately, "Blessed are the eyes that see

o 15 Greek *Hades*

10:9
m Mt 3:2

10:11
n Mt 10:14

10:12
o Mt 10:15

10:16
p Mt 10:40

10:18
q Rev 9:1

10:19
r Mk 16:18

10:8, 9 Jesus gave two rules for the disciples to follow as they traveled. They were to eat what was set before them—that is, they were to accept hospitality without being picky—and they were to heal the sick. Because of the healings, people would be willing to listen to the gospel.

10:12 Sodom was an evil city that God destroyed because of its great sinfulness (Genesis 19). The city's name is often used to symbolize wickedness and immorality. Sodom will suffer at judgment day, but cities who saw the Messiah and rejected him will suffer even more.

10:13 Korazin was a city near the Sea of Galilee, probably about two miles north of Capernaum. Tyre and Sidon were cities destroyed by God as punishment for their wickedness (see Ezekiel 26—28).

10:15 Capernaum was Jesus' base for his Galilean ministry. The city was located at an important crossroads used by traders and the Roman army, so a message proclaimed in Capernaum was likely to go far. But many people of Capernaum did not understand Jesus' miracles or believe his teaching, and the city was included among those who would be judged for rejecting him.

10:17-20 The disciples had seen tremendous results as they ministered in Jesus' name and with his authority. They were elated by the victories they had witnessed, and Jesus shared their enthusiasm. He helped them get their priorities right, however, by reminding them of their most important victory—that their names were written in heaven. This honor was more important than any of their accomplishments. As we see God's wonders at work in and through us, we should not lose sight of the greatest wonder of all—our heavenly citizenship.

10:18, 19 Jesus may have been looking ahead to his victory over Satan at the cross. John 12:31, 32 indicates that Satan would be judged and driven out at the time of Jesus' death. On the other hand, Jesus may have been warning his disciples against pride. Perhaps he was referring to Isaiah 14:12-17, which begins, "How you have fallen from heaven, O morning star, son of the dawn!" Some interpreters identify this verse with Satan and explain that Satan's pride led to all the evil we see on earth today. To Jesus' disciples, who were thrilled with their power over evil spirits ("snakes and scorpions"), he may have been giving this stern warning: "Yours is the kind of pride that led to Satan's downfall. Be careful!"

10:21 Jesus thanked God that spiritual truth was for everyone, and not just for the elite. Many of life's rewards seem to go to the intelligent, the rich, the good-looking, or the powerful, but the kingdom of God is equally available to all, regardless of position or abilities. We come to Jesus not through strength or brains, but through childlike trust. Jesus is not opposed to engaging in scholarly pursuits; he is opposed to spiritual pride (being wise in one's own eyes). Join Jesus in thanking God that we all have equal access to him. Trust in God's grace, not in your personal qualifications, for your citizenship in the kingdom.

10:22 Christ's mission was to reveal God the Father to people. His words brought difficult ideas down to earth. He explained God's love through parables, teachings, and, most of all, his life. By examining Jesus' actions, principles, and attitudes, we can understand God more clearly.

● **10:23, 24** The disciples had a fantastic opportunity—they were eyewitnesses of Christ, the Son of God. But for many months they took Jesus for granted, not really listening to him or obeying him.

what you see. 24For I tell you that many prophets and kings wanted to see what you see but did not see it, and to hear what you hear but did not hear it."

Jesus Tells the Parable of the Good Samaritan
(132)

25On one occasion an expert in the law stood up to test Jesus. "Teacher," he asked, "what must I do to inherit eternal life?"ˢ

26"What is written in the Law?" he replied. "How do you read it?"

27He answered: " 'Love the Lord your God with all your heart and with all your soul and with all your strength and with all your mind'ᴾ;ᵗ and, 'Love your neighbor as yourself.'ᑫ"ᵘ

28"You have answered correctly," Jesus replied. "Do this and you will live."

29But he wanted to justify himself,ᵛ so he asked Jesus, "And who is my neighbor?"

30In reply Jesus said: "A man was going down from Jerusalem to Jericho, when he fell into the hands of robbers. They stripped him of his clothes, beat him and went away, leaving him half dead. 31A priest happened to be going down the same road, and when he saw the man, he passed by on the other side. 32So too, a Levite, when he came to the place and saw him, passed by on the other side. 33But a Samaritan, as he traveled, came where the man was; and when he saw him, he took pity on him. 34He went to him and bandaged his wounds, pouring on oil and wine. Then he put the man on his own donkey, took him to an inn and took care of him. 35The next day he took out two silver coinsʳ and gave them to the innkeeper. 'Look after him,' he said, 'and when I return, I will reimburse you for any extra expense you may have.'

p *27* Deut. 6:5   q *27* Lev. 19:18   r *35* Greek *two denarii*

10:25
ˢMt 19:16

10:27
ᵗDt 6:5
ᵘLev 19:18

10:29
ᵛLk 16:15

A COLLECTION OF ATTITUDES

To the expert in the law, the wounded man was a subject to discuss.

To the robbers, the wounded man was someone to use and exploit.

To the religious men, the wounded man was a problem to be avoided.

To the innkeeper, the wounded man was a customer to serve for a fee.

To the Samaritan, the wounded man was a human being worth being cared for and loved.

To Jesus, all of them and all of us were worth dying for.

Confronting the needs of others brings out various attitudes in us. Jesus used the story of the good but despised Samaritan to make clear what attitude was acceptable to him. If we are honest, we often will find ourselves in the place of the expert in the law, needing to learn again who our neighbor is. Note these different attitudes toward the wounded man.

We also have a privileged position, with knowledge of 2,000 years of church history, availability of the Bible in hundreds of languages and translations, and access to many excellent pastors and speakers. Yet often we take these for granted. Remember, with privilege comes responsibility. Because we are privileged to know so much about Christ, we must be careful to follow him.

10:24 Old Testament men of God such as David and the prophet Isaiah made many God-inspired predictions that Jesus fulfilled. As Peter later wrote, these prophets wondered what their words meant and when they would be fulfilled (1 Peter 1:10–13). In Jesus' words, they "wanted to see what you see" — the coming of God's kingdom.

10:27 This expert in the law was quoting Deuteronomy 6:5 and Leviticus 19:18. He correctly understood that the law demanded total devotion to God and love for one's neighbor. Jesus talked more about these laws elsewhere (see Matthew 19:16–22 and Mark 10:17–22).

10:27-37 The law expert treated the wounded man as a topic for discussion; the robbers, as an object to exploit; the priest, as a problem to avoid; and the Levite, as an object of curiosity. Only the Samaritan treated him as a person to love.

● **10:27-37** From the parable we learn three principles about loving our neighbor: (1) lack of love is often easy to justify, even though it is never right; (2) our neighbor is anyone of any race, creed, or social background who is in need; and (3) love means acting to meet the person's need. Wherever you live, there are needy people close by. There is no good reason for refusing to help.

● **10:33** There was deep hatred between Jews and Samaritans. The Jews saw themselves as pure descendants of Abraham, while the Samaritans were a mixed race produced when Jews from the northern kingdom intermarried with other peoples after Israel's exile. To this law expert, the person least likely to act correctly would be the Samaritan. In fact, he could not bear to say "Samaritan" in answer to Jesus' question. This "expert's" attitude betrayed his lack of the very thing that he had earlier said the law commanded — love.

36"Which of these three do you think was a neighbor to the man who fell into the hands of robbers?"

37The expert in the law replied, "The one who had mercy on him."

Jesus told him, "Go and do likewise."

Jesus Visits Mary and Martha
(133)

38As Jesus and his disciples were on their way, he came to a village where a woman named Martha opened her home to him. 39She had a sister called Mary, who sat at the Lord's feet[w] listening to what he said. 40But Martha was distracted by all the preparations that had to be made. She came to him and asked, "Lord, don't you care that my sister has left me to do the work by myself? Tell her to help me!"

41"Martha, Martha," the Lord answered, "you are worried[x] and upset about many things, 42but only one thing is needed.[s][y] Mary has chosen what is better, and it will not be taken away from her."

10:39
[w] Lk 8:35

10:41
[x] Mt 6:25-34

10:42
[y] Ps 27:4

Jesus Teaches His Disciples about Prayer
(134)

11 One day Jesus was praying[z] in a certain place. When he finished, one of his disciples said to him, "Lord, teach us to pray, just as John taught his disciples."

2He said to them, "When you pray, say:

" 'Father,[t]
hallowed be your name,
your kingdom come.[u]
3Give us each day our daily bread.
4Forgive us our sins,
for we also forgive everyone who sins against us.[v][a]
And lead us not into temptation.[w]' "

11:1
[z] Lk 3:21

11:4
[a] Mt 18:35;
Mk 11:25

[s] 42 Some manuscripts *but few things are needed—or only one*   [t] 2 Some manuscripts *Our Father in heaven*
[u] 2 Some manuscripts *come. May your will be done on earth as it is in heaven.*   [v] 4 Greek *everyone who is indebted to us*   [w] 4 Some manuscripts *temptation but deliver us from the evil one*

● **10:38-42** Mary and Martha both loved Jesus. On this occasion they were both serving him. But Martha thought Mary's style of serving was inferior to hers. She didn't realize that in her desire to serve, she was actually neglecting her guest. Are you so busy doing things *for* Jesus that you're not spending any time *with* him? Don't let your service become self-serving.

10:41, 42 Jesus did not blame Martha for being concerned about household chores. He was only asking her to set priorities. It is possible for service to Christ to degenerate into mere busywork that is no longer full of devotion to God.

11:1-4 Notice the order in this prayer. First Jesus praised God; then he made his requests. Praising God first puts us in the right frame of mind to tell him about our needs. Too often our prayers are more like shopping lists than conversations.

11:2-13 These verses focus on three aspects of prayer: its content (11:2-4), our persistence (11:5-10), and God's faithfulness (11:11-13).

11:3 God's provision is daily, not all at once. We cannot store it up and then cut off communication with God. And we dare not be self-satisfied. If you are running low on strength, ask yourself—how long have I been away from the Source?

● **11:4** When Jesus taught his disciples to pray, he made forgiveness the cornerstone of their relationship with God. God has forgiven our sins; we must now forgive those who have wronged us. To remain unforgiving shows we have not understood that we ourselves deeply need to be forgiven. Think of some people who have wronged you. Have you forgiven them? How will God deal with you if he treats you as you treat others?

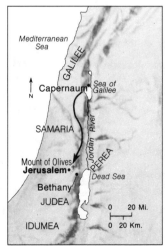

JESUS VISITS MARY AND MARTHA
After teaching throughout Galilee, Jesus returned to Jerusalem for the Feast of Tabernacles (John 7:2). He spoke in Jerusalem and then visited his friends Mary and Martha in the tiny village of Bethany on the slope of the Mount of Olives.

⁵Then he said to them, "Suppose one of you has a friend, and he goes to him at midnight and says, 'Friend, lend me three loaves of bread, ⁶because a friend of mine on a journey has come to me, and I have nothing to set before him.'

⁷"Then the one inside answers, 'Don't bother me. The door is already locked, and my children are with me in bed. I can't get up and give you anything.' ⁸I tell you, though he will not get up and give him the bread because he is his friend, yet because of the man's boldnessˣ he will get up and give him as much as he needs. ᵇ

⁹"So I say to you: Ask and it will be given to you;ᶜ seek and you will find; knock and the door will be opened to you. ¹⁰For everyone who asks receives; he who seeks finds; and to him who knocks, the door will be opened.

ˣ 8 Or *persistence*

11:8
ᵇ Lk 18:1-6

11:9
ᶜ Mt 7:7

MARTHA

Many older brothers and sisters have an irritating tendency to take charge, a habit developed while growing up. We can easily see this pattern in Martha, the older sister of Mary and Lazarus. She was used to being in control.

The fact that Martha, Mary, and Lazarus are remembered for their hospitality takes on added significance when we note that hospitality was a social requirement in their culture. It was considered shameful to turn anyone away from your door. Apparently Martha's family met this requirement very well.

Martha worried about details. She wished to please, to serve, to do the right thing—but she often succeeded in making everyone around her uncomfortable. Perhaps as the oldest she feared shame if her home did not measure up to expectations. She tried to do everything she could to make sure that wouldn't happen. As a result, she found it hard to relax and enjoy her guests, and even harder to accept Mary's lack of cooperation in all the preparations. Martha's frustration was so intense that she finally asked Jesus to settle the matter. He gently corrected her attitude and showed her that her priorities, though good, were not the best. The personal attention she gave her guests should be more important than the comforts she tried to provide for them.

Later, following her brother Lazarus's death, Martha could hardly help being herself. When she heard Jesus was finally coming, she rushed out to meet him and expressed her inner conflict of disappointment and hope. Jesus pointed out that her hope was too limited. He was not only Lord beyond death, he was Lord over death—the resurrection and the life! Moments later, Martha again spoke without thinking, pointing out that four-day-old corpses are well on their way to decomposition. Her awareness of details sometimes kept her from seeing the whole picture, but Jesus was consistently patient with her.

In our last picture of Martha, she is once again serving a meal to Jesus and his disciples. She has not stopped serving. But the Bible records her silence this time. She has begun to learn what her younger sister already knew—that worship begins with silence and listening.

Strengths and accomplishments:
• Known as a hospitable homemaker
• Believed in Jesus with growing faith
• Had a strong desire to do everything exactly right

Weaknesses and mistakes:
• Expected others to agree with her priorities
• Was overly concerned with details
• Tended to feel sorry for herself when her efforts were not recognized
• Limited Jesus' power to this life

Lessons from her life:
• Getting caught up in details can make us forget the main reasons for our actions
• There is a proper time to listen to Jesus and a proper time to work for him

Vital statistics:
• Where: Bethany
• Relatives: Sister: Mary. Brother: Lazarus

Key verse:
"But Martha was distracted by all the preparations that had to be made. She came to him and asked, 'Lord, don't you care that my sister has left me to do the work by myself? Tell her to help me!' " (Luke 10:40).

Martha's story is told in Luke 10:38–42 and John 11:17–45.

11:8 Persistence, or boldness, in prayer overcomes our insensitivity, not God's. To practice persistence does more to change our hearts and minds than his, and it helps us understand and express the intensity of our need. Persistence in prayer helps us recognize God's work.

11"Which of you fathers, if your son asks forʸ a fish, will give him a snake instead? 12Or if he asks for an egg, will give him a scorpion? 13If you then, though you are evil, know how to give good gifts to your children, how much more will your Father in heaven give the Holy Spirit to those who ask him!"

Jesus Answers Hostile Accusations
(135)

14Jesus was driving out a demon that was mute. When the demon left, the man who had been mute spoke, and the crowd was amazed.ᵈ 15But some of them said, "By Beelzebub,ᶻ the prince of demons, he is driving out demons."ᵉ 16Others tested him by asking for a sign from heaven.ᶠ

17Jesus knew their thoughts and said to them: "Any kingdom divided against itself will be ruined, and a house divided against itself will fall. 18If Satanᵍ is divided against himself, how can his kingdom stand? I say this because you claim that I drive out demons by Beelzebub. 19Now if I drive out demons by Beelzebub, by whom do your followers drive them out? So then, they will be your judges. 20But if I drive out demons by the finger of God,ʰ then the kingdom of Godⁱ has come to you.

21"When a strong man, fully armed, guards his own house, his possessions are safe. 22But when someone stronger attacks and overpowers him, he takes away the armor in which the man trusted and divides up the spoils.

23"He who is not with me is against me, and he who does not gather with me, scatters.ʲ

24"When an evilᵃ spirit comes out of a man, it goes through arid places seeking rest and does not find it. Then it says, 'I will return to the house I left.' 25When it arrives, it finds the house swept clean and put in order. 26Then it goes and takes seven other spirits more wicked than itself, and they go in and live there. And the final condition of that man is worse than the first."ᵏ

11:14
ᵈMt 9:32, 33
11:15
ᵉMt 9:34
11:16
ᶠMt 12:38
11:18
ᵍMt 4:10
11:20
ʰEx 8:19
ⁱMt 3:2
11:23
ʲMt 12:30;
Lk 9:50
11:26
ᵏ2Pe 2:20

ʸ 11 Some manuscripts *for bread, will give him a stone; or if he asks for* ᶻ 15 Greek *Beezeboul* or *Beelzeboul*; also in verses 18 and 19 ᵃ 24 Greek *unclean*

11:13 Even though good fathers make mistakes, they treat their children well. How much better our perfect heavenly Father treats his children! The most important gift he could ever give us is the Holy Spirit (Acts 2:1–4), whom he promised to give all believers after his death, resurrection, and return to heaven (John 15:26).

11:14–23 A similar and possibly separate event is reported in Matthew 12:22–45 and Mark 3:20–30. The event described by Luke happened in Judea while the other took place in Galilee. According to Luke, Jesus spoke to the crowds; in Matthew and Mark, he accused the Pharisees.

11:15–20 There are two common interpretations of these verses. (1) Some of the Pharisees' followers drove out demons. If this was so, the Pharisees' accusations were becoming more desperate. To accuse Jesus of being empowered by Beelzebub, the prince of demons (or Satan himself), because Jesus was driving out demons was also to say that the Pharisees' own followers were doing Satan's work. Jesus turned the religious leaders' accusation against them. (2) Another possibility is that the Pharisees' followers were *not* driving out demons; and even if they tried, they did not succeed. Jesus first dismissed their claim as absurd (Why would the devil drive out his own demons?). Then he engaged in a little irony ("By whom do your followers drive them out?"). Finally he concluded that his work of driving out demons proves that the kingdom of God had arrived.

Satan, who had controlled the kingdom of this world for thousands of years, was now being controlled and overpowered by Jesus and the kingdom of heaven. Jesus' kingdom began to come into power at Jesus' birth, grew as he resisted the desert temptations, established itself through his teachings and healings, blos-

somed in victory at his resurrection and at Pentecost, and will become permanent and universal at his second coming. Though these two interpretations may differ, they arrive at the same conclusion — the kingdom of God has arrived with the coming of Jesus Christ.

11:21, 22 Jesus may have been referring to Isaiah 49:24–26. Regardless of how great Satan's power is, Jesus is stronger still. He will bind Satan and dispose of him for eternity (see Revelation 20:2, 10).

11:23 How does this verse relate to 9:50: "Whoever is not against you is for you"? In the earlier passage, Jesus was talking about a person who was driving out demons in Jesus' name. Those who fight evil, he was saying, are on the same side as one driving out demons in Jesus' name. Here, by contrast, he was talking about the conflict between God and the devil. In this battle, if a person is not on God's side, he or she is on Satan's. There is no neutral ground. Because God has already won the battle, why be on the losing side? If you aren't actively for Christ, you are against him.

11:24–26 Jesus was illustrating an unfortunate human tendency — our desire to reform often does not last long. In Israel's history, almost as soon as a good king would pull down idols, a bad king would set them up again. It is not enough to be emptied of evil; we must then be filled with the power of the Holy Spirit to accomplish God's new purpose in our lives (see also Matthew 12:43–45; Galatians 5:22).

11:27, 28 Jesus was speaking to people who put extremely high value on family ties. Their genealogies were important guarantees that they were part of God's chosen people. A man's value came from his ancestors, and a woman's value came from the sons she

11:27
/Lk 23:29

11:28
mLk 8:21

27As Jesus was saying these things, a woman in the crowd called out, "Blessed is the mother who gave you birth and nursed you."/

28He replied, "Blessed rather are those who hear the word of God and obey it."m

Jesus Warns against Unbelief
(136)

11:29
nMt 12:38

11:31
o1Ki 10:1

11:32
pJnh 3:5

29As the crowds increased, Jesus said, "This is a wicked generation. It asks for a miraculous sign,n but none will be given it except the sign of Jonah. 30For as Jonah was a sign to the Ninevites, so also will the Son of Man be to this generation. 31The Queen of the South will rise at the judgment with the men of this generation and condemn them; for she came from the ends of the earth to listen to Solomon's wisdom,o and now oneb greater than Solomon is here. 32The men of Nineveh will stand up at the judgment with this generation and condemn it; for they repented at the preaching of Jonah,p and now one greater than Jonah is here.

Jesus Teaches about the Light Within
(137)

11:33
qMt 5:15

33"No one lights a lamp and puts it in a place where it will be hidden, or under a bowl. Instead he puts it on its stand, so that those who come in may see the light.q 34Your eye is the lamp of your body. When your eyes are good, your whole body also is full of light. But when they are bad, your body also is full of darkness. 35See to it, then, that the light within you is not darkness. 36Therefore, if your whole body is full of light, and no part of it dark, it will be completely lighted, as when the light of a lamp shines on you."

Jesus Criticizes the Religious Leaders
(138)

11:38
rMk 7:3, 4

11:39
sMt 23:25, 26

11:41
tLk 12:33

37When Jesus had finished speaking, a Pharisee invited him to eat with him; so he went in and reclined at the table. 38But the Pharisee, noticing that Jesus did not first wash before the meal,r was surprised.

39Then the Lord said to him, "Now then, you Pharisees clean the outside of the cup and dish, but inside you are full of greed and wickedness.s 40You foolish people! Did not the one who made the outside make the inside also? 41But give what is inside the dish,c to the poor,t and everything will be clean for you.

b 31 Or *something*; also in verse 32   c 41 Or *what you have*

bore. Jesus' response to the woman meant that a person's obedience to God is more important than his or her place on the family tree. The patient work of consistent obedience is even more important than the honor of bearing a respected son.

11:29, 30 What was the sign of Jonah? God had asked Jonah to preach repentance to the Gentiles (non-Jews). Jesus was affirming Jonah's message. Salvation is not only for Jews, but for all people. Matthew 12:40 adds another explanation: Jesus would die and rise after three days, just as the prophet Jonah was rescued after three days in the belly of the great fish.

11:29–32 The cruel, warlike men of Nineveh, capital of Assyria, repented when Jonah preached to them—and Jonah did not even care about them. The pagan Queen of the South (Sheba) praised the God of Israel when she heard Solomon's wisdom, and Solomon was full of faults. By contrast, Jesus, the perfect Son of God, had come to people that he loved dearly—but they rejected him. Thus God's chosen people made themselves more liable to judgment than either a notoriously wicked nation or a powerful pagan queen. Compare 10:12–15 where Jesus says the evil cities of Sodom, Tyre, and Sidon will be judged less harshly than the cities in Judea and Galilee that rejected Jesus' message.

11:31, 32 The Ninevites and the Queen of the South had turned

to God with far less evidence than Jesus was giving his listeners — and far less than we have today. We have eyewitness reports of the risen Jesus, the continuing power of the Holy Spirit unleashed at Pentecost, easy access to the Bible, and knowledge of 2,000 years of Christ's acts through his church. With the knowledge and insight available to us, our response to Christ ought to be even more complete and wholehearted.

11:33–36 The lamp is Christ; the eye represents spiritual understanding and insight. Evil desires make the eye less sensitive and blot out the light of Christ's presence. If you have a hard time seeing God at work in the world and in your life, check your vision. Are any sinful desires blinding you to Christ?

● **11:37–39** This washing was done not for health reasons, but as a symbol of washing away any contamination from touching anything unclean. Not only did the Pharisees make a public show of their washing, but they also commanded everyone else to follow a practice originally intended only for the priests.

● **11:41** The Pharisees loved to think of themselves as "clean," but their stinginess toward God and the poor proved that they were not as clean as they thought. How do you use the resources God has entrusted to you? Are you generous in meeting the needs around you? Your generosity reveals much about the purity of your heart.

42"Woe to you Pharisees, because you give God a tenth[u] of your mint, rue and all other kinds of garden herbs, but you neglect justice and the love of God. You should have practiced the latter without leaving the former undone.[v]

43"Woe to you Pharisees, because you love the most important seats in the synagogues and greetings in the marketplaces.[w]

44"Woe to you, because you are like unmarked graves,[x] which men walk over without knowing it."

45One of the experts in the law answered him, "Teacher, when you say these things, you insult us also."

46Jesus replied, "And you experts in the law, woe to you, because you load people down with burdens they can hardly carry, and you yourselves will not lift one finger to help them.[y]

47"Woe to you, because you build tombs for the prophets, and it was your forefathers who killed them. 48So you testify that you approve of what your forefathers did; they killed the prophets, and you build their tombs. 49Because of this, God in his wisdom[z] said, 'I will send them prophets and apostles, some of whom they will kill and others they will persecute.'[a] 50Therefore this generation will be held responsible for the blood of all the prophets that has been shed since the beginning of the world, 51from the blood of Abel[b] to the blood of Zechariah,[c] who was killed between the altar and the sanctuary. Yes, I tell you, this generation will be held responsible for it all.

52"Woe to you experts in the law, because you have taken away the key to knowledge. You yourselves have not entered, and you have hindered those who were entering."[d]

53When Jesus left there, the Pharisees and the teachers of the law began to oppose him fiercely and to besiege him with questions, 54waiting to catch him in something he might say.

11:42
u Lk 18:12
v Mt 23:23

11:43
w Mt 23:6, 7

11:44
x Mt 23:27

11:46
y Mt 23:4

11:49
z 1Co 1:24, 30
a Mt 23:34

11:51
b Ge 4:8
c 2Ch 24:20, 21

11:52
d Mt 23:13

11:42 It is easy to rationalize not helping others because we have already given to the church, but a person who follows Jesus should share with needy neighbors. While tithing is important to the life of the church, our compassion must not stop there. Where we can help, we should help.

●**11:42-52** Jesus criticized the Pharisees and the experts in the law harshly because they (1) washed their outsides but not their insides, (2) remembered to give a tenth of even their garden herbs, but neglected justice, (3) loved praise and attention, (4) loaded people down with burdensome religious demands, (5) would not accept the truth about Jesus, and (6) prevented others from believing the truth as well. They went wrong by focusing on outward appearances and ignoring the inner condition of their hearts. We do the same when our service comes from a desire to be seen rather than from a pure heart and out of a love for others. People may sometimes be fooled, but God isn't. Don't be a Christian on the outside only. Bring your inner life under God's control, and your outer life will naturally reflect him.

●**11:44** The Old Testament laws said a person who touched a grave was unclean (Numbers 19:16). Jesus accused the Pharisees of making others unclean by their spiritual rottenness. Like unmarked graves hidden in a field, the Pharisees corrupted everyone who came in contact with them.

●**11:46** These "burdens" were the details the Pharisees had added to God's law. To the commandment, "Remember the Sabbath day by keeping it holy" (Exodus 20:8), for example, they had added instructions regarding how far a person could walk on the Sabbath, which kinds of knots could be tied, and how much weight could be carried. Healing a person was considered unlawful work on the

Sabbath, although rescuing a trapped animal was permitted (14:5). No wonder Jesus condemned their additions to the law.

11:49 God's prophets have been persecuted and murdered throughout history. But this generation was rejecting more than a human prophet—they were rejecting God himself. This quotation is not from the Old Testament. Jesus, the greatest Prophet of all, was directly giving them God's message.

11:51 Abel's death is recorded in Genesis 4:8. For more about him, see his Profile in Genesis 6. Zechariah's death is recorded in 2 Chronicles 24:20-22 (the last book in the Hebrew canon). Why would all these sins come upon this particular generation? Because they were rejecting the Messiah himself, the One to whom all their history and prophecy were pointing.

●**11:52** How did the law experts take away the "key to knowledge"? Through their erroneous interpretations of Scripture and their added man-made rules, they made God's truth hard to understand and practice. On top of that, these men were bad examples, arguing their way out of the demanding rules they placed on others. Caught up in a religion of their own making, they could no longer lead the people to God. They had closed the door of God's love to the people and had thrown away the key.

11:53, 54 The teachers of the law and the Pharisees hoped to arrest Jesus for blasphemy, heresy, and lawbreaking. They were enraged by Jesus' words about them, but they couldn't arrest him for merely speaking words. They had to find a legal way to get rid of Jesus.

●**12:1, 2** As Jesus watched the huge crowds waiting to hear him, he warned his disciples against hypocrisy—trying to appear good when one's heart is far from God. The Pharisees could not keep their attitudes hidden forever. Their selfishness would act like yeast, and soon they would expose themselves for what they really were—power-hungry impostors, not devoted religious leaders. It is

Jesus Speaks against Hypocrisy
(139)

12 Meanwhile, when a crowd of many thousands had gathered, so that they were trampling on one another, Jesus began to speak first to his disciples, saying: "Be on your guard against the yeast of the Pharisees, which is hypocrisy.*e* ²There is nothing concealed that will not be disclosed, or hidden that will not be made known.*f* ³What you have said in the dark will be heard in the daylight, and what you have whispered in the ear in the inner rooms will be proclaimed from the roofs.

⁴"I tell you, my friends,*g* do not be afraid of those who kill the body and after that can do no more. ⁵But I will show you whom you should fear: Fear him who, after the killing of the body, has power to throw you into hell. Yes, I tell you, fear him.*h* ⁶Are not five sparrows sold for two pennies*d*? Yet not one of them is forgotten by God. ⁷Indeed, the very hairs of your head are all numbered.*i* Don't be afraid; you are worth more than many sparrows.*j*

⁸"I tell you, whoever acknowledges me before men, the Son of Man will also acknowledge him before the angels of God. ⁹But he who disowns me before men will be disowned before the angels of God. ¹⁰And everyone who speaks a word against the Son of Man will be forgiven, but anyone who blasphemes against the Holy Spirit will not be forgiven.*k*

¹¹"When you are brought before synagogues, rulers and authorities, do not worry about how you will defend yourselves or what you will say,*l* ¹²for the Holy Spirit will teach you at that time what you should say."*m*

Jesus Tells the Parable of the Rich Fool
(140)

¹³Someone in the crowd said to him, "Teacher, tell my brother to divide the inheritance with me."

¹⁴Jesus replied, "Man, who appointed me a judge or an arbiter between you?"

d 6 Greek two assaria

12:1
e Mt 16:6, 11, 12

12:2
f Mk 4:22

12:4
g Jn 15:14, 15

12:5
h Heb 10:31

12:7
i Mt 10:30
j Mt 12:12

12:10
k Mt 12:31, 32;
1Jn 5:16

12:11
l Mt 10:17, 19

12:12
m Mt 10:20

---

easy to be angry at the blatant hypocrisy of the Pharisees, but each of us must resist the temptation to settle for the appearance of respectability when our hearts are far from God.

12:4, 5 Fear of opposition or ridicule can weaken our witness for Christ. Often we cling to peace and comfort, even at the cost of our walk with God. Jesus reminds us here that we should fear God, who controls eternal, not merely temporal, consequences. Don't allow fear of a person or group to keep you from standing up for Christ.

12:7 Our true value is God's estimate of our worth, not our peers'. Other people evaluate and categorize us according to how we perform, what we achieve, and how we look. But God cares for us, as he does for all of his creatures, because we belong to him. So we can face life without fear.

12:8, 9 We disown Jesus when we (1) hope no one will think we are Christians, (2) decide *not* to speak up for what is right, (3) are silent about our relationship with God, (4) blend into society, (5) accept our culture's non-Christian values. By contrast, we acknowledge him when we (1) live moral, upright, Christ-honoring lives, (2) look for opportunities to share our faith with others, (3) help others in need, (4) take a stand for justice, (5) love others, (6) acknowledge our loyalty to Christ, (7) use our lives and resources to carry out his desires rather than our own.

12:10 Jesus said that blasphemy against the Holy Spirit is unforgivable. This has worried many sincere Christians, but it does not need to. The unforgivable sin means attributing to Satan the work that the Holy Spirit accomplishes (see the notes on Matthew 12:31, 32; Mark 3:28, 29). Thus it is deliberate and ongoing rejection of the

Holy Spirit's work and even of God himself. A person who has committed this sin has shut himself or herself off from God so thoroughly that he or she is unaware of any sin at all. A person who fears having committed it shows, by his or her very concern, that he or she has not sinned in this way.

12:11, 12 The disciples knew they could never dominate a religious dispute with the well-educated Jewish leaders. Nevertheless, they would not be left unprepared. Jesus promised that the Holy Spirit would supply the needed words. The disciples' testimony might not make them look impressive, but it would still point out God's work in the world through Jesus' life. We need to pray for opportunities to speak for God, and then trust him to help us with our words. This promise of the Spirit's help, however, does not compensate for lack of preparation. Remember that these disciples had three years of teaching and practical application. We too must study God's Word. Then God will bring his truths to mind when we most need them, helping us present them in the most effective way.

12:13ff Problems like this were often brought to rabbis for them to settle. Jesus' response, though not directly to the topic, is not a change of subject. Rather, Jesus is pointing to a higher issue — a correct attitude toward the accumulation of wealth. Life is more than material goods; far more important is our relationship with God. Jesus put his finger on this questioner's heart. When we bring problems to God in prayer, he often does the same — showing us how we need to change and grow in our attitude toward the problem. This answer is often not the one we were looking for, but it is more effective in helping us trace God's hand in our lives.

15Then he said to them, "Watch out! Be on your guard against all kinds of greed; a man's life does not consist in the abundance of his possessions."

16And he told them this parable: "The ground of a certain rich man produced a good crop. 17He thought to himself, 'What shall I do? I have no place to store my crops.'

18"Then he said, 'This is what I'll do. I will tear down my barns and build bigger ones, and there I will store all my grain and my goods. 19And I'll say to myself, "You have plenty of good things laid up for many years. Take life easy; eat, drink and be merry." '

20"But God said to him, 'You fool!n This very night your life will be demanded from you. o Then who will get what you have prepared for yourself?' p

21"This is how it will be with anyone who stores up things for himself but is not rich toward God."q

12:20
n Jer 17:11
o Job 27:8
p Ps 39:6

12:21
q ver 33

Jesus Warns about Worry
(141)

22Then Jesus said to his disciples: "Therefore I tell you, do not worry about your life, what you will eat; or about your body, what you will wear. 23Life is more than food, and the body more than clothes. 24Consider the ravens: They do not sow or reap, they have no storeroom or barn; yet God feeds them.r And how much more valuable you are than birds! 25Who of you by worrying can add a single hour to his lifee? 26Since you cannot do this very little thing, why do you worry about the rest?

27"Consider how the lilies grow. They do not labor or spin. Yet I tell you, not even Solomon in all his splendors was dressed like one of these. 28If that is how God clothes the grass of the field, which is here today, and tomorrow is thrown into the fire, how much more will he clothe you, O you of little faith!t 29And do not set your heart on what you will eat or drink; do not worry about it. 30For the pagan world runs after all such things, and your Father knows that you need them. u 31But seek his kingdom, and these things will be given to you as well.

32"Do not be afraid,v little flock, for your Father has been pleased to give you the kingdom. 33Sell your possessions and give to the poor. Provide purses for yourselves that will not wear out, a treasure in heavenw that will not be exhausted, where no thief comes near and no moth destroys. 34For where your treasure is, there your heart will be also. x

12:24
r Job 38:41

12:27
s 1Ki 10:4-7

12:28
t Mt 6:30

12:30
u Mt 6:8

12:32
v Mt 14:27

12:33
w Mt 6:20

12:34
x Mt 6:21

e 25 Or *single cubit to his height*

12:15 Jesus says that the good life has nothing to do with being wealthy, so be on guard against greed (desire for what we don't have). This is the exact opposite of what society usually says. Advertisers spend millions of dollars to entice us to think that if we buy more and more of their products, we will be happier, more fulfilled, more comfortable. How do you respond to the constant pressure to buy? Learn to tune out expensive enticements and concentrate instead on the truly good life — living in a relationship with God and doing his work.

12:16–21 The rich man in Jesus' story died before he could begin to use what was stored in his big barns. Planning for retirement — preparing for life *before* death — is wise, but neglecting life *after* death is disastrous. If you accumulate wealth only to enrich yourself, with no concern for helping others, you will enter eternity empty-handed.

12:18–20 Why do you save money? To retire? To buy more expensive cars or toys? To be secure? Jesus challenges us to think beyond earthbound goals and to use what we have been given for God's kingdom. Faith, service, and obedience are the way to become rich toward God.

12:22–34 Jesus commands us not to worry. But how can we avoid it? Only faith can free us from the anxiety caused by greed and covetousness. It is good to work and plan responsibly; it is bad to dwell on all the ways our planning could go wrong. Worry is

pointless because it can't fill any of our needs; worry is foolish because the Creator of the universe loves us and knows what we need. He promises to meet all our real needs, but not necessarily all our desires.

12:31 Seeking the kingdom of God means making Jesus the Lord and King of your life. He must control every area — your work, play, plans, relationships. Is the kingdom only one of your many concerns, or is it central to all you do? Are you holding back any areas of your life from God's control? As Lord and Creator, he wants to help provide what you need as well as guide how you use what he provides.

12:33 Money seen as an end in itself quickly traps us and cuts us off from both God and the needy. The key to using money wisely is to see how much we can use for God's purposes, not how much we can accumulate for ourselves. Does God's love touch your wallet? Does your money free you to help others? If so, you are storing up lasting treasures in heaven. If your financial goals and possessions hinder you from giving generously, loving others, or serving God, sell what you must to bring your life into perspective.

12:34 If you concentrate your money in your business, your thoughts will center on making the business profitable. If you direct it toward other people, you will become concerned with their welfare. Where do you put your time, money, and energy? What do you think about most? How should you change the way you use your resources in order to reflect kingdom values more accurately?

Jesus Warns about Preparing for His Coming
(142)

35"Be dressed ready for service and keep your lamps burning, 36like men waiting for their master to return from a wedding banquet, so that when he comes and knocks they can immediately open the door for him. 37It will be good for those servants whose master finds them watching when he comes.*y* I tell you the truth, he will dress himself to serve, will have them recline at the table and will come and wait on them. 38It will be good for those servants whose master finds them ready, even if he comes in the second or third watch of the night. 39But understand this: If the owner of the house had known at what hour the thief*z* was coming, he would not have let his house be broken into. 40You also must be ready,*a* because the Son of Man will come at an hour when you do not expect him."

41Peter asked, "Lord, are you telling this parable to us, or to everyone?"

42The Lord*b* answered, "Who then is the faithful and wise manager, whom the master puts in charge of his servants to give them their food allowance at the proper time? 43It will be good for that servant whom the master finds doing so when he returns. 44I tell you the truth, he will put him in charge of all his possessions. 45But suppose the servant says to himself, 'My master is taking a long time in coming,' and he then begins to beat the menservants and maidservants and to eat and drink and get drunk. 46The master of that servant will come on a day when he does not expect him and at an hour he is not aware of. He will cut him to pieces and assign him a place with the unbelievers.

47"That servant who knows his master's will and does not get ready or does not do what his master wants will be beaten with many blows.*c* 48But the one who does not know and does things deserving punishment will be beaten with few blows.*d* From everyone who has been given much, much will be demanded; and from the one who has been entrusted with much, much more will be asked.

Jesus Warns about Coming Division
(143)

49"I have come to bring fire on the earth, and how I wish it were already kindled! 50But I have a baptism*e* to undergo, and how distressed I am until it is completed! 51Do you think I came to bring peace on earth? No, I tell you, but division. 52From now on there will be five in one family divided against each other, three against two and two against three. 53They will be divided, father against son and son against father, mother against daughter and daughter against mother, mother-in-law against daughter-in-law and daughter-in-law against mother-in-law."*f*

12:37
*y*Mt 24:42, 46

12:39
*z*Mt 6:19;
1Th 5:2;
2Pe 3:10;
Rev 3:3; 16:15

12:40
*a*Mk 13:33;
Lk 21:36

12:42
*b*Lk 7:13

12:47
*c*Dt 25:2

12:48
*d*Lev 5:17;
Nu 15:27-30

12:50
*e*Mk 10:38

12:53
*f*Mic 7:6;
Mt 10:21

12:35-40 Jesus repeatedly said that he would leave this world but would return at some future time (see Matthew 24; 25; John 14:1–3). He also said that a kingdom is being prepared for his followers. Many Greeks envisioned this as a heavenly, idealized, spiritual kingdom. Jews — like Isaiah and John, the writer of Revelation — saw it as a restored earthly kingdom.

12:40 Christ's return at an unexpected time is not a trap, a trick by which God hopes to catch us off guard. In fact, God is delaying his return so more people will have the opportunity to follow him (see 2 Peter 3:9). Before Christ's return, we have time to live out our beliefs and to reflect Jesus' love as we relate to others.

People who are ready for their Lord's return are (1) not hypocritical, but sincere (12:1), (2) not fearful, but ready to witness (12:4–9), (3) not worried, but trusting (12:25, 26), (4) not greedy, but generous (12:34), (5) not lazy, but diligent (12:37). May your life be more like Christ's so that when he comes, you will be ready to greet him joyfully.

12:42-44 Jesus promises a reward for those who have been faithful to the Master. While we sometimes experience immediate and material rewards for our obedience to God, this is not always the case. If so, we would be tempted to boast about our achievements and do good only for what we get. Jesus said that if we look

for rewards now, we will lose them later (see Mark 8:36). Our heavenly rewards will be the most accurate reflection of what we have done on earth, and they will be far greater than we can imagine.

12:48 Jesus has told us how to live until he comes: we must watch for him, work diligently, and obey his commands. Such attitudes are especially necessary for leaders. Watchful and faithful leaders will be given increased opportunities and responsibilities. The more resources, talents, and understanding we have, the more we are responsible to use them effectively. God will not hold us responsible for gifts he has not given us, but all of us have enough gifts and duties to keep us busy until Jesus comes.

12:50 The "baptism" to which Jesus referred was his coming crucifixion. Jesus was dreading the physical pain, of course, but even worse would be the spiritual pain of complete separation from God that would accompany his death for the sins of the world.

12:51-53 In these strange and unsettling words, Jesus revealed that his coming often results in conflict. He demands a response, so intimate groups may be torn apart when some choose to follow him and others refuse to do so. There is no middle ground with Jesus. Loyalties must be declared and commitments made, sometimes to the point of severing other relationships. Are you willing to risk your family's approval in order to gain eternal life?

Jesus Warns about the Future Crisis
(144)

⁵⁴He said to the crowd: "When you see a cloud rising in the west, immediately you say, 'It's going to rain,' and it does. ⁹ ⁵⁵And when the south wind blows, you say, 'It's going to be hot,' and it is. ⁵⁶Hypocrites! You know how to interpret the appearance of the earth and the sky. How is it that you don't know how to interpret this present time?ʰ

⁵⁷"Why don't you judge for yourselves what is right? ⁵⁸As you are going with your adversary to the magistrate, try hard to be reconciled to him on the way, or he may drag you off to the judge, and the judge turn you over to the officer, and the officer throw you into prison. ⁱ ⁵⁹I tell you, you will not get out until you have paid the last penny.ᶠ"ʲ

12:54
⁹Mt 16:2

12:56
ʰMt 16:3

12:58
ⁱMt 5:25

12:59
ʲMk 12:42

Jesus Calls the People to Repent
(145)

13 Now there were some present at that time who told Jesus about the Galileans whose blood Pilateᵏ had mixed with their sacrifices. ²Jesus answered, "Do you think that these Galileans were worse sinners than all the other Galileans because they suffered this way?ˡ ³I tell you, no! But unless you repent, you too will all perish. ⁴Or those eighteen who died when the tower in Siloamᵐ fell on them—do you think they were more guilty than all the others living in Jerusalem? ⁵I tell you, no! But unless you repent, you too will all perish."

⁶Then he told this parable: "A man had a fig tree, planted in his vineyard, and he went to look for fruit on it, but did not find any.ⁿ ⁷So he said to the man who took care of the vineyard, 'For three years now I've been coming to look for fruit on this fig tree and haven't found any. Cut it down!ᵒ Why should it use up the soil?'

⁸"'Sir,' the man replied, 'leave it alone for one more year, and I'll dig around it and fertilize it. ⁹If it bears fruit next year, fine! If not, then cut it down.'"

13:1
ᵏMt 27:2

13:2
ˡJn 9:2, 3

13:4
ᵐJn 9:7, 11

13:6
ⁿIsa 5:2;
Mt 21:19

13:7
ᵒMt 3:10

Jesus Heals the Crippled Woman
(146)

¹⁰On a Sabbath Jesus was teaching in one of the synagogues,ᵖ ¹¹and a woman was there who had been crippled by a spirit for eighteen years.ᵠ She was bent over and could not straighten up at all. ¹²When Jesus saw her, he called her forward and said to her, "Woman, you are set free from your infirmity." ¹³Then he put his hands on her,ʳ and immediately she straightened up and praised God.

13:10
ᵖMt 4:23

13:11
ᵠver 16

13:13
ʳMk 5:23

ᶠ 59 Greek *lepton*

12:54-57 For most of recorded history, the world's principal occupation was farming. The farmer depended directly on the weather for his livelihood. He needed just the right amounts of sun and rain—not too much, not too little—to make his living, and he grew skilled at interpreting natural signs. Jesus was announcing an earthshaking event that would be much more important than the year's crops—the coming of God's kingdom. Like a rainstorm or a sunny day, there were signs that the kingdom would soon arrive. But Jesus' hearers, though skilled at interpreting weather signs, were intentionally ignoring the signs of the times.

13:1-5 Pilate may have killed the Galileans because he thought they were rebelling against Rome; those killed by the tower of Siloam may have been working for the Romans on an aqueduct there. The Pharisees, who were opposed to using force to deal with Rome, would have said that the Galileans deserved to die for rebelling. The Zealots, a group of anti-Roman terrorists, would have said the aqueduct workers deserved to die for cooperating. Jesus said that neither the Galileans nor the workers should be blamed for their calamity. And instead of blaming others, everyone should look to his or her own day of judgment.

13:5 Whether a person is killed in a tragic accident or miraculously survives is not a measure of righteousness. Everyone has to

die; that's part of being human. But not everyone needs to stay dead. Jesus promises that those who believe in him will not perish but have eternal life (John 3:16).

13:6-9 In the Old Testament, a fruitful tree was often used as a symbol of godly living (see, for example, Psalm 1:3 and Jeremiah 17:7, 8). Jesus pointed out what would happen to the other kind of tree—the kind that took valuable time and space and still produced nothing for the patient gardener. This was one way Jesus warned his listeners that God would not tolerate forever their lack of productivity. (Luke 3:9 records John the Baptist's version of the same message.) Have you been enjoying God's special treatment without giving anything in return? If so, respond to the Gardener's patient care, and begin to bear the fruit God has created you to produce.

•**13:10-17** Why was healing considered work? The religious leaders saw healing as part of a doctor's profession, and practicing one's profession on the Sabbath was prohibited. The synagogue ruler could not see beyond the law to Jesus' compassion in healing this crippled woman. Jesus shamed him and the other leaders by pointing out their hypocrisy. They would untie their animals and care for them, but they refused to rejoice when a human being was freed from Satan's bondage.

13:14
s Mk 5:22
t Ex 20:9

14Indignant because Jesus had healed on the Sabbath, the synagogue ruler s said to the people, "There are six days for work. t So come and be healed on those days, not on the Sabbath."

13:15
u Lk 14:5

15The Lord answered him, "You hypocrites! Doesn't each of you on the Sabbath untie his ox or donkey from the stall and lead it out to give it water? u 16Then should not this woman, a daughter of Abraham, v whom Satan w has kept bound for eighteen long years, be set free on the Sabbath day from what bound her?"

13:16
v Lk 3:8
w Mt 4:10

17When he said this, all his opponents were humiliated, but the people were delighted with all the wonderful things he was doing.

Jesus Teaches about the Kingdom of God
(147)

18Then Jesus asked, "What is the kingdom of God like? What shall I compare it to? 19It is like a mustard seed, which a man took and planted in his garden. It grew and became a tree, and the birds of the air perched in its branches."

20Again he asked, "What shall I compare the kingdom of God to? 21It is like yeast that a woman took and mixed into a large amount g of flour until it worked all through the dough."

Jesus Teaches about Entering the Kingdom
(153)

13:22
x Lk 9:51

22Then Jesus went through the towns and villages, teaching as he made his way to Jerusalem. x 23Someone asked him, "Lord, are only a few people going to be saved?"

13:24
y Mt 7:13

He said to them, 24"Make every effort to enter through the narrow door, y because many, I tell you, will try to enter and will not be able to. 25Once the owner

g 21 Greek *three satas* (probably about 1/2 bushel or 22 liters)

**SEVEN
SABBATH
MIRACLES**

Jesus sends a demon out of a man	Mark 1:21–28
Jesus heals Peter's mother-in-law	Mark 1:29–31
Jesus heals a lame man by Bethesda Pool	John 5:1–18
Jesus heals a man with a shriveled hand	Mark 3:1–6
Jesus restores a crippled woman	Luke 13:10–17
Jesus heals a man with dropsy	Luke 14:1–6
Jesus heals a man born blind	John 9:1–16

Over the centuries, the Jewish religious leaders had added rule after rule to God's law. For example, God's law said the Sabbath is a day of rest (Exodus 20:10, 11). But the religious leaders added to that law, creating one that said, "you cannot heal on the Sabbath" because that is "work." Seven times Jesus healed people on the Sabbath. In doing this, he was challenging these religious leaders to look beneath their rules to their true purpose—to honor God by helping those in need. Would God have been pleased if Jesus had ignored these people?

• **13:15, 16** The Pharisees hid behind their own set of laws to avoid love's obligations. We too can use the letter of the law to rationalize away our obligation to care for others (for example, by tithing regularly and then refusing to help a needy neighbor). But people's needs are more important than rules and regulations. Take time to help others, even if doing so might compromise your public image.

13:16 In our fallen world, disease and disability are common. Their causes are many and often multiple — inadequate nutrition, contact with a source of infection, lowered defenses, and even direct attack by Satan. Whatever the immediate cause of our illness, we can trace its original source to Satan, the author of all the evil in our world. The good news is that Jesus is more powerful than any devil or any disease. He often brings physical healing in this life; and when he returns, he will put an end to all disease and disability.

13:18–21 The general expectation among Jesus' hearers was that the Messiah would come as a great king and leader, freeing the nation from Rome and restoring Israel's former glory. But Jesus said his kingdom was beginning quietly. Like the tiny mustard seed that grows into an enormous tree, or the spoonful of yeast that makes the bread dough double in size, the kingdom of God would eventually push outward until the whole world was changed.

13:22 This is the second time Luke reminds us that Jesus was intentionally going to Jerusalem (the other time is in 9:51). Jesus knew he was on his way to die, but he continued preaching to large crowds. The prospect of death did not deter Jesus from his mission.

13:24, 25 Finding salvation requires more concentrated effort than most people are willing to put forth. Obviously we cannot save ourselves — there is no way we can work ourselves into God's favor. The effort we must put out "to enter through the narrow door" is earnestly desiring to know Jesus and diligently striving to follow him whatever the cost. We dare not put off making this decision because the door will not stay open forever.

of the house gets up and closes the door, you will stand outside knocking and pleading, 'Sir, open the door for us.'

"But he will answer, 'I don't know you or where you come from.'*z*

26"Then you will say, 'We ate and drank with you, and you taught in our streets.'

27"But he will reply, 'I don't know you or where you come from. Away from me, all you evildoers!'*a*

28"There will be weeping there, and gnashing of teeth,*b* when you see Abraham, Isaac and Jacob and all the prophets in the kingdom of God, but you yourselves thrown out. 29People will come from east and west*c* and north and south, and will take their places at the feast in the kingdom of God. 30Indeed there are those who are last who will be first, and first who will be last."*d*

13:25
z Mt 7:23; 25:10-12

13:27
a Mt 7:23

13:28
b Mt 8:12

13:29
c Mt 8:11

13:30
d Mt 19:30

Jesus Grieves over Jerusalem
(154)

31At that time some Pharisees came to Jesus and said to him, "Leave this place and go somewhere else. Herod wants to kill you."

32He replied, "Go tell that fox, 'I will drive out demons and heal people today and tomorrow, and on the third day I will reach my goal.'*e* 33In any case, I must keep going today and tomorrow and the next day—for surely no prophet*f* can die outside Jerusalem!

34"O Jerusalem, Jerusalem, you who kill the prophets and stone those sent to you, how often I have longed to gather your children together, as a hen gathers her chicks under her wings,*g* but you were not willing! 35Look, your house is left to you desolate. I tell you, you will not see me again until you say, 'Blessed is he who comes in the name of the Lord.'*h*"*h*

13:32
e Heb 2:10

13:33
f Mt 21:11

13:34
g Mt 23:37

13:35
h Ps 118:26;
Lk 19:38

Jesus Heals a Man with Dropsy
(155)

14 One Sabbath, when Jesus went to eat in the house of a prominent Pharisee, he was being carefully watched. 2There in front of him was a man suffering from dropsy. 3Jesus asked the Pharisees and experts in the law,*i* "Is it lawful to heal on the Sabbath or not?"*j* 4But they remained silent. So taking hold of the man, he healed him and sent him away.

14:3
i Mt 22:35
j Mt 12:2

h 35 Psalm 118:26

13:26, 27 The kingdom of God will not necessarily be populated with the people we expect to find there. Some perfectly respectable religious leaders claiming allegiance to Jesus will not be there because secretly they were morally corrupt.

13:27 The people were eager to know who would be in God's kingdom. Jesus explained that although many people know something about God, only a few have acknowledged their sins and accepted his forgiveness. Just listening to Jesus' words or admiring his miracles is not enough—we must turn from sin and trust in God to save us.

13:29 God's kingdom will include people from every part of the world. Israel's rejection of Jesus as Messiah would not stop God's plan. True Israel includes all people who believe in God. This was an important fact for Luke to stress as he was directing his Gospel to a Gentile audience (see also Romans 4:16-25; Galatians 3:6-9).

● **13:30** There will be many surprises in God's kingdom. Some who are despised now will be greatly honored then; some influential people here will be left outside the gates. Many "great" people on this earth (in God's eyes) are virtually ignored by the rest of the world. What matters to God is not a person's earthly popularity, status, wealth, heritage, or power, but his or her commitment to Christ. How do your values match what the Bible tells you to value? Put God in first place, and you will join people from all over the world who will take their places at the feast in the kingdom of heaven.

13:31-33 The Pharisees weren't interested in protecting Jesus from danger. They were trying to trap him themselves. The Pharisees urged Jesus to leave because they wanted to stop him from going to Jerusalem, not because they feared Herod. But Jesus' life, work, and death were not to be determined by Herod or the Pharisees. His life was planned and directed by God himself, and his mission would unfold in God's time and according to God's plan.

13:33, 34 Why was Jesus focusing on Jerusalem? Jerusalem, the city of God, symbolized the entire nation. It was Israel's largest city and the nation's spiritual and political capital, and Jews from around the world visited it frequently. But Jerusalem had a history of rejecting God's prophets (1 Kings 19:10; 2 Chronicles 24:19; Jeremiah 2:30; 26:20-23), and it would reject the Messiah just as it had rejected his forerunners.

14:1-6 Earlier Jesus had been invited to a Pharisee's home for discussion (7:36). This time a prominent Pharisee invited Jesus to his home specifically to trap him into saying or doing something for which he could be arrested. It may be surprising to see Jesus on the Pharisees' turf after he had denounced them so many times. But he was not afraid to face them, even though he knew that their purpose was to trick him into breaking their laws.

14:2 Luke, the physician, identifies this man's disease—he was suffering from *dropsy*, an abnormal accumulation of fluid in bodily tissues and cavities.

14:5
*k*Lk 13:15

5Then he asked them, "If one of you has a son[i] or an ox that falls into a well on the Sabbath day, will you not immediately pull him out?"[k] 6And they had nothing to say.

Jesus Teaches about Seeking Honor
(156)

7When he noticed how the guests picked the places of honor at the table, he told them this parable: 8"When someone invites you to a wedding feast, do not take the place of honor, for a person more distinguished than you may have been invited. 9If so, the host who invited both of you will come and say to you, 'Give this man your seat.' Then, humiliated, you will have to take the least important place. 10But when you are invited, take the lowest place, so that when your host comes, he will say to you, 'Friend, move up to a better place.' Then you will be honored in the presence of all your fellow guests. 11For everyone who exalts himself will be humbled, and he who humbles himself will be exalted."[l]

14:11
*l*Mt 23:12

12Then Jesus said to his host, "When you give a luncheon or dinner, do not invite your friends, your brothers or relatives, or your rich neighbors; if you do, they may invite you back and so you will be repaid. 13But when you give a banquet, invite the poor, the crippled, the lame, the blind,[m] 14and you will be blessed. Although they cannot repay you, you will be repaid at the resurrection of the righteous."[n]

14:13
*m*ver 21

14:14
*n*Ac 24:15

Jesus Tells the Parable of the Great Feast
(157)

15When one of those at the table with him heard this, he said to Jesus, "Blessed is the man who will eat at the feast[o] in the kingdom of God."

14:15
*o*Rev 19:9

16Jesus replied: "A certain man was preparing a great banquet and invited many guests. 17At the time of the banquet he sent his servant to tell those who had been invited, 'Come, for everything is now ready.'

18"But they all alike began to make excuses. The first said, 'I have just bought a field, and I must go and see it. Please excuse me.'

19"Another said, 'I have just bought five yoke of oxen, and I'm on my way to try them out. Please excuse me.'

i 5 Some manuscripts *donkey*

● **14:7-11** Jesus advised people not to rush for the best places at a feast. People today are just as eager to raise their social status, whether by being with the right people, dressing for success, or driving the right car. Whom do you try to impress? Rather than aiming for prestige, look for a place where you can serve. If God wants you to serve on a wider scale, he will invite you to take a higher place.

● **14:7-14** Jesus taught two lessons here. First, he spoke to the guests, telling them not to seek places of honor. Service is more important in God's kingdom than status. Second, he told the host not to be exclusive about whom he invites. God opens his kingdom to everyone.

● **14:11** How can we humble ourselves? Some people try to give the appearance of humility in order to manipulate others. Others think that humility means putting themselves down. Truly humble people compare themselves only with Christ, realize their sinfulness, and understand their limitations. On the other hand, they also recognize their gifts and strengths and are willing to use them as Christ directs. Humility is not self-degradation; it is realistic assessment and commitment to serve.

14:15-24 The man sitting at the table with Jesus saw the glory of God's kingdom, but he did not yet understand how to get in. In Jesus' story, many people turned down the invitation to the banquet because the timing was inconvenient. We too can resist or delay responding to God's invitation, and our excuses may sound reasonable — work duties, family responsibilities, financial needs, or whatever they may be. Nevertheless, God's invitation is the most important event in our lives, no matter how inconveniently it may be timed. Are you making excuses to avoid responding to God's call? Jesus reminds us that the time will come when God will pull his invitation and offer it to others — then it will be too late to get into the banquet.

14:16ff It was customary to send two invitations to a party — the first to announce the event, the second to tell the guests that everything was ready. The guests in Jesus' story insulted the host by making excuses when he issued the second invitation. In Israel's history, God's first invitation came from Moses and the prophets; the second came from his Son. The religious leaders accepted the first invitation. They believed that God had called them to be his people, but they insulted God by refusing to accept his Son. Thus, as the master in the story sent his servant into the streets to invite the needy to his banquet, so God sent his Son to the whole world of needy people to tell them that God's kingdom had arrived and was ready for them.

● **14:16ff** In this chapter we read Jesus' words against seeking status, and in favor of hard work and even suffering. Let us not lose sight of the end result of all our humility and self-sacrifice — a joyous banquet with our Lord! God never asks us to suffer for the sake of suffering. He never asks us to give up something good unless he plans to replace it with something even better. Jesus is not calling us to join him in a labor camp but in a feast — the wedding supper of the Lamb (Revelation 19:6-9), when God and his beloved church will be joined forever.

20"Still another said, 'I just got married, so I can't come.'

21"The servant came back and reported this to his master. Then the owner of the house became angry and ordered his servant, 'Go out quickly into the streets and alleys of the town and bring in the poor, the crippled, the blind and the lame.'*p*

22"'Sir,' the servant said, 'what you ordered has been done, but there is still room.'

23"Then the master told his servant, 'Go out to the roads and country lanes and make them come in, so that my house will be full. 24I tell you, not one of those men who were invited will get a taste of my banquet.' "*q*

14:21
p ver 13

14:24
q Mt 21:43;
Ac 13:46

Jesus Teaches about the Cost of Being a Disciple
(158)

25Large crowds were traveling with Jesus, and turning to them he said: 26"If anyone comes to me and does not hate his father and mother, his wife and children, his brothers and sisters — yes, even his own life — he cannot be my disciple.*r* 27And anyone who does not carry his cross and follow me cannot be my disciple.*s*

28"Suppose one of you wants to build a tower. Will he not first sit down and estimate the cost to see if he has enough money to complete it? 29For if he lays the foundation and is not able to finish it, everyone who sees it will ridicule him, 30saying, 'This fellow began to build and was not able to finish.'

31"Or suppose a king is about to go to war against another king. Will he not first sit down and consider whether he is able with ten thousand men to oppose the one coming against him with twenty thousand? 32If he is not able, he will send a delegation while the other is still a long way off and will ask for terms of peace. 33In the same way, any of you who does not give up everything he has cannot be my disciple.*t*

34"Salt is good, but if it loses its saltiness, how can it be made salty again?*u* 35It is fit neither for the soil nor for the manure pile; it is thrown out.*v*

"He who has ears to hear, let him hear."*w*

14:26
r Mt 10:37

14:27
s Mt 10:38;
Lk 9:23

14:33
t Php 3:7, 8

14:34
u Mk 9:50

14:35
v Mt 5:13
w Mt 11:15

Jesus Tells the Parable of the Lost Sheep
(159)

15 Now the tax collectors*x* and "sinners" were all gathering around to hear him. 2But the Pharisees and the teachers of the law muttered, "This man welcomes sinners and eats with them."*y*

3Then Jesus told them this parable: 4"Suppose one of you has a hundred sheep

15:1
x Lk 5:29

15:2
y Mt 9:11

14:27 Jesus' audience was well aware of what it meant to carry one's own cross. When the Romans led a criminal to his execution site, he was forced to carry the cross on which he would die. This showed his submission to Rome and warned observers that they had better submit too. Jesus spoke this teaching to get the crowds to think through their enthusiasm for him. He encouraged those who were superficial either to go deeper or to turn back. Following Christ means total submission to him — perhaps even to the point of death.

● **14:28-30** When a builder doesn't count the cost or estimates it inaccurately, his building may be left half completed. Will your Christian life be only half built and then abandoned because you did not count the cost of commitment to Jesus? What are those costs? Christians may face loss of social status or wealth. They may have to give up control over their money, their time, or their career. They may be hated, separated from their family, and even put to death. Following Christ does not mean a trouble-free life. We must carefully count the cost of becoming Christ's disciples so that we will know what we are getting into and won't be tempted later to turn back.

14:34 Salt can lose its flavor. When it gets wet and then dries, nothing is left but a tasteless residue. Many Christians blend into the world and avoid the cost of standing up for Christ. But Jesus says if Christians lose their distinctive saltiness, they become

worthless. Just as salt flavors and preserves food, we are to preserve the good in the world, help keep it from spoiling, and bring new flavor to life. This requires careful planning, willing sacrifice, and unswerving commitment to Christ's kingdom. Being "salty" is not easy, but if a Christian fails in this function, he or she fails to represent Christ in the world. How salty are you?

● **15:2** Why were the Pharisees and teachers of the law bothered that Jesus associated with these people? The religious leaders were always careful to stay "clean" according to Old Testament law. In fact, they went well beyond the law in their avoidance of certain people and situations and in their ritual washings. By contrast, Jesus took their concept of "cleanness" lightly. He risked defilement by touching those who had leprosy and by neglecting to wash in the Pharisees' prescribed manner, and he showed complete disregard for their sanctions against associating with certain classes of people. He came to offer salvation to sinners, to show that God loves them. Jesus didn't worry about the accusations. Instead he continued going to those who needed him, regardless of the effect these rejected people might have on his reputation. What keeps you away from people who need Christ?

● **15:3-6** It may seem foolish for the shepherd to leave 99 sheep to go search for just one. But the shepherd knew that the 99 would be safe in the sheepfold, whereas the lost sheep was in danger. Because each sheep was of high value, the shepherd knew that it

and loses one of them. Does he not leave the ninety-nine in the open country and go after the lost sheep until he finds it? 5And when he finds it, he joyfully puts it on his shoulders 6and goes home. Then he calls his friends and neighbors together and says, 'Rejoice with me; I have found my lost sheep.' 7I tell you that in the same way there will be more rejoicing in heaven over one sinner who repents than over ninety-nine righteous persons who do not need to repent.z

15:7
zver 10

Jesus Tells the Parable of the Lost Coin
(160)

8"Or suppose a woman has ten silver coinsj and loses one. Does she not light a lamp, sweep the house and search carefully until she finds it? 9And when she finds it, she calls her friends and neighbors together and says, 'Rejoice with me; I have found my lost coin.' 10In the same way, I tell you, there is rejoicing in the presence of the angels of God over one sinner who repents."a

15:10
aver 7

Jesus Tells the Parable of the Lost Son
(161)

15:11
bMt 21:28
15:12
cDt 21:17
dver 30

11Jesus continued: "There was a man who had two sons.b 12The younger one said to his father, 'Father, give me my share of the estate.'c So he divided his propertyd between them.

13"Not long after that, the younger son got together all he had, set off for a distant country and there squandered his wealth in wild living. 14After he had spent everything, there was a severe famine in that whole country, and he began to be in need. 15So he went and hired himself out to a citizen of that country, who sent him to his fields to feed pigs. 16He longed to fill his stomach with the pods that the pigs were eating, but no one gave him anything.

17"When he came to his senses, he said, 'How many of my father's hired men have food to spare, and here I am starving to death! 18I will set out and go back to my father and say to him: Father, I have sinned against heaven and against you. 19I am no longer worthy to be called your son; make me like one of your hired men.' 20So he got up and went to his father.

j 8 Greek ten drachmas, each worth about a day's wages

---

was worthwhile to search diligently for the lost one. God's love for each individual is so great that he seeks each one out and rejoices when he or she is "found." Jesus associated with sinners because he wanted to bring the lost sheep — people considered beyond hope — the gospel of God's kingdom. Before you were a believer, God sought you; and his love is still seeking those who are yet lost.

• **15:4, 5** We may be able to understand a God who would forgive sinners who come to him for mercy. But a God who tenderly searches for sinners and then joyfully forgives them must possess an extraordinary love! This is the kind of love that prompted Jesus to come to earth to search for lost people and save them. This is the kind of extraordinary love that God has for you. If you feel far from God, don't despair. He is seaching for you.

• **15:8-10** Palestinian women received ten silver coins as a wedding gift. Besides their monetary value, these coins held sentimental value like that of a wedding ring, and to lose one would be extremely distressing. Just as a woman would rejoice at finding her lost coin or ring, so the angels rejoice over a repentant sinner. Each individual is precious to God. He grieves over every loss and rejoices whenever one of his children is found and brought into the kingdom. Perhaps we would have more joy in our churches if we shared Jesus' love and concern for the lost.

15:12 The younger son's share of the estate would have been one-third, with the older son receiving two-thirds (Deuteronomy 21:17). In most cases he would have received this at his father's death, although fathers sometimes chose to divide up their inheritance early and retire from managing their estates. What is unusual

here is that the younger one initiated the division of the estate. This showed arrogant disregard for his father's authority as head of the family.

15:15, 16 According to Moses' law, pigs were unclean animals (Leviticus 11:2-8; Deuteronomy 14:8). This meant that pigs could not be eaten or used for sacrifices. To protect themselves from defilement, Jews would not even touch pigs. For a Jew to stoop to feeding pigs was a great humiliation, and for this young man to eat food that the pigs had touched was to be degraded beyond belief. The younger son had truly sunk to the depths.

15:17 The younger son, like many who are rebellious and immature, wanted to be free to live as he pleased, and he had to hit bottom before he came to his senses. It often takes great sorrow and tragedy to cause people to look to the only One who can help them. Are you trying to live life your own way, selfishly pushing aside any responsibility or commitment that gets in your way? Stop and look before you hit bottom. You will save yourself and your family much grief.

• **15:20** In the two preceding stories, the seeker actively looked for the coin and the sheep, which could not return by themselves. In this story, the father watched and waited. He was dealing with a human being with a will of his own, but he was ready to greet his son if he returned. In the same way, God's love is constant and patient and welcoming. He will search for us and give us opportunities to respond, but he will not force us to come to him. Like the father in this story, God waits patiently for us to come to our senses.

"But while he was still a long way off, his father saw him and was filled with compassion for him; he ran to his son, threw his arms around him and kissed him. *e*

21"The son said to him, 'Father, I have sinned against heaven and against you. *f* I am no longer worthy to be called your son. *k*'

22"But the father said to his servants, 'Quick! Bring the best robe *g* and put it on him. Put a ring on his finger *h* and sandals on his feet. 23Bring the fattened calf and kill it. Let's have a feast and celebrate. 24For this son of mine was dead and is alive again; *i* he was lost and is found.' So they began to celebrate. *j*

25"Meanwhile, the older son was in the field. When he came near the house, he heard music and dancing. 26So he called one of the servants and asked him what was going on. 27'Your brother has come,' he replied, 'and your father has killed the fattened calf because he has him back safe and sound.'

28"The older brother became angry and refused to go in. So his father went out and pleaded with him. 29But he answered his father, 'Look! All these years I've been slaving for you and never disobeyed your orders. Yet you never gave me even a young goat so I could celebrate with my friends. 30But when this son of yours who has squandered your property *k* with prostitutes *l* comes home, you kill the fattened calf for him!'

31"'My son,' the father said, 'you are always with me, and everything I have is yours. 32But we had to celebrate and be glad, because this brother of yours was dead and is alive again; he was lost and is found.' "*m*

Jesus Tells the Parable of the Shrewd Manager
(162)

16 Jesus told his disciples: "There was a rich man whose manager was accused of wasting his possessions. *n* 2So he called him in and asked him, 'What is this I hear about you? Give an account of your management, because you cannot be manager any longer.'

3"The manager said to himself, 'What shall I do now? My master is taking away my job. I'm not strong enough to dig, and I'm ashamed to beg— 4I know what I'll do so that, when I lose my job here, people will welcome me into their houses.'

5"So he called in each one of his master's debtors. He asked the first, 'How much do you owe my master?'

6"'Eight hundred gallons *l* of olive oil,' he replied.

"The manager told him, 'Take your bill, sit down quickly, and make it four hundred.'

7"Then he asked the second, 'And how much do you owe?'

"'A thousand bushels *m* of wheat,' he replied.

"He told him, 'Take your bill and make it eight hundred.'

k 21 Some early manuscripts *son. Make me like one of your hired men.* *l 6* Greek *one hundred batous* (probably about 3 kiloliters) *m 7* Greek *one hundred korous* (probably about 35 kiloliters)

15:20 *e*Ge 45:14, 15; 46:29; Ac 20:37

15:21 *f*Ps 51:4

15:22 *g*Zec 3:4; Rev 6:11 *h*Ge 41:42

15:24 *i*Eph 2:1, 5; 5:14; 1Ti 5:6 *j*ver 32

15:30 *k*ver 12, 13 *l*Pr 29:3

15:32 *m*ver 24

16:1 *n*Lk 15:13, 30

● **15:24** The sheep was lost because it may have foolishly wandered away (15:4); the coin was lost through no fault of its own (15:8); and the son left out of selfishness (15:12). God's great love reaches out and finds sinners no matter why or how they got lost.

● **15:25-31** It was hard for the older brother to accept his younger brother when he returned, and it is just as difficult to accept "younger brothers" today. People who repent after leading notoriously sinful lives are often held in suspicion; churches are sometimes unwilling to admit them to membership. Instead, we should rejoice like the angels in heaven when an unbeliever repents and turns to God. Like the father, accept repentant sinners wholeheartedly and give them the support and encouragement that they need to grow in Christ.

● **15:30** In the story of the lost son, the father's response is contrasted with the older brother's. The father forgave because he was filled with love. The son refused to forgive because he was bitter about the injustice of it all. His resentment rendered him just as lost to the father's love as his younger brother had been. Don't let anything keep you from forgiving others. If you are refusing to forgive people, you are missing a wonderful opportunity to experience joy and share it with others. Make your joy grow: forgive somebody who has hurt you.

● **15:32** In Jesus' story, the older brother represented the Pharisees, who were angry and resentful that sinners were being welcomed into God's kingdom. After all, the Pharisees must have thought, we have sacrificed and done *so much* for God. How easy it is to resent God's gracious forgiveness of others whom we consider to be far worse sinners than ourselves. But when our self-righteousness gets in the way of rejoicing when others come to Jesus, we are no better than the Pharisees.

16:1-8 Our use of money is a good test of the lordship of Christ. (1) Let us use our resources wisely because they belong to God, and not to us. (2) Money can be used for good or evil; let us use ours for good. (3) Money has a lot of power, so we must use it carefully and thoughtfully. (4) We must use our material goods in a way that will foster faith and obedience (see 12:33, 34).

8“The master commended the dishonest manager because he had acted
shrewdly. For the people of this world are more shrewd in dealing with their own
kind than are the people of the light.[o] 9I tell you, use worldly wealth to gain friends
for yourselves, so that when it is gone, you will be welcomed into eternal dwellings.[p]
10“Whoever can be trusted with very little can also be trusted with much,[q] and
whoever is dishonest with very little will also be dishonest with much. 11So if you
have not been trustworthy in handling worldly wealth, who will trust you with true
riches? 12And if you have not been trustworthy with someone else’s property, who
will give you property of your own?
13“No servant can serve two masters. Either he will hate the one and love the
other, or he will be devoted to the one and despise the other. You cannot serve both
God and Money.”[r]
14The Pharisees, who loved money, heard all this and were sneering at Jesus.[s]
15He said to them, “You are the ones who justify yourselves[t] in the eyes of men,
but God knows your hearts. What is highly valued among men is detestable in
God’s sight.
16“The Law and the Prophets were proclaimed until John.[u] Since that time, the
good news of the kingdom of God is being preached,[v] and everyone is forcing his
way into it. 17It is easier for heaven and earth to disappear than for the least stroke
of a pen to drop out of the Law.[w]
18“Anyone who divorces his wife and marries another woman commits adultery,
and the man who marries a divorced woman commits adultery.[x]

Jesus Tells about the Rich Man and the Beggar
(163)

19“There was a rich man who was dressed in purple and fine linen and lived in
luxury every day. 20At his gate was laid a beggar[y] named Lazarus, covered with

16:8 [o]Jn 12:36; Eph 5:8; 1Th 5:5
16:9 [p]Mt 19:21
16:10 [q]Mt 25:21, 23
16:13 [r]Mt 6:24
16:14 [s]Lk 23:35
16:15 [t]Lk 10:29
16:16 [u]Mt 11:12, 13 [v]Mt 4:23
16:17 [w]Mt 5:18
16:18 [x]Mt 5:31, 32; Mk 10:11; 1Co 7:10, 11
16:20 [y]Ac 3:2

16:9 We are to make wise use of the financial opportunities we have, not to earn heaven, but so that heaven (“eternal dwellings”) will be a welcome experience for those we help. If we use our money to help those in need or to help others find Christ, our earthly investment will bring eternal benefit. When we obey God’s will, the unselfish use of possessions will follow.

16:10, 11 Our integrity often meets its match in money matters. God calls us to be honest even in small details we could easily rationalize away. Heaven’s riches are far more valuable than earthly wealth. But if we are not trustworthy with our money here (no matter how much or little we have), we will be unfit to handle the vast riches of God’s kingdom. Don’t let your integrity slip in small matters, and it will not fail you in crucial decisions either.

16:13 Money has the power to take God’s place in your life. It can become your master. How can you tell if you are a slave to Money? (1) Do you think and worry about it frequently? (2) Do you give up doing what you should do or would like to do in order to make more money? (3) Do you spend a great deal of your time caring for your possessions? (4) Is it hard for you to give money away? (5) Are you in debt?

Money is a hard master and a deceptive one. Wealth promises power and control, but often it cannot deliver. Great fortunes can be made—and lost—overnight, and no amount of money can provide health, happiness, or eternal life. How much better it is to let God be your Master. His servants have peace of mind and security, both now and forever.

16:14 Because the Pharisees loved money, they took exception to Jesus’ teaching. We live in an age that measures people’s worth by how much money they make. Do we laugh at Jesus’ warnings against serving Money? Do we try to explain them away? Do we apply them to someone else—the Pharisees, for example? Unless we take Jesus’ statements seriously, we may be acting like Pharisees ourselves.

16:15 The Pharisees acted piously to get praise from others, but God knew what was in their hearts. They considered their wealth to be a sign of God’s approval. God detested their wealth because it caused them to abandon true spirituality. Though prosperity may earn people’s praise, it must never substitute for devotion and service to God.

16:16, 17 John the Baptist’s ministry was the dividing line between the Old and New Testaments (John 1:15–18). With the arrival of Jesus came the realization of all the prophets’ hopes. Jesus emphasized that his kingdom fulfilled the law (the Old Testament); it did not cancel it (Matthew 5:17). His was not a new system but the culmination of the old. The same God who worked through Moses was working through Jesus.

16:18 Most religious leaders of Jesus’ day permitted a man to divorce his wife for nearly any reason. Jesus’ teaching about divorce went beyond Moses’ (Deuteronomy 24:1–4). Stricter than any of the then-current schools of thought, Jesus’ teachings shocked his hearers (see Matthew 19:10) just as they shake today’s readers. Jesus says in no uncertain terms that marriage is a lifetime commitment. To leave your spouse for another person may be legal, but it is adultery in God’s eyes. As you think about marriage, remember that God intends it to be a permanent commitment.

16:19–31 The Pharisees considered wealth to be a proof of a person’s righteousness. Jesus startled them with this story where a diseased beggar is rewarded and a rich man is punished. The rich man did not go to hell because of his wealth but because he was selfish, refusing to feed Lazarus, take him in, or care for him. The rich man was hardhearted in spite of his great blessings. The amount of money we have is not as important as the way we use it. What is your attitude toward your money and possessions? Do you hoard them selfishly, or do you use them to help others?

16:20 This Lazarus should not be confused with the Lazarus whom Jesus raised from the dead in John 11.

sores [21]and longing to eat what fell from the rich man's table. Even the dogs came and licked his sores.

[22]"The time came when the beggar died and the angels carried him to Abraham's side. The rich man also died and was buried. [23]In hell,[n] where he was in torment, he looked up and saw Abraham far away, with Lazarus by his side. [24]So he called to him, 'Father Abraham, have pity on me and send Lazarus to dip the tip of his finger in water and cool my tongue, because I am in agony in this fire.'

[25]"But Abraham replied, 'Son, remember that in your lifetime you received your good things, while Lazarus received bad things, but now he is comforted here and you are in agony.[z] [26]And besides all this, between us and you a great chasm has been fixed, so that those who want to go from here to you cannot, nor can anyone cross over from there to us.'

[27]"He answered, 'Then I beg you, father, send Lazarus to my father's house, [28]for I have five brothers. Let him warn them, so that they will not also come to this place of torment.'

[29]"Abraham replied, 'They have Moses[a] and the Prophets;[b] let them listen to them.'

[30]" 'No, father Abraham,' he said, 'but if someone from the dead goes to them, they will repent.'

[31]"He said to him, 'If they do not listen to Moses and the Prophets, they will not be convinced even if someone rises from the dead.' "

Jesus Tells about Forgiveness and Faith
(164)

17 Jesus said to his disciples: "Things that cause people to sin are bound to come, but woe to that person through whom they come.[c] [2]It would be better for him to be thrown into the sea with a millstone tied around his neck than for him to cause one of these little ones to sin. [3]So watch yourselves.

"If your brother sins, rebuke him,[d] and if he repents, forgive him. [4]If he sins against you seven times in a day, and seven times comes back to you and says, 'I repent,' forgive him."[e]

[5]The apostles[f] said to the Lord, "Increase our faith!"

[6]He replied, "If you have faith as small as a mustard seed,[g] you can say to this mulberry tree, 'Be uprooted and planted in the sea,' and it will obey you.

[7]"Suppose one of you had a servant plowing or looking after the sheep. Would

[n] *23 Greek* Hades

16:25
[z]Lk 6:21, 24, 25

16:29
[a]Jn 5:45-47; Ac 15:21
[b]Lk 4:17

17:1
[c]Mt 18:7

17:3
[d]Mt 18:15

17:4
[e]Mt 18:21, 22

17:5
[f]Mk 6:30

17:6
[g]Mt 17:20

16:29-31 The rich man thought that his five brothers would surely believe a messenger who had been raised from the dead. But Jesus said that if they did not believe Moses and the prophets, who spoke constantly of the duty to care for the poor, not even a resurrection would convince them. Notice the irony in Jesus' statement; on his way to Jerusalem to die, he was fully aware that even when he had risen from the dead, most of the religious leaders would not accept him. They were set in their ways, and neither Scripture nor God's Son himself would shake them loose.

17:1-3 Jesus may have been directing this warning at the religious leaders who taught their converts their own hypocritical ways (see Matthew 23:15). They were perpetuating an evil system. A person who teaches others has a solemn responsibility (James 3:1). Like physicians, a teacher should keep this ancient oath in mind: "First, do no harm."

17:3, 4 To rebuke does not mean to point out every sin we see; it means to bring sin to a person's attention with the purpose of restoring him or her to God and to fellow humans. When you feel you must rebuke another Christian for a sin, check your attitudes before you speak. Do you love the person? Are you willing to forgive? Unless rebuke is tied to forgiveness, it will not help the sinning person.

17:5, 6 The disciples' request was genuine; they wanted the faith necessary for such radical forgiveness. But Jesus didn't directly answer their question because the amount of faith is not as important as its genuineness. What is faith? It is total dependence on God and a willingness to do his will. Faith is not something we use to put on a show for others. It is complete and humble obedience to God's will, readiness to do whatever he calls us to do. The amount of faith isn't as important as the right kind of faith — faith in our all-powerful God.

17:6 A mustard seed is small, but it is alive and growing. Like a tiny seed, a small amount of genuine faith in God will take root and grow. Almost invisible at first, it will begin to spread, first under the ground and then visibly. Although each change will be gradual and imperceptible, soon this faith will have produced major results that will uproot and destroy competing loyalties. We don't need more faith; a tiny seed of faith is enough, if it is alive and growing.

17:7-10 If we have obeyed God, we have only done our duty and we should regard it as a privilege. Do you sometimes feel that you deserve extra credit for serving God? Remember, obedience is not something extra we do; it is our duty. Jesus is not rendering our service as meaningless or useless, nor is he doing away with rewards. He is attacking unwarranted self-esteem and spiritual pride.

he say to the servant when he comes in from the field, 'Come along now and sit down to eat'? 8Would he not rather say, 'Prepare my supper, get yourself ready and wait on me[h] while I eat and drink; after that you may eat and drink'? 9Would he thank the servant because he did what he was told to do? 10So you also, when you have done everything you were told to do, should say, 'We are unworthy servants; we have only done our duty.' "

17:8
[h]Lk 12:37

Jesus Heals Ten Men with Leprosy
(169)

17:11
[i]Lk 9:51
[j]Jn 4:3, 4

17:12
[k]Lev 13:45, 46

17:14
[l]Mt 8:4

17:15
[m]Mt 9:8

17:16
[n]Mt 10:5

17:19
[o]Mt 9:22

11Now on his way to Jerusalem,[i] Jesus traveled along the border between Samaria and Galilee.[j] 12As he was going into a village, ten men who had leprosy[o] met him. They stood at a distance[k] 13and called out in a loud voice, "Jesus, Master, have pity on us!"

14When he saw them, he said, "Go, show yourselves to the priests."[l] And as they went, they were cleansed.

15One of them, when he saw he was healed, came back, praising God[m] in a loud voice. 16He threw himself at Jesus' feet and thanked him — and he was a Samaritan.[n]

17Jesus asked, "Were not all ten cleansed? Where are the other nine? 18Was no one found to return and give praise to God except this foreigner?" 19Then he said to him, "Rise and go; your faith has made you well."[o]

Jesus Teaches about the Coming of the Kingdom of God
(170)

17:21
[p]ver 23

20Once, having been asked by the Pharisees when the kingdom of God would come, Jesus replied, "The kingdom of God does not come with your careful observation, 21nor will people say, 'Here it is,' or 'There it is,'[p] because the kingdom of God is within[p] you."

22Then he said to his disciples, "The time is coming when you will long to see

[o] 12 The Greek word was used for various diseases affecting the skin—not necessarily leprosy. [p] 21 Or *among*

17:11-14 People who had leprosy were required to try to stay away from other people and to announce their presence if they had to come near. Sometimes leprosy went into remission. If a leper thought his leprosy had gone away, he was supposed to present himself to a priest who could declare him clean (Leviticus 14). Jesus sent the ten lepers to the priest *before* they were healed — and they went! They responded in faith, and Jesus healed them on the way. Is your trust in God so strong that you act on what he says even before you see evidence that it will work?

17:16 Jesus healed all ten lepers, but only one returned to thank him. It is possible to receive God's great gifts with an ungrateful spirit — nine of the ten men did so. Only the thankful man, however, learned that his faith had played a role in his healing; and only grateful Christians grow in understanding God's grace. God does not demand that we thank him, but he is pleased when we do so. And he uses our responsiveness to teach us more about himself.

17:16 Not only was this man a leper, he was also a Samaritan — a race despised by the Jews as idolatrous half-breeds (see the note on 10:33). Once again Luke is pointing out that God's grace is for everybody.

17:20, 21 The Pharisees asked when God's kingdom would come, not knowing that it had already arrived. The kingdom of God is not like an earthly kingdom with geographical boundaries. Instead, it begins with the work of God's Spirit in people's lives and in relationships. Still today we must resist looking to institutions or programs for evidence of the progress of God's kingdom. Instead, we should look for what God is doing in people's hearts.

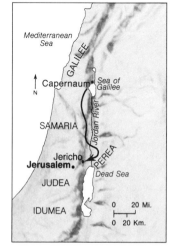

LAST TRIP FROM GALILEE Jesus left Galilee for the last time—he would not return before his death. He passed through Samaria, met and healed ten men who had leprosy, and continued to Jerusalem. He spent some time east of the Jordan (Mark 10:1) before going to Jericho (19:1).

one of the days of the Son of Man, but you will not see it. 23Men will tell you, 'There he is!' or 'Here he is!' Do not go running off after them.q 24For the Son of Man in his dayq will be like the lightning,r which flashes and lights up the sky from one end to the other. 25But first he must suffer many things and be rejecteds by this generation.

26"Just as it was in the days of Noah,t so also will it be in the days of the Son of Man. 27People were eating, drinking, marrying and being given in marriage up to the day Noah entered the ark. Then the flood came and destroyed them all.

28"It was the same in the days of Lot. People were eating and drinking, buying and selling, planting and building. 29But the day Lot left Sodom, fire and sulfur rained down from heaven and destroyed them all.

30"It will be just like this on the day the Son of Man is revealed.u 31On that day no one who is on the roof of his house, with his goods inside, should go down to get them. Likewise, no one in the field should go back for anything.v 32Remember Lot's wife!w 33Whoever tries to keep his life will lose it, and whoever loses his life will preserve it. 34I tell you, on that night two people will be in one bed; one will be taken and the other left. 35Two women will be grinding grain together; one will be taken and the other left.r"x

37"Where, Lord?" they asked.

He replied, "Where there is a dead body, there the vultures will gather."y

17:23
q Mt 24:23;
Lk 21:8
17:24
r Mt 24:27
17:25
s Lk 9:22
17:26
t Ge 7:6-24
17:30
u 2Th 1:7
17:31
v Mt 24:17, 18
17:32
w Ge 19:26
17:35
x Mt 24:41
17:37
y Mt 24:28

Jesus Tells the Parable of the Persistent Widow
(171)

18 Then Jesus told his disciples a parable to show them that they should always pray and not give up.z 2He said: "In a certain town there was a judge who neither feared God nor cared about men. 3And there was a widow in that town who kept coming to him with the plea, 'Grant me justice against my adversary.'

4"For some time he refused. But finally he said to himself, 'Even though I don't fear God or care about men, 5yet because this widow keeps bothering me, I will see that she gets justice, so that she won't eventually wear me out with her coming!' "a

6And the Lord said, "Listen to what the unjust judge says. 7And will not God bring about justice for his chosen ones, who cry outb to him day and night? Will he keep putting them off? 8I tell you, he will see that they get justice, and quickly. However, when the Son of Man comes, will he find faith on the earth?"

18:1
z Lk 11:5-8

18:5
a Lk 11:8

18:7
b Rev 6:10

q 24 Some manuscripts do not have *in his day*. r 35 Some manuscripts *left. 36Two men will be in the field; one will be taken and the other left.*

17:23, 24 Many will claim to be the Messiah and many will claim that Jesus has returned — and people will believe them. Jesus warns us never to take such reports seriously, no matter how convincing they may sound. When Jesus returns, his power and presence will be evident to everyone. No one will need to spread the message because all will see for themselves.

17:23-36 Life will be going on as usual on the day Christ returns. There will be no warning. Most people will be going about their everyday tasks, indifferent to the demands of God. They will be as surprised by Christ's return as the people in Noah's day were by the flood (Genesis 6 – 8) or the people in Lot's day by the destruction of Sodom (Genesis 19). We don't know the time of Christ's return, but we do know that he is coming. He may come today, tomorrow, or centuries in the future. Whenever he comes, we must be morally and spiritually ready. Live as if Jesus were returning today.

17:26-35 Jesus warned against false security. We are to abandon the values and attachments of this world in order to be ready for Christ's return. His return will happen suddenly, and when he comes, there will be no second chances. Some will be taken to be with him; the rest will be left behind.

17:37 To answer the disciples' question, Jesus quoted a familiar proverb. One vulture circling overhead does not mean much, but a gathering of vultures means that a dead body is nearby. Likewise, one sign of the end may not be significant, but when many signs occur, the second coming is near.

18:1 To persist in prayer and not give up does not mean endless repetition or painfully long prayer sessions. Always praying means keeping our requests constantly before God as we live for him day by day, believing he will answer. When we live by faith, we are not to give up. God may delay answering, but his delays always have good reasons. As we persist in prayer we grow in character, faith, and hope.

18:3 Widows and orphans were among the most vulnerable of all God's people, and both Old Testament prophets and New Testament apostles insisted that these needy people be properly cared for. See, for example, Exodus 22:22 – 24; Isaiah 1:17; 1 Timothy 5:3; James 1:27.

18:6, 7 If unjust judges respond to constant pressure, how much more will a great and loving God respond to us. If we know he loves us, we can believe he will hear our cries for help.

Jesus Tells the Parable of Two Men Who Prayed (172)

18:9
c Lk 16:15

9To some who were confident of their own righteousness[c] and looked down on everybody else, Jesus told this parable: 10"Two men went up to the temple to pray, one a Pharisee and the other a tax collector. 11The Pharisee stood up[d] and prayed about[s] himself: 'God, I thank you that I am not like other men — robbers, evildoers, adulterers — or even like this tax collector. 12I fast[e] twice a week and give a tenth[f] of all I get.'

18:11
d Mk 11:25

18:12
e Mt 9:14
f Lk 11:42

13"But the tax collector stood at a distance. He would not even look up to heaven, but beat his breast[g] and said, 'God, have mercy on me, a sinner.'

18:13
g Lk 23:48

14"I tell you that this man, rather than the other, went home justified before God. For everyone who exalts himself will be humbled, and he who humbles himself will be exalted."[h]

18:14
h Mt 23:12

Jesus Blesses Little Children (174/Matthew 19:13–15; Mark 10:13–16)

15People were also bringing babies to Jesus to have him touch them. When the disciples saw this, they rebuked them. 16But Jesus called the children to him and said, "Let the little children come to me, and do not hinder them, for the kingdom of God belongs to such as these. 17I tell you the truth, anyone who will not receive the kingdom of God like a little child[i] will never enter it."

18:17
i Mt 18:3

Jesus Speaks to the Rich Young Man (175/Matthew 19:16–30; Mark 10:17–31)

18A certain ruler asked him, "Good teacher, what must I do to inherit eternal life?"[j]

18:18
j Lk 10:25

19"Why do you call me good?" Jesus answered. "No one is good — except God alone. 20You know the commandments: 'Do not commit adultery, do not murder, do not steal, do not give false testimony, honor your father and mother.'[t]"[k]

18:20
k Ex 20:12-16;
Dt 5:16-20;
Ro 13:9

21"All these I have kept since I was a boy," he said.

22When Jesus heard this, he said to him, "You still lack one thing. Sell everything you have and give to the poor, and you will have treasure in heaven.[l] Then come, follow me."

18:22
l Mt 6:20

23When he heard this, he became very sad, because he was a man of great

s 11 Or to   t 20 Exodus 20:12-16; Deut. 5:16-20

18:10   The people who lived near Jerusalem often went to the temple to pray. The temple was the center of their worship.

18:11–14   The Pharisee did not go to the temple to pray to God but to announce to all within earshot how good he was. The tax collector went recognizing his sin and begging for mercy. Self-righteousness is dangerous. It leads to pride, causes a person to despise others, and prevents him or her from learning anything from God. The tax collector's prayer should be our prayer because we all need God's mercy every day. Don't let pride in your achievements cut you off from God.

18:15–17   It was customary for a mother to bring her children to a rabbi for a blessing, and that is why these mothers gathered around Jesus. The disciples, however, thought the children were unworthy of the Master's time — less important than whatever else he was doing. But Jesus welcomed them, because little children have the kind of faith and trust needed to enter God's kingdom. It is important that we introduce our children to Jesus and that we ourselves approach him with childlike attitudes of acceptance, faith, and trust.

●**18:18ff**   This ruler sought reassurance, some way of knowing for sure that he had eternal life. He wanted Jesus to measure and grade his qualifications, or to give him some task he could do to assure his own immortality. So Jesus gave him a task — the one thing the rich ruler knew he could not do. "Who then can be saved?" the bystanders asked. "No one can, by his or her own achievements," Jesus' answer implied. "What is impossible with men is possible with God." Salvation cannot be earned — it is God's gift (see Ephesians 2:8–10).

18:18, 19   Jesus' question to the ruler who came and called him "Good teacher" was, in essence, "Do you know who I am?" Undoubtedly the man did not catch the implications of Jesus' reply — that the man was right in calling him good because Jesus truly is God.

●**18:22, 23**   This man's wealth made his life comfortable and gave him power and prestige. When Jesus told him to sell everything he owned, Jesus was touching the very basis of his security and identity. The man did not understand that he would be even more secure if he followed Jesus than he was with all his wealth. Jesus does not ask all believers to sell everything they have, although this may be his will for some. He does ask us all, however, to get rid of anything that has become more important than God. If your basis for security has shifted from God to what you own, it would be better for you to get rid of those possessions.

wealth. 24Jesus looked at him and said, "How hard it is for the rich to enter the kingdom of God!*m* 25Indeed, it is easier for a camel to go through the eye of a needle than for a rich man to enter the kingdom of God."

26Those who heard this asked, "Who then can be saved?"

27Jesus replied, "What is impossible with men is possible with God."*n*

28Peter said to him, "We have left all we had to follow you!"

29"I tell you the truth," Jesus said to them, "no one who has left home or wife or brothers or parents or children for the sake of the kingdom of God 30will fail to receive many times as much in this age and, in the age to come,*o* eternal life."

Jesus Predicts His Death the Third Time
(177/Matthew 20:17–19; Mark 10:32–34)

31Jesus took the Twelve aside and told them, "We are going up to Jerusalem,*p* and everything that is written by the prophets*q* about the Son of Man will be fulfilled. 32He will be handed over to the Gentiles.*r* They will mock him, insult him, spit on him, flog him*s* and kill him. 33On the third day he will rise again."

34The disciples did not understand any of this. Its meaning was hidden from them, and they did not know what he was talking about.*t*

Jesus Heals a Blind Beggar
(179/Matthew 20:29–34; Mark 10:46–52)

35As Jesus approached Jericho, a blind man was sitting by the roadside begging. 36When he heard the crowd going by, he asked what was happening. 37They told him, "Jesus of Nazareth is passing by."

38He called out, "Jesus, Son of David,*u* have mercy on me!"

39Those who led the way rebuked him and told him to be quiet, but he shouted all the more, "Son of David, have mercy on me!"

40Jesus stopped and ordered the man to be brought to him. When he came near, Jesus asked him, 41"What do you want me to do for you?"

"Lord, I want to see," he replied.

42Jesus said to him, "Receive your sight; your faith has healed you."*v* 43Immediately he received his sight and followed Jesus, praising God. When all the people saw it, they also praised God.*w*

18:24 *m*Pr 11:28
18:27 *n*Mt 19:26
18:30 *o*Mt 12:32
18:31 *p*Lk 9:51 *q*Ps 22
18:32 *r*Lk 23:1 *s*Mt 16:21
18:34 *t*Mk 9:32
18:38 *u*Mt 9:27
18:42 *v*Mt 9:22
18:43 *w*Mt 9:8

● **18:24-27** Because money represents power, authority, and success, often it is difficult for wealthy people to realize their need and their powerlessness to save themselves. The rich in talent or intelligence suffer the same difficulty. Unless God reaches down into their lives, they will not come to him. Jesus surprised some of his hearers by offering salvation to the poor; he may surprise some people today by offering it to the rich. It is difficult for a self-sufficient person to realize his or her need and come to Jesus, but "What is impossible with men is possible with God."

18:26-30 Peter and the other disciples had paid a high price — leaving their homes and jobs — to follow Jesus. But Jesus reminded Peter that following him has its benefits as well as its sacrifices. Any believer who has had to give up something to follow Christ will be paid back in this life as well as in the next. For example, if you must give up a secure job, you will find that God offers a secure relationship with himself now and forever. If you must give up your family's approval, you will gain the love of the family of God. The disciples had begun to pay the price of following Jesus, and Jesus said they would be rewarded. Don't dwell on what you have given up; think about what you have gained and give thanks for it. You can never outgive God.

18:31-34 Some predictions about what would happen to Jesus are found in Psalm 41:9 (betrayal); Psalm 22:16–18 and Isaiah 53:4–7 (crucifixion); Psalm 16:10 (resurrection). The disciples didn't understand Jesus, apparently because they focused on what he said about his death and ignored what he said about his resurrection. Even though Jesus spoke plainly, they would not grasp the significance of his words until they saw the risen Christ face to face.

18:35 Beggars often waited along the roads near cities, because that was where they were able to contact the most people. Usually disabled in some way, beggars were unable to earn a living. Medical help was not available for their problems, and people tended to ignore their obligation to care for the needy (Leviticus 25:35–38). Thus beggars had little hope of escaping their degrading way of life. But this blind beggar took hope in the Messiah. He shamelessly cried out for Jesus' attention, and Jesus said that his faith allowed him to see. No matter how desperate your situation may seem, if you call out to Jesus in faith, he will help you.

18:38 The blind man called Jesus "Son of David," a title for the Messiah (Isaiah 11:1–3). This means that he understood Jesus to be the long-awaited Messiah. A poor and blind beggar could *see* that Jesus was the Messiah, while the religious leaders who saw his miracles were blinded to his identity and refused to recognize him as the Messiah.

Jesus Brings Salvation to Zacchaeus's Home
(180)

19:1
xLk 18:35

19 Jesus entered Jericho[x] and was passing through. ²A man was there by the name of Zacchaeus; he was a chief tax collector and was wealthy. ³He wanted to see who Jesus was, but being a short man he could not, because of the crowd. ⁴So he ran ahead and climbed a sycamore-fig[y] tree to see him, since Jesus was coming that way.

19:4
y1Ki 10:27;
1Ch 27:28

⁵When Jesus reached the spot, he looked up and said to him, "Zacchaeus, come down immediately. I must stay at your house today." ⁶So he came down at once and welcomed him gladly.

⁷All the people saw this and began to mutter, "He has gone to be the guest of a 'sinner.'"[z]

19:7
zMt 9:11

19:8
aLk 7:13
bEx 22:1;
Lev 6:4, 5;
Nu 5:7;
2Sa 12:6

⁸But Zacchaeus stood up and said to the Lord,[a] "Look, Lord! Here and now I give half of my possessions to the poor, and if I have cheated anybody out of anything, I will pay back four times the amount."[b]

⁹Jesus said to him, "Today salvation has come to this house, because this man, too, is a son of Abraham.[c] ¹⁰For the Son of Man came to seek and to save what was lost."

19:9
cLk 3:8

GOSPEL ACCOUNTS FOUND ONLY IN LUKE		
	1:5–80	Special events leading up to birth of John the Baptist and Jesus
	2:1–52	Events from Jesus' childhood
	3:19, 20	Herod puts John in prison
	4:16–30	Jesus is rejected at Nazareth
	5:1–11	Jesus provides a miraculous catch of fish
	7:11–17	Jesus raises a widow's son from the dead
	7:36–50	A sinful woman anoints Jesus' feet
	8:1–3	Women travel with Jesus
	10:1–18:14	Events, miracles, and teachings during the months prior to Christ's death
	19:1–27	Jesus meets Zacchaeus and later tells the parable of the king's ten servants
	23:6–12	Jesus' trial before Herod
	24:44–49	Some of Jesus' last words before his ascension

19:1-10 To finance their great world empire, the Romans levied heavy taxes on all nations under their control. The Jews opposed these taxes because they supported a secular government and its pagan gods, but they were still forced to pay. Tax collectors were among the most unpopular people in Israel. Jews by birth, they chose to work for Rome and were considered traitors. Besides, it was common knowledge that tax collectors were making themselves rich by gouging their fellow Jews. No wonder the people muttered when Jesus went home with the tax collector Zacchaeus. But despite the fact that Zacchaeus was both a cheater and a turncoat, Jesus loved him; and in response, the little tax collector was converted. In every society, certain groups of people are considered "untouchable" because of their political views, their immoral behavior, or their life-style. We should not give in to social pressure to avoid these people. Jesus loves them, and they need to hear his Good News.

● **19:8** Judging from the crowd's reaction to him, Zacchaeus must

have been a very crooked tax collector. But after he met Jesus, he realized that his life needed straightening out. By giving to the poor and making restitution — with generous interest — to those he had cheated, Zacchaeus demonstrated inward change by outward action. It is not enough to follow Jesus in your head or heart alone. You must show your faith by changed behavior. Has your faith resulted in action? What changes do you need to make?

19:9, 10 When Jesus said Zacchaeus was a son of Abraham and yet was lost, he must have shocked his hearers in at least two ways. They would not have liked to acknowledge that this unpopular tax collector was a fellow son of Abraham, and they would not have wished to admit that sons of Abraham could be lost. But a person is not saved by a good heritage or condemned by a bad one; faith is more important than genealogy. Jesus still loves to bring the lost into his kingdom, no matter what their background or previous way of life. Through faith, the lost can be forgiven and made new.

Jesus Tells the Parable of the King's Ten Servants
(181)

¹¹While they were listening to this, he went on to tell them a parable, because he was near Jerusalem and the people thought that the kingdom of God was going to appear at once. *d* ¹²He said: "A man of noble birth went to a distant country to have himself appointed king and then to return. ¹³So he called ten of his servants and gave them ten minas. ᵘ 'Put this money to work,' he said, 'until I come back.'

¹⁴"But his subjects hated him and sent a delegation after him to say, 'We don't want this man to be our king.'

¹⁵"He was made king, however, and returned home. Then he sent for the servants to whom he had given the money, in order to find out what they had gained with it.

¹⁶"The first one came and said, 'Sir, your mina has earned ten more.'

¹⁷" 'Well done, my good servant!' his master replied. 'Because you have been trustworthy in a very small matter, take charge of ten cities.' *e*

¹⁸"The second came and said, 'Sir, your mina has earned five more.'

¹⁹"His master answered, 'You take charge of five cities.'

²⁰"Then another servant came and said, 'Sir, here is your mina; I have kept it laid away in a piece of cloth. ²¹I was afraid of you, because you are a hard man. You take out what you did not put in and reap what you did not sow.' *f*

²²"His master replied, 'I will judge you by your own words, *g* you wicked servant! You knew, did you, that I am a hard man, taking out what I did not put in, and reaping what I did not sow? *h* ²³Why then didn't you put my money on deposit, so that when I came back, I could have collected it with interest?'

²⁴"Then he said to those standing by, 'Take his mina away from him and give it to the one who has ten minas.'

²⁵" 'Sir,' they said, 'he already has ten!'

²⁶"He replied, 'I tell you that to everyone who has, more will be given, but as for the one who has nothing, even what he has will be taken away. *i* ²⁷But those enemies of mine who did not want me to be king over them — bring them here and kill them in front of me.' "

3. Jesus' ministry in Jerusalem

Jesus Rides into Jerusalem on a Donkey
(183/Matthew 21:1–11; Mark 11:1–11; John 12:12–19)

²⁸After Jesus had said this, he went on ahead, going up to Jerusalem. *j* ²⁹As he approached Bethphage and Bethany at the hill called the Mount of Olives, *k* he sent two of his disciples, saying to them, ³⁰"Go to the village ahead of you, and as you enter it, you will find a colt tied there, which no one has ever ridden. Untie it and bring it here. ³¹If anyone asks you, 'Why are you untying it?' tell him, 'The Lord needs it.' "

³²Those who were sent ahead went and found it just as he had told them. ³³As they were untying the colt, its owners asked them, "Why are you untying the colt?"

³⁴They replied, "The Lord needs it."

ᵘ *13* A mina was about three months' wages.

19:11
d Ac 1:6

19:17
e Lk 16:10

19:21
f Mt 25:24
19:22
g 2Sa 1:16;
Job 15:6
h Mt 25:26

19:26
i Mt 25:29

19:28
j Mk 10:32
19:29
k Mt 21:1

19:11ff The people still hoped for a political leader who would set up an earthly kingdom and get rid of Roman domination. Jesus' parable showed that his kingdom would not take this form right away. First he would go away for a while, and his followers would need to be faithful and productive during his absence. Upon his return, Jesus would inaugurate a kingdom more powerful and just than anything they could expect.

● **19:11ff** This story showed Jesus' followers what they were to do during the time between Jesus' departure and his second coming. Because we live in that time period, it applies directly to us. We have been given excellent resources to build and expand God's kingdom. Jesus expects us to use these talents so that they multi-

ply and the kingdom grows. He asks each of us to account for what we do with his gifts. While awaiting the coming of the kingdom of God in glory, we must do Christ's work.

● **19:20–27** Why was the king so hard on this man who had not increased the money? He punished the man because (1) he didn't share his master's interest in the kingdom; (2) he didn't trust his master's intentions; (3) his only concern was for himself, and (4) he did nothing to use the money. Like the king in this story, God has given you gifts to use for the benefit of his kingdom. Do you want the kingdom to grow? Do you trust God to govern it fairly? Are you as concerned for others' welfare as you are for your own? Are you willing to use faithfully what he has entrusted to you?

19:36
l2Ki 9:13

35They brought it to Jesus, threw their cloaks on the colt and put Jesus on it. 36As he went along, people spread their cloaks[l] on the road.

37When he came near the place where the road goes down the Mount of Olives, the whole crowd of disciples began joyfully to praise God in loud voices for all the miracles they had seen:

19:38
mPs 118:26;
Lk 13:35
nLk 2:14

38"Blessed is the king who comes in the name of the Lord!"[v][m]

"Peace in heaven and glory in the highest!"[n]

19:39
oMt 21:15, 16

39Some of the Pharisees in the crowd said to Jesus, "Teacher, rebuke your disciples!"[o]

19:40
pHab 2:11

40"I tell you," he replied, "if they keep quiet, the stones will cry out."[p]

19:41
qLk 13:34, 35

41As he approached Jerusalem and saw the city, he wept over it[q] 42and said, "If you, even you, had only known on this day what would bring you peace — but now it is hidden from your eyes. 43The days will come upon you when your enemies will build an embankment against you and encircle you and hem you in on every side.[r] 44They will dash you to the ground, you and the children within your walls. They will not leave one stone on another,[s] because you did not recognize the time of God's coming[t] to you."

19:43
rIsa 29:3;
Jer 6:6;
Eze 4:2;
Lk 21:20

19:44
sLk 21:6
t1Pe 2:12

Jesus Clears the Temple Again
(184/Matthew 21:12–17; Mark 11:12–19)

45Then he entered the temple area and began driving out those who were selling. 46"It is written," he said to them, " 'My house will be a house of prayer'[w];[u] but you have made it 'a den of robbers.'[x]"[v]

19:46
uIsa 56:7
vJer 7:11

v 38 Psalm 118:26   w 46 Isaiah 56:7   x 46 Jer. 7:11

LAST WEEK IN JERUSALEM
As they approached Jerusalem from Jericho (19:1), Jesus and the disciples came to the villages of Bethany and Bethphage, nestled on the eastern slope of the Mount of Olives, only a few miles outside Jerusalem. Jesus stayed in Bethany during the nights of that last week, entering Jerusalem during the day.

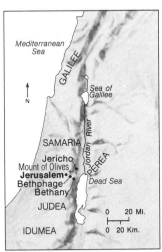

chose a *time* when all Israel would be gathered at Jerusalem, a *place* where huge crowds could see him, and a *way* of proclaiming his mission that was unmistakable. The people went wild. They were sure their liberation was at hand.

●**19:38** The people who were praising God for giving them a king had the wrong idea about Jesus. They expected him to be a national leader who would restore their nation to its former glory, and thus they were deaf to the words of their prophets and blind to Jesus' real mission. When it became apparent that Jesus was not going to fulfill their hopes, many people would turn against him.

19:39, 40 The Pharisees thought the crowd's words were sacrilegious and blasphemous. They didn't want someone challenging their power and authority, and they didn't want a revolt that would bring the Roman army down on them. So they asked Jesus to keep his people quiet. But Jesus said that if the people were quiet, the stones would immediately cry out. Why? Not because Jesus was setting up a powerful political kingdom, but because he was establishing God's eternal kingdom, a reason for the greatest celebration of all.

19:41-44 The Jewish leaders had rejected their King (19:47). They had gone too far. They had refused God's offer of salvation in Jesus Christ when they were visited by God himself ("the time of God's coming"), and soon their nation would suffer. God did not turn away from the Jewish people who obeyed him, however. He continues to offer salvation to the people he loves, both Jews and Gentiles. Eternal life is within your reach — accept it while the opportunity is still offered.

19:30-35 By this time Jesus was extremely well known. Everyone coming to Jerusalem for the Passover feast had heard of him, and, for a time, the popular mood was favorable toward him. "The Lord needs it" was all the disciples had to say, and the colt's owners gladly turned their animal over to them.

19:35-38 Christians celebrate this event on Palm Sunday. The people lined the road, praising God, waving palm branches, and throwing their cloaks in front of the colt as it passed before them. "Long live the King" was the meaning behind their joyful shouts, because they knew that Jesus was intentionally fulfilling the prophecy in Zechariah 9:9: "See, your king comes to you, righteous and having salvation, gentle and riding on a donkey, on a colt, the foal of a donkey." To announce that he was indeed the Messiah, Jesus

19:43, 44 About 40 years after Jesus said these words, they came true. In A.D. 66, the Jews revolted against Roman control. Three years later Titus, son of the Emperor Vespasian, was sent to crush the rebellion. Roman soldiers attacked Jerusalem and broke through the northern wall but still couldn't take the city. Finally they laid siege to it, and in A.D. 70 they were able to enter the severely weakened city and burn it. Six hundred thousand Jews were killed during Titus' onslaught.

47Every day he was teaching at the temple.ᵂ But the chief priests, the teachers of the law and the leaders among the people were trying to kill him.ˣ 48Yet they could not find any way to do it, because all the people hung on his words.

Religious Leaders Challenge Jesus' Authority
(189/Matthew 21:23–27; Mark 11:27–33)

20 One day as he was teaching the people in the temple courtsʸ and preaching the gospel,ᶻ the chief priests and the teachers of the law, together with the elders, came up to him. 2"Tell us by what authority you are doing these things," they said. "Who gave you this authority?"ᵃ

3He replied, "I will also ask you a question. Tell me, 4John's baptism—was it from heaven, or from men?"

5They discussed it among themselves and said, "If we say, 'From heaven,' he will ask, 'Why didn't you believe him?' 6But if we say, 'From men,' all the people will stone us, because they are persuaded that John was a prophet."

7So they answered, "We don't know where it was from."

8Jesus said, "Neither will I tell you by what authority I am doing these things."

Jesus Tells the Parable of the Wicked Tenants
(191/Matthew 21:33–46; Mark 12:1–12)

9He went on to tell the people this parable: "A man planted a vineyard, rented it to some farmers and went away for a long time. 10At harvest time he sent a servant to the tenants so they would give him some of the fruit of the vineyard. But the tenants beat him and sent him away empty-handed. 11He sent another servant, but that one also they beat and treated shamefully and sent away empty-handed. 12He sent still a third, and they wounded him and threw him out.

13"Then the owner of the vineyard said, 'What shall I do? I will send my son, whom I love; perhaps they will respect him.'

14"But when the tenants saw him, they talked the matter over. 'This is the heir,' they said. 'Let's kill him, and the inheritance will be ours.' 15So they threw him out of the vineyard and killed him.

"What then will the owner of the vineyard do to them? 16He will come and kill those tenantsᵇ and give the vineyard to others."

When the people heard this, they said, "May this never be!"

17Jesus looked directly at them and asked, "Then what is the meaning of that which is written:

" 'The stone the builders rejected
has become the capstoneʸ'ᶻ?ᶜ

18Everyone who falls on that stone will be broken to pieces, but he on whom it falls will be crushed."

19The teachers of the law and the chief priests looked for a way to arrest himᵈ

ʸ 17 Or cornerstone ᶻ 17 Psalm 118:22

19:47 ᵂMt 26:55 ˣMk 11:18
20:1 ʸMt 26:55 ᶻLk 8:1
20:2 ᵃAc 4:7; 7:27
20:16 ᵇLk 19:27
20:17 ᶜPs 118:22
20:19 ᵈLk 19:47

●**19:47** Who were the "leaders among the people"? This group probably included wealthy leaders in politics, commerce, and law. They had several reasons for wanting to get rid of Jesus. He had damaged business in the temple by driving the merchants out. In addition, he was preaching against injustice, and his teachings often favored the poor over the rich. Further, his great popularity was in danger of attracting Rome's attention, and the leaders of Israel wanted as little as possible to do with Rome.

● **20:1-8** This group of leaders wanted to get rid of Jesus, so they tried to trap him with their question. If Jesus would answer that his authority came from God—if he stated openly that he was the Messiah and the Son of God—they would accuse him of blasphemy and bring him to trial. Jesus did not let himself be caught. Instead, he turned the question on them. Thus he exposed their motives and avoided their trap.

● **20:9-16** The characters in this story are easily identified. Even the religious leaders understood it. The owner of the vineyard is God; the vineyard is Israel; the tenants are the religious leaders; the servants are the prophets and priests God sent to Israel; the son is the Messiah, Jesus; and the others are the Gentiles. Jesus' parable indirectly answered the religious leaders' question about his authority; it also showed them that he knew about their plan to kill him.

20:17-19 Quoting Psalm 118:22, Jesus showed the unbelieving leaders that even their rejection of the Messiah had been prophesied in Scripture. Ignoring the capstone, or cornerstone, was dangerous. A person could be tripped or crushed (judged and punished). Jesus' comments were veiled, but the religious leaders had no trouble interpreting them. They immediately wanted to arrest him.

immediately, because they knew he had spoken this parable against them. But they were afraid of the people.

Religious Leaders Question Jesus about Paying Taxes
(193/Matthew 22:15–22; Mark 12:13–17)

20:20
e Mt 12:10
f Mt 27:2

20:21
g Jn 3:2

20:25
h Lk 23:2;
Ro 13:7

20:27
i Ac 23:8

20:28
j Dt 25:5

20:35
k Mt 12:32

20:36
l Jn 1:12

20Keeping a close watch on him, they sent spies, who pretended to be honest. They hoped to catch Jesus in something he said*e* so that they might hand him over to the power and authority of the governor.*f* 21So the spies questioned him: "Teacher, we know that you speak and teach what is right, and that you do not show partiality but teach the way of God in accordance with the truth.*g* 22Is it right for us to pay taxes to Caesar or not?"

23He saw through their duplicity and said to them, 24"Show me a denarius. Whose portrait and inscription are on it?"

25"Caesar's," they replied.

He said to them, "Then give to Caesar what is Caesar's,*h* and to God what is God's."

26They were unable to trap him in what he had said there in public. And astonished by his answer, they became silent.

Religious Leaders Question Jesus about the Resurrection
(194/Matthew 22:23–33; Mark 12:18–27)

27Some of the Sadducees, who say there is no resurrection,*i* came to Jesus with a question. 28"Teacher," they said, "Moses wrote for us that if a man's brother dies and leaves a wife but no children, the man must marry the widow and have children for his brother.*j* 29Now there were seven brothers. The first one married a woman and died childless. 30The second 31and then the third married her, and in the same way the seven died, leaving no children. 32Finally, the woman died too. 33Now then, at the resurrection whose wife will she be, since the seven were married to her?"

34Jesus replied, "The people of this age marry and are given in marriage. 35But those who are considered worthy of taking part in that age*k* and in the resurrection from the dead will neither marry nor be given in marriage, 36and they can no longer die; for they are like the angels. They are God's children,*l* since they are children of the resurrection. 37But in the account of the bush, even Moses showed that the dead rise, for he calls the Lord 'the God of Abraham, and the God of Isaac, and the

---

20:20-26 Jesus turned his enemies' attempt to trap him into a powerful lesson: As God's followers, we have legitimate obligations to both God and the government. But it is important to keep our priorities straight. When the two authorities conflict, our duty to God always must come before our duty to the government.

20:21 These spies, pretending to be honest men, flattered Jesus before asking him their trick question, hoping to catch him off guard. But Jesus knew what they were trying to do and stayed out of their trap. Beware of flattery. With God's help, you can detect it and avoid the trap that often follows.

20:22 This was a loaded question. The Jews were enraged at having to pay taxes to Rome, thus supporting the pagan government and its gods. They hated the system that allowed tax collectors to charge exorbitant rates and keep the extra for themselves. If Jesus said they should pay taxes, they would call him a traitor to their nation and their religion. But if he said they should not, they could report him to Rome as a rebel. Jesus' questioners thought they had him this time, but he outwitted them again.

20:24 The denarius was the usual pay for one day's work.

20:27-38 The Sadducees, a group of conservative religious leaders, honored only the Pentateuch — Genesis through Deuteronomy — as Scripture. They also did not believe in a resurrection of the dead because they could find no mention of it in those books. The Sadducees decided to try their hand at tricking Jesus, so they brought him a question that had always stumped the Pharisees. After addressing their question about marriage, Jesus answered their *real* question about resurrection. Basing his answer on the writings of Moses — an authority they respected — he upheld belief in resurrection.

20:34, 35 Jesus' statement does not mean that people will not recognize their partners in heaven. It simply means that we must not think of heaven as an extension of life as we now know it. Our relationships in this life are limited by time, death, and sin. We don't know everything about our resurrection life, but Jesus affirms that relationships will be different from what we are used to here and now.

20:37, 38 The Sadducees came to Jesus with a trick question. Not believing in the resurrection, they wanted Jesus to say something they could refute. Even so, Jesus did not ignore or belittle their question. He answered it, and then he went beyond it to the real issue. When people ask you tough religious questions — "How can a loving God allow people to starve?" "If God knows what I'm going to do, do I have any free choice?" — follow Jesus' example. First answer the question to the best of your ability; then look for the real issue — hurt over a personal tragedy, for example, or difficulty in making a decision. Often the spoken question is only a test, not of your ability to answer hard questions, but of your willingness to listen and care.

God of Jacob.' **a**m 38He is not the God of the dead, but of the living, for to him all
are alive."

39Some of the teachers of the law responded, "Well said, teacher!" 40And no one
dared to ask him any more questions. n

20:37
mEx 3:6

20:40
nMt 22:46;
Mk 12:34

Religious Leaders Cannot Answer Jesus' Question
(196/Matthew 22:41–46; Mark 12:35–37)

41Then Jesus said to them, "How is it that they say the Christ**b** is the Son of
David? 42David himself declares in the Book of Psalms:

> " 'The Lord said to my Lord:
> "Sit at my right hand
> 43until I make your enemies
> a footstool for your feet." ' **c**o

20:43
oPs 110:1

44David calls him 'Lord.' How then can he be his son?"

Jesus Warns against the Religious Leaders
(197/Matthew 23:1–12; Mark 12:38–40)

45While all the people were listening, Jesus said to his disciples, 46"Beware of
the teachers of the law. They like to walk around in flowing robes and love to be
greeted in the marketplaces and have the most important seats in the synagogues
and the places of honor at banquets. p 47They devour widows' houses and for a
show make lengthy prayers. Such men will be punished most severely."

20:46
pLk 11:43

A Poor Widow Gives All She Has
(200/Mark 12:41–44)

21 As he looked up, Jesus saw the rich putting their gifts into the temple treasury. q 2He also saw a poor widow put in two very small copper coins.**d** 3"I
tell you the truth," he said, "this poor widow has put in more than all the others.
4All these people gave their gifts out of their wealth; but she out of her poverty put
in all she had to live on."r

21:1
qMt 27:6

21:4
r2Co 8:12

Jesus Tells about the Future
(201/Matthew 24:1–25; Mark 13:1–23)

5Some of his disciples were remarking about how the temple was adorned with
beautiful stones and with gifts dedicated to God. But Jesus said, 6"As for what you

a 37 Exodus 3:6   b 41 Or *Messiah*   c 43 Psalm 110:1   d 2 Greek *two lepta*

● **20:41–44** The Pharisees and Sadducees had asked their questions. Then Jesus turned the tables and asked them a question that
went right to the heart of the matter — what they thought about the
Messiah's identity. The Pharisees knew that the Messiah would be
a descendant of David, but they did not understand that he would
be more than a human descendant — he was God in the flesh. Jesus quoted from Psalm 110:1 to show that David knew that the
Messiah would be both human and divine. The Pharisees expected only a human ruler to restore Israel's greatness as in the
days of David and Solomon.

The central issue of life is what we believe about Jesus. Other
spiritual questions are irrelevant unless we first decide to believe
that Jesus is who he said he is. The Pharisees and Sadducees
could not do this. They remained confused over Jesus' identity.

20:45–47 The teachers of the law loved the benefits associated
with their position, and they sometimes cheated the poor in order
to get even more benefits. Every job has its rewards, but gaining
rewards should never become more important than doing the job
faithfully. God will punish people who use their position of responsibility to cheat others. Whatever resources you have been given,
use them to help others and not just yourself.

● **20:47** How strange to think that the teachers of the law would receive the worst punishment. But behind their appearance of holiness and respectability, they were arrogant, crafty, selfish, and
uncaring. Jesus exposed their evil hearts. He showed that despite
their pious words, they were neglecting God's laws and doing as
they pleased. Religious deeds do not cancel sin. Jesus said that
God's most severe judgment awaited these teachers because they
should have been living examples of mercy and justice.

21:1, 2 Jesus was in the area of the temple called the court of
women. The treasury was located there or in an adjoining walkway.
In this area were seven boxes in which worshipers could deposit
their temple tax and six boxes for freewill offerings like the one this
woman gave. Not only was she poor; as a widow she had few resources for making money. Her small gift was a sacrifice, but she
gave it willingly.

21:1–4 This widow gave all she had to live on, in contrast to the
way most of us handle our money. When we consider giving a certain percentage of our income a great accomplishment, we resem-
ble those who gave "out of their wealth." Here, Jesus was admiring
generous and sacrificial giving. As believers, we should consider
increasing our giving — whether of money, time, or talents — to a
point beyond convenience or safety.

21:6
sLk 19:44

see here, the time will come when not one stone will be left on another;s every one of them will be thrown down."

7"Teacher," they asked, "when will these things happen? And what will be the sign that they are about to take place?"

8He replied: "Watch out that you are not deceived. For many will come in my name, claiming, 'I am he,' and, 'The time is near.' Do not follow them.t 9When you hear of wars and revolutions, do not be frightened. These things must happen first, but the end will not come right away."

21:8
tLk 17:23

10Then he said to them: "Nation will rise against nation, and kingdom against kingdom.u 11There will be great earthquakes, famines and pestilences in various places, and fearful events and great signs from heaven.

21:10
u2Ch 15:6

12"But before all this, they will lay hands on you and persecute you. They will deliver you to synagogues and prisons, and you will be brought before kings and governors, and all on account of my name. 13This will result in your being witnesses to them.v 14But make up your mind not to worry beforehand how you will defend yourselves.w 15For I will give youx words and wisdom that none of your adversaries will be able to resist or contradict. 16You will be betrayed even by parents, brothers, relatives and friends,y and they will put some of you to death. 17All men will hate you because of me. 18But not a hair of your head will perish.z 19By standing firm you will gain life.

21:13
vPhp 1:12

21:14
wLk 12:11

21:15
xLk 12:12

21:16
yLk 12:52, 53

21:18
zMt 10:30

21:20
aLk 19:43

20"When you see Jerusalem being surrounded by armies,a you will know that its desolation is near. 21Then let those who are in Judea flee to the mountains, let those

---

21:5, 6 The temple the disciples were admiring was not Solomon's temple — that had been destroyed by the Babylonians in the seventh century B.C. This temple had been built by Ezra after the return from exile in the sixth century B.C., desecrated by the Seleucids in the second century B.C., reconsecrated by the Maccabees soon afterward, and enormously expanded by Herod the Great over a 46-year period. It was a beautiful, imposing structure with a significant history, but Jesus said that it would be completely destroyed. This happened in A.D. 70 when the Roman army burned Jerusalem.

21:7ff Jesus did not leave his disciples unprepared for the difficult years ahead. He warned them about false messiahs, natural disasters, and persecutions; but he assured them that he would be with them to protect them and make his kingdom known through them. In the end, Jesus promised that he would return in power and glory to save them. Jesus' warnings and promises to his disciples also apply to us as we look forward to his return.

21:12, 13 These persecutions soon began. Luke recorded many of them in the book of Acts. Paul wrote from prison that he suffered gladly because it helped him know Christ better and do Christ's work for the church (Philippians 3:10; Colossians 1:24). The early church thrived despite intense persecution. In fact, late in the second century the church father Tertullian wrote, "The blood of Christians is seed," because opposition helped spread Christianity.

21:14–19 Jesus warned that in the coming persecutions his followers would be betrayed by their family members and friends. Christians of every age have had to face this possibility. It is reassuring to know that even when we feel completely abandoned, the Holy Spirit will stay with us. He will comfort us, protect us, and give us the words we need. This assurance can give us the courage and hope to stand firm for Christ no matter how difficult the situation.

21:18 Jesus was *not* saying that believers would be exempt from physical harm or death during the persecutions. Remember that most of the disciples were martyred. Rather he was saying that none of his followers would suffer spiritual or eternal loss. On earth, everyone will die, but believers in Jesus will be saved for eternal life.

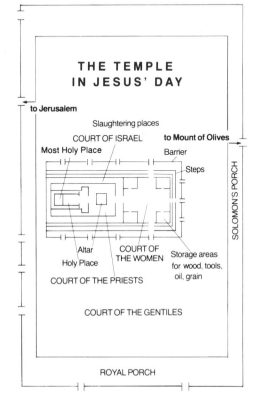

THE TEMPLE
IN JESUS' DAY

to Jerusalem

Slaughtering places

COURT OF ISRAEL   to Mount of Olives

Most Holy Place   Barrier

Steps

Altar   COURT OF   Storage areas
Holy Place THE WOMEN   for wood, tools,
                          oil, grain
COURT OF THE PRIESTS

COURT OF THE GENTILES

SOLOMON'S PORCH

ROYAL PORCH

in the city get out, and let those in the country not enter the city. *b* 22For this is the time of punishment*c* in fulfillment of all that has been written. 23How dreadful it will be in those days for pregnant women and nursing mothers! There will be great distress in the land and wrath against this people. 24They will fall by the sword and will be taken as prisoners to all the nations. Jerusalem will be trampled*d* on by the Gentiles until the times of the Gentiles are fulfilled.

21:21
b Lk 17:31

21:22
c Isa 63:4;
Da 9:24-27

21:24
d Isa 63:18;
Da 8:13;
Rev 11:2

Jesus Tells about His Return
(202/Matthew 24:26–35; Mark 13:24–31)

25"There will be signs in the sun, moon and stars. On the earth, nations will be in anguish and perplexity at the roaring and tossing of the sea. *e* 26Men will faint from terror, apprehensive of what is coming on the world, for the heavenly bodies will be shaken. 27At that time they will see the Son of Man coming in a cloud*f* with power and great glory. 28When these things begin to take place, stand up and lift up your heads, because your redemption is drawing near."*g*

29He told them this parable: "Look at the fig tree and all the trees. 30When they sprout leaves, you can see for yourselves and know that summer is near. 31Even so, when you see these things happening, you know that the kingdom of God*h* is near.

32"I tell you the truth, this generation*e* will certainly not pass away until all these things have happened. 33Heaven and earth will pass away, but my words will never pass away.

21:25
e 2Pe 3:10, 12

21:27
f Rev 1:7

21:28
g Lk 18:7

21:31
h Mt 3:2

Jesus Tells about Remaining Watchful
(203/Matthew 24:36–51; Mark 13:32–37)

34"Be careful, or your hearts will be weighed down with dissipation, drunkenness and the anxieties of life,*i* and that day will close on you unexpectedly*j* like a trap. 35For it will come upon all those who live on the face of the whole earth. 36Be always on the watch, and pray that you may be able to escape all that is about to happen, and that you may be able to stand before the Son of Man."

37Each day Jesus was teaching at the temple, and each evening he went out*k* to spend the night on the hill called the Mount of Olives, 38and all the people came early in the morning to hear him at the temple.

e 32 Or race

21:34
i Mk 4:19
j 1Th 5:2-7

21:37
k Mk 11:19

21:24 The "times of the Gentiles" began with Babylon's destruction of Jerusalem in 586 B.C. and the exile of the Jewish people. Israel was no longer an independent nation but was under the control of Gentile rulers. In Jesus' day, Israel was governed by the Roman empire, and a Roman general would destroy the city in A.D. 70. Jesus was saying that the domination of God's people by his enemies would continue until God decided to end it. The "times of the Gentiles" refers not just to the repeated destructions of Jerusalem, but also to the continuing and mounting persecution of God's people until the end.

● **21:28** The picture of the coming persecutions and natural disasters is gloomy, but ultimately it is a cause not for worry but for great joy. When believers see these events happening, they will know that the return of their Messiah is near, and they can look forward to his reign of justice and peace. Rather than being terrified by what is happening in our world, we should confidently await Christ's return to bring justice and restoration to his people.

21:34-36 Jesus told the disciples to keep a constant watch for his return. Although nearly 2,000 years have passed since he spoke these words, their truth remains: Christ is coming again, and we need to watch and be spiritually fit. This means working faithfully at the tasks God has given us. Don't let your mind and spirit be dulled by careless living, drinking, or the foolish pursuit of pleasure. Don't let life's anxieties overburden you, so that you will be ready to move at God's command.

● **21:36** Only days after telling the disciples to pray that they might escape persecution, Jesus himself asked God to spare him the agonies of the cross, if that was God's will (22:41, 42). It is abnormal to *want* to suffer, but as Jesus' followers we are willing to suffer if by doing so we can help build God's kingdom. We have two wonderful promises to help us as we suffer: God will always be with us (Matthew 28:20), and he will one day rescue us and give us eternal life (Revelation 21:1–4).

22:1 All Jewish males over the age of 12 were required to go to Jerusalem for the Passover festival, followed by a seven-day festi-

C. DEATH AND RESURRECTION OF JESUS, THE SAVIOR (22:1–24:53)

The perfect man was a high ideal in Greek culture. Written with Greeks in mind, Luke's Gospel shows how Jesus was the perfect man given as the perfect sacrifice for the sin of all mankind. Christ is the ideal human—the perfect model for us to follow. We must stand in awe of his character, which met humanity's highest ideals as well as God's demand for an atonement for sin. He is, at one and the same time, our model and our Savior.

Religious Leaders Plot to Kill Jesus
(207/Matthew 26:1–5; Mark 14:1, 2)
Judas Agrees to Betray Jesus
(208/Matthew 26:14–16; Mark 14:10, 11)

22 Now the Feast of Unleavened Bread, called the Passover, was approaching, 2and the chief priests and the teachers of the law were looking for some way to get rid of Jesus, *l* for they were afraid of the people. 3Then Satan entered Judas, called Iscariot, one of the Twelve. 4And Judas went to the chief priests and the officers of the temple guard and discussed with them how he might betray Jesus. 5They were delighted and agreed to give him money.*m* 6He consented, and watched for an opportunity to hand Jesus over to them when no crowd was present.

22:2
*l*Mt 12:14

22:5
*m*Zec 11:12

Disciples Prepare for the Passover
(209/Matthew 26:17–19; Mark 14:12–16)

7Then came the day of Unleavened Bread on which the Passover lamb had to be sacrificed. 8Jesus sent Peter and John,*n* saying, "Go and make preparations for us to eat the Passover."

22:8
*n*Ac 3:1, 11

9"Where do you want us to prepare for it?" they asked.

10He replied, "As you enter the city, a man carrying a jar of water will meet you. Follow him to the house that he enters, 11and say to the owner of the house, 'The Teacher asks: Where is the guest room, where I may eat the Passover with my disciples?' 12He will show you a large upper room, all furnished. Make preparations there."

13They left and found things just as Jesus had told them. So they prepared the Passover.

Jesus and the Disciples Have the Last Supper
(211/Matthew 26:20–30; Mark 14:17–26; John 13:21–30)

14When the hour came, Jesus and his apostles reclined at the table.*o* 15And he said to them, "I have eagerly desired to eat this Passover with you before I suffer. 16For I tell you, I will not eat it again until it finds fulfillment in the kingdom of God."*p*

22:14
*o*Mt 26:20;
Mk 14:17, 18

22:16
*p*Lk 14:15

---

val called the Feast of Unleavened Bread. For these feasts, Jews from all over the Roman empire converged on Jerusalem to celebrate one of the most important events in their history. To learn more about the Passover and the Feast of Unleavened Bread, see the first note on Mark 14:1.

22:3 Satan's part in the betrayal of Jesus does not remove any of the responsibility from Judas. Disillusioned because Jesus was talking about dying rather than about setting up his kingdom, Judas may have been trying to force Jesus' hand and make him use his power to prove he was the Messiah. Or perhaps Judas, not understanding Jesus' mission, no longer believed that Jesus was God's chosen one. (For more information on Judas, see his Profile in Mark 14.) Whatever Judas thought, Satan assumed that Jesus' death would end Jesus' mission and thwart God's plan. Like Judas, he did not know that Jesus' death and resurrection were the most important parts of God's plan all along.

22:7, 8 The Passover meal included the sacrifice of a lamb because of the association with the Jews' exodus from Egypt. When the Jews were getting ready to leave, God told them to kill a lamb and paint its blood on the doorframes of their houses. They then were to prepare the meat for food. Peter and John had to buy and prepare the lamb as well as the unleavened bread, herbs, wine, and other ceremonial food.

22:10 Ordinarily women, not men, went to the well and brought home the water. So this man would have stood out in the crowd.

●**22:14-18** The Passover commemorated Israel's escape from Egypt when the blood of a lamb painted on their doorframes saved their firstborn sons from death. This event foreshadowed Jesus' work on the cross. As the spotless Lamb of God, his blood would be spilled in order to save his people from the penalty of death brought by sin.

17 After taking the cup, he gave thanks and said, "Take this and divide it among you. 18 For I tell you I will not drink again of the fruit of the vine until the kingdom of God comes."

19 And he took bread, gave thanks and broke it, and gave it to them, saying, "This is my body given for you; do this in remembrance of me."

20 In the same way, after the supper he took the cup, saying, "This cup is the new covenant in my blood, which is poured out for you. 21 But the hand of him who is going to betray me is with mine on the table. 22 The Son of Man will go as it has been decreed, *q* but woe to that man who betrays him." 23 They began to question among themselves which of them it might be who would do this.

24 Also a dispute arose among them as to which of them was considered to be greatest. *r* 25 Jesus said to them, "The kings of the Gentiles lord it over them; and those who exercise authority over them call themselves Benefactors. 26 But you are not to be like that. Instead, the greatest among you should be like the youngest, *s* and the one who rules like the one who serves. 27 For who is greater, the one who is at the table or the one who serves? Is it not the one who is at the table? But I am among you as one who serves. *t* 28 You are those who have stood by me in my trials. 29 And I confer on you a kingdom, *u* just as my Father conferred one on me, 30 so that you may eat and drink at my table in my kingdom and sit on thrones, judging the twelve tribes of Israel. *v*

Jesus Predicts Peter's Denial
(212/John 13:31–38)

31 "Simon, Simon, Satan has asked to sift you*f* as wheat. *w* 32 But I have prayed for you, *x* Simon, that your faith may not fail. And when you have turned back, strengthen your brothers." *y*

f 31 The Greek is plural.

22:22 *q* Ac 2:23; 4:28
22:24 *r* Mk 9:34; Lk 9:46
22:26 *s* 1Pe 5:5
22:27 *t* Mt 20:28
22:29 *u* 2Ti 2:12
22:30 *v* Mt 19:28
22:31 *w* Am 9:9
22:32 *x* Jn 17:9, 15 *y* Jn 21:15-17

22:17, 20 Luke mentions two cups of wine, while Matthew and Mark mention only one. In the traditional Passover meal, the wine is served four times. Christ spoke the words about his body and his blood when he offered the fourth and last cup.

22:17-20 Christians differ in their interpretation of the meaning of the commemoration of the Lord's Supper. There are three main views: (1) the bread and wine actually become Christ's body and blood; (2) the bread and wine remain unchanged, yet Christ is spiritually present by faith in and through them; (3) the bread and wine, which remain unchanged, are lasting memorials of Christ's sacrifice. No matter which view they favor, all Christians agree that the Lord's Supper commemorates Christ's death on the cross for our sins and points to the coming of his kingdom in glory. When we partake of it, we show our deep gratitude for Christ's work on our behalf, and our faith is strengthened.

● **22:19** Jesus asked the disciples to eat the broken bread "in remembrance of me." He wanted them to remember his sacrifice, the basis for forgiveness of sins, and also his friendship that they could continue to enjoy through the work of the Holy Spirit. Although the exact meaning of Communion has been strongly debated throughout church history, Christians still take bread and wine in remembrance of their Lord and Savior, Jesus Christ. Do not neglect participating in the Lord's Supper. Let it remind you of what Christ did for you.

● **22:20** In Old Testament times, God agreed to forgive people's sins if they brought animals for the priests to sacrifice. When this sacrificial system was inaugurated, the agreement between God and man was sealed with the blood of animals (Exodus 24:8). But animal blood did not in itself remove sin (only God can forgive sin), and animal sacrifices had to be repeated day by day and year after year. Jesus instituted a "new covenant" or agreement between humans and God. Under this new covenant, Jesus would die in the place of sinners. Unlike the blood of animals, his blood (because

he is God) would truly remove the sins of all who put their faith in him. And Jesus' sacrifice would never have to be repeated; it would be good for all eternity (Hebrews 9:23–28). The prophets looked forward to this new covenant that would fulfill the old sacrificial agreement (Jeremiah 31:31–34), and John the Baptist called Jesus "the Lamb of God, who takes away the sin of the world" (John 1:29).

22:21 From the accounts of Mark and John we know that the betrayer was Judas Iscariot. Although the other disciples were confused by Jesus' words, Judas knew what he meant.

22:24 The most important event in human history was about to take place, and the disciples were still arguing about their prestige in the kingdom! Looking back, we say, "This was no time to worry about status." But the disciples, wrapped up in their own concerns, did not perceive what Jesus had been trying to tell them about his approaching death and resurrection. What are your major concerns today? Twenty years from now, as you look back, will these worries look petty and inappropriate? Get your eyes off yourself and get ready for Christ's coming into human history for the second time.

22:24-27 The world's system of leadership is very different from leadership in God's kingdom. Worldly leaders are often selfish and arrogant as they claw their way to the top. (Some kings in the ancient world gave themselves the title "Benefactor.") But among Christians, the leader is to be the one who *serves* best. There are different styles of leadership—some lead through public speaking, some through administering, some through relationships—but every Christian leader needs a servant's heart. Ask the people you lead how you can serve them better.

22:31, 32 Satan wanted to crush Simon Peter and the other disciples like grains of wheat. He hoped to find only chaff and blow it away. But Jesus assured Peter that his faith, although it would falter, would not be destroyed. It would be renewed, and Peter would become a powerful leader.

33But he replied, "Lord, I am ready to go with you to prison and to death."

34Jesus answered, "I tell you, Peter, before the rooster crows today, you will deny three times that you know me."

22:35
zMt 10:9, 10;
Lk 9:3; 10:4

35Then Jesus asked them, "When I sent you without purse, bag or sandals,z did you lack anything?"

"Nothing," they answered.

36He said to them, "But now if you have a purse, take it, and also a bag; and if you don't have a sword, sell your cloak and buy one. 37It is written: 'And he was numbered with the transgressors'9;a and I tell you that this must be fulfilled in me. Yes, what is written about me is reaching its fulfillment."

22:37
a Isa 53:12

38The disciples said, "See, Lord, here are two swords."

"That is enough," he replied.

Jesus Agonizes in the Garden
(223/Matthew 26:36–46; Mark 14:32–42)

22:39
bLk 21:37

22:40
cMt 6:13

22:43
dMt 4:11

39Jesus went out as usualb to the Mount of Olives, and his disciples followed him. 40On reaching the place, he said to them, "Pray that you will not fall into temptation."c 41He withdrew about a stone's throw beyond them, knelt down and prayed, 42"Father, if you are willing, take this cup from me; yet not my will, but yours be done." 43An angel from heaven appeared to him and strengthened him.d

9 37 Isaiah 53:12

JESUS' TRIAL	Event	Probable reasons	References
Jesus' trial was actually a series of hearings, carefully controlled to accomplish the death of Jesus. The verdict was predecided, but certain "legal" procedures were necessary. A lot of effort went into condemning and crucifying an innocent man. Jesus went through an unfair trial in our place so that we would not have to face a fair trial and receive the well-deserved punishment for our sins.	Trial before Annas (powerful ex-high priest)	Although no longer the high priest, he may have still wielded much power	John 18:13–23
	Trial before Caiaphas (the ruling high priest)	To gather evidence for the full council hearing to follow	Matthew 26:57–68 Mark 14:53–65 Luke 22:54, 63–65 John 18:24
	Trial before the council (Sanhedrin)	Formal religious trial and condemnation to death	Matthew 27:1 Mark 15:1 Luke 22:66–71
	Trial before Pilate (highest Roman authority)	All death sentences needed Roman approval	Matthew 27:2, 11–14 Mark 15:1–5 Luke 23:1–6 John 18:28–38
	Trial before Herod (ruler of Galilee)	A courteous and guilt-sharing act by Pilate because Jesus was from Galilee, Herod's district	Luke 23:7–12
	Trial before Pilate	Pilate's last effort to avoid condemning an obviously innocent man	Matthew 27:15–26 Mark 15:6–15 Luke 23:13–25 John 18:39 – 19:16

22:33, 34 Jesus predicted that Judas would betray him, and he said that calamity awaited the traitor (22:22). Jesus then predicted that Peter would deny that he knew Jesus, but later Peter would repent and receive a commission to feed Jesus' lambs (John 21:15). Betraying and denying — one is just about as bad as the other. But the two men had entirely different fates because one repented.

22:35-38 Here Jesus reversed his earlier advice regarding how to travel (9:3). The disciples were to bring bags, money, and swords. They would be facing hatred and persecution and would need to be prepared. When Jesus said "That is enough," he may have meant it was not time to think of using swords. In either case, mention of a sword vividly communicated the trials they were soon to face.

22:39 The Mount of Olives was located just to the east of Jerusalem. Jesus went up the southwestern slope to an olive grove called Gethsemane, which means "oil press."

22:40 Jesus asked the disciples to pray that they would not fall into temptation because he knew that he would soon be leaving them. Jesus also knew that they would need extra strength to face the temptations ahead — temptations to run away or to deny their relationship with him. They were about to see Jesus die. Would they still think he was the Messiah? The disciples' strongest temptation would undoubtedly be to think they had been deceived.

● **22:41, 42** Was Jesus trying to get out of his mission? It is never wrong to express our true feelings to God. Jesus exposed his dread of the coming trials, but he also reaffirmed his commitment to do what God wanted. The cup he spoke of meant the terrible agony he knew he would endure — not only the horror of the crucifixion but, even worse, the total separation from God that he would have to experience in order to die for the world's sins.

44And being in anguish, he prayed more earnestly, and his sweat was like drops of blood falling to the ground. h

45When he rose from prayer and went back to the disciples, he found them asleep, exhausted from sorrow. 46"Why are you sleeping?" he asked them. "Get up and pray so that you will not fall into temptation." e

22:46
e ver 40

Jesus Is Betrayed and Arrested
(224/Matthew 26:47–56; Mark 14:43–52; John 18:1–11)

47While he was still speaking a crowd came up, and the man who was called Judas, one of the Twelve, was leading them. He approached Jesus to kiss him, 48but Jesus asked him, "Judas, are you betraying the Son of Man with a kiss?"

49When Jesus' followers saw what was going to happen, they said, "Lord, should we strike with our swords?" f 50And one of them struck the servant of the high priest, cutting off his right ear.

22:49
f ver 38

51But Jesus answered, "No more of this!" And he touched the man's ear and healed him.

52Then Jesus said to the chief priests, the officers of the temple guard, g and the elders, who had come for him, "Am I leading a rebellion, that you have come with swords and clubs? 53Every day I was with you in the temple courts, and you did not lay a hand on me. But this is your hour h — when darkness reigns."

22:52
g ver 4

22:53
h Jn 12:27

Peter Denies Knowing Jesus
(227/Matthew 26:69–75; Mark 14:66–72; John 18:25–27)

54Then seizing him, they led him away and took him into the house of the high priest. i Peter followed at a distance. j 55But when they had kindled a fire in the middle of the courtyard and had sat down together, Peter sat down with them. 56A servant girl saw him seated there in the firelight. She looked closely at him and said, "This man was with him."

22:54
i Mt 26:57; Mk 14:53;
j Mt 26:58; Mk 14:54; Jn 18:15

57But he denied it. "Woman, I don't know him," he said.

58A little later someone else saw him and said, "You also are one of them."

"Man, I am not!" Peter replied.

59About an hour later another asserted, "Certainly this fellow was with him, for he is a Galilean."

60Peter replied, "Man, I don't know what you're talking about!" Just as he was speaking, the rooster crowed. 61The Lord k turned and looked straight at Peter. Then Peter remembered the word the Lord had spoken to him: "Before the rooster crows today, you will disown me three times." l 62And he went outside and wept bitterly.

22:61
k Lk 7:13
l ver 34

63The men who were guarding Jesus began mocking and beating him. 64They blindfolded him and demanded, "Prophesy! Who hit you?" 65And they said many other insulting things to him.

h 44 Some early manuscripts do not have verses 43 and 44.

●**22:44** Only Luke tells us that Jesus' sweat resembled drops of blood. Jesus was in extreme agony, but he did not give up or give in. He went ahead with the mission for which he had come.

22:46 These disciples were asleep. How tragic it is that many Christians act as if they are asleep when it comes to devotion to Christ and service for him. Don't be found insensitive to or unprepared for Christ's work.

22:47 A kiss was and still is the traditional greeting among men in certain parts of the world. In this case, it was also the agreed-upon signal to point out Jesus (Matthew 26:48). It is ironic that a gesture of greeting would be the means of betrayal. It was a hollow gesture because of Judas's treachery. Have any of your religious practices become empty gestures? We still betray Christ when our acts of service or giving are insincere or carried out merely for show.

22:50 We learn from the Gospel of John that the man who cut off the servant's ear was Peter (John 18:10).

●**22:53** The religious leaders had not arrested Jesus in the temple for fear of a riot. Instead, they came secretly at night, under the influence of the prince of darkness, Satan himself. Although it looked as if Satan was getting the upper hand, everything was proceeding according to God's plan. It was time for Jesus to die.

●**22:54** Jesus was immediately taken to the high priest's house, even though this was the middle of the night. The Jewish leaders were in a hurry—they wanted to complete the execution before the Sabbath and get on with the Passover celebration. This residence was a palace with outer walls enclosing a courtyard where servants and soldiers warmed themselves around a fire.

22:55 Peter's experiences in the next few hours would change his life. He would change from a halfhearted follower to a repentant disciple, and finally to the kind of person Christ could use to build his church. For more information on Peter, see his Profile in Matthew 27.

The Council of Religious Leaders Condemns Jesus
(228/Matthew 27:1, 2; Mark 15:1)

22:66
*m*Mt 27:1;
Mk 15:1

66At daybreak the council of the elders of the people, both the chief priests and teachers of the law, met together, *m* and Jesus was led before them. 67"If you are the Christ,¹" they said, "tell us."

Jesus answered, "If I tell you, you will not believe me, 68and if I asked you, you would not answer. 69But from now on, the Son of Man will be seated at the right hand of the mighty God."

70They all asked, "Are you then the Son of God?"

22:70
*n*Mt 27:11;
Lk 23:3

He replied, "You are right in saying I am."*n*

71Then they said, "Why do we need any more testimony? We have heard it from his own lips."

Jesus Stands Trial before Pilate
(230/Matthew 27:11–14; Mark 15:2–5; John 18:28–37)

23:1
*o*Mt 27:2

23:2
*p*Lk 20:22
*q*Jn 19:12

23 Then the whole assembly rose and led him off to Pilate.*o* 2And they began to accuse him, saying, "We have found this man subverting our nation. He opposes payment of taxes to Caesar*p* and claims to be Christ,ʲ a king."*q*

3So Pilate asked Jesus, "Are you the king of the Jews?"

"Yes, it is as you say," Jesus replied.

4Then Pilate announced to the chief priests and the crowd, "I find no basis for a charge against this man."

5But they insisted, "He stirs up the people all over Judeaᵏ by his teaching. He started in Galilee and has come all the way here."

ⁱ67 Or *Messiah* ʲ2 Or *Messiah*; also in verses 35 and 39 ᵏ5 Or *over the land of the Jews*

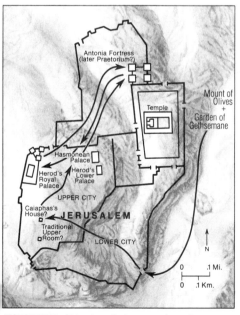

JESUS' TRIAL Taken from Gethsemane, Jesus first appeared before the Jewish council, which had convened at daybreak at Caiaphas's house. From there he went first to Pilate, the Roman governor; then to Herod, tetrarch of Galilee, who was visiting in Jerusalem; and back to Pilate, who, in desperation, sentenced Jesus to die.

22:62 Peter wept bitterly, not only because he realized that he had denied his Lord, the Messiah, but also because he had turned away from a very dear friend, a person who had loved and taught him for three years. Peter had said that he would *never* disown Christ, despite Jesus' prediction (Mark 14:29–31; Luke 22:33, 34). But when frightened, he went against all he had boldly promised. Unable to stand up for his Lord for even 12 hours, he had failed as a disciple and as a friend. We need to be aware of our own breaking points and not become overconfident or self-sufficient. If we fail him, we must remember that Christ can use those who recognize their failure. From this humiliating experience Peter learned much that would help him later when he assumed leadership of the young church.

● **22:70** Jesus in effect agreed that he was the Son of God when he simply turned the high priest's question around by saying, "You are right in saying I am." And Jesus identified himself with God by using a familiar title for God found in the Old Testament: "I am" (Exodus 3:14). The high priest recognized Jesus' claim and accused him of blasphemy. For any other human this claim would have been blasphemy, but in this case it was true. Blasphemy, the sin of claiming to be God or of attacking God's authority and majesty in any way, was punishable by death. The Jewish leaders had the evidence they wanted.

23:1 Pilate was the Roman governor of Judea, where Jerusalem was located. He seemed to take special pleasure in harassing the Jews. For example, Pilate had taken money from the temple treasury and had used it to build an aqueduct. And he had insulted the Jewish religion by bringing imperial images into the city. As Pilate well knew, such acts could backfire. If the people were to lodge a formal complaint against his administration, Rome might remove him from his post. Pilate was already beginning to feel insecure in his position when the Jewish leaders brought Jesus to trial. Would he continue to badger the Jews and risk his political future, or would he give in to their demands and condemn a man who, he was quite sure, was innocent? That was the question facing Pilate that springtime Friday morning nearly 2,000 years ago. For more about Pilate, see his Profile in Mark 15.

Jesus Stands Trial before Herod

(231)

6On hearing this, Pilate asked if the man was a Galilean. 7When he learned that Jesus was under Herod's jurisdiction, he sent him to Herod,ʳ who was also in Jerusalem at that time.

8When Herod saw Jesus, he was greatly pleased, because for a long time he had been wanting to see him. ˢ From what he had heard about him, he hoped to see him perform some miracle. 9He plied him with many questions, but Jesus gave him no answer. 10The chief priests and the teachers of the law were standing there, vehemently accusing him. 11Then Herod and his soldiers ridiculed and mocked him. Dressing him in an elegant robe,ᵗ they sent him back to Pilate. 12That day Herod and Pilate became friendsᵘ — before this they had been enemies.

Pilate Hands Jesus Over to Be Crucified

(232/Matthew 27:15–26; Mark 15:6–15; John 18:38 – 19:16)

13Pilate called together the chief priests, the rulers and the people, 14and said to them, "You brought me this man as one who was inciting the people to rebellion. I have examined him in your presence and have found no basis for your charges against him. ᵛ 15Neither has Herod, for he sent him back to us; as you can see, he has done nothing to deserve death. 16Therefore, I will punish himʷ and then release him.ˡ"

18With one voice they cried out, "Away with this man! Release Barabbas to us!"ˣ 19(Barabbas had been thrown into prison for an insurrection in the city, and for murder.)

ˡ 16 Some manuscripts *him." 17Now he was obliged to release one man to them at the Feast.*

23:7
ʳMt 14:1

23:8
ˢLk 9:9

23:11
ᵗMk 15:17-19;
Jn 19:2, 3

23:12
ᵘAc 4:27

23:14
ᵛver 4

23:16
ʷMt 27:26;
Jn 19:1

23:18
ˣAc 3:13, 14

23:7 Herod, also called Herod Antipas, was in Jerusalem that weekend for the Passover celebration. (This was the Herod who killed John the Baptist.) Pilate hoped to pass Jesus off on Herod because he knew that Jesus had lived and worked in Galilee. But Herod was not much help. He was curious about Jesus and enjoyed making fun of him. But when Herod sent Jesus back to Pilate, it was with the verdict of "not guilty." For more about Herod Antipas, see his Profile in Mark 6.

23:12 Herod was the part-Jewish ruler of Galilee and Perea. Pilate was the Roman governor of Judea and Samaria. Those four provinces, together with several others, had been united under Herod the Great. But when Herod died in 4 B.C., the kingdom was divided among his sons, each of whom was called "tetrarch" (meaning "ruler of a fourth part of a region"). Archelaus, the son who had received Judea and Samaria, was removed from office within ten years, and his provinces were then ruled by a succession of Roman governors, of whom Pilate was the fifth.

Herod Antipas had two advantages over Pilate: he came from a hereditary, part-Jewish monarchy, and he had held his position much longer. But Pilate had two advantages over Herod: he was a Roman citizen and an envoy of the emperor, and his position was created to replace that of Herod's ineffective half brother. It is not surprising that the two men were uneasy around each other. Jesus' trial, however, brought them together. Because Pilate had recognized Herod's authority over Galilee, Herod stopped feeling threatened by the Roman politician. And because neither man knew what to do in this predicament, their common problem united them.

23:13–25 Pilate wanted to release Jesus, but the crowd loudly demanded his death; so Pilate sentenced Jesus to die. No doubt Pilate did not want to risk losing his position, which may already have been shaky, by allowing a riot to occur in his province. As a career politician, he knew the importance of compromise, and he saw Jesus more as a political threat than as a human being with rights and dignity.

When the stakes are high, it is difficult to stand up for what is right, and it is easy to see our opponents as problems to be solved rather than as people to be respected. Had Pilate been a man of real courage, he would have released Jesus no matter what the consequences. But the crowd roared, and Pilate buckled. We are like Pilate when we know what is right, but decide not to do it. When you have a difficult decision to make, don't discount the effects of peer pressure. Realize beforehand that the right decision could have unpleasant consequences: social rejection, career derailment, public ridicule. Then think of Pilate and resolve to stand up for what is right no matter what other people pressure you to do.

● **23:15** Jesus was tried six times, by both Jewish and Roman authorities, but he was never convicted of a crime deserving death. Even when condemned to execution, he had been convicted of no felony. Today, no one can find fault in Jesus. But just like Pilate, Herod, and the religious leaders, many still refuse to acknowledge him as Lord.

23:18, 19 Barabbas had been part of a rebellion against the Roman government (Mark 15:7). As a political insurgent, he was no doubt a hero among some of the Jews. How ironic it is that Barabbas, who was released, was guilty of the very crime Jesus was accused of (23:14).

23:18, 19 Who was Barabbas? Jewish men had names that identified them with their fathers. Simon Peter, for example, is called Simon son of Jonah (Matthew 16:17). Because Jesus is never identified by his given name, and this name is not much help either — *bar-abbas* means "son of *Abba*" (or "son of daddy"). He could have been anybody's son — and that's just the point. Barabbas, son of an unnamed father, committed a crime. Because Jesus died in his place, this man was set free. We too are sinners and criminals who have broken God's holy law. Like Barabbas, we deserve to die. But Jesus has died in our place, for our sins, and we have been set free. We don't have to be "very important people" to accept our freedom in Christ. In fact, thanks to Jesus, God adopts us all as his own sons and daughters and gives us the right to call him *Abba* — "daddy" (see Galatians 4:4–6).

20Wanting to release Jesus, Pilate appealed to them again. 21But they kept shouting, "Crucify him! Crucify him!"

22For the third time he spoke to them: "Why? What crime has this man committed? I have found in him no grounds for the death penalty. Therefore I will have him punished and then release him."

23But with loud shouts they insistently demanded that he be crucified, and their shouts prevailed. 24So Pilate decided to grant their demand. 25He released the man who had been thrown into prison for insurrection and murder, the one they asked for, and surrendered Jesus to their will.

Jesus Is Led Away to Be Crucified
(234/Matthew 27:32–34; Mark 15:21–24; John 19:17)

23:26
yMt 27:32
zJn 19:17

26As they led him away, they seized Simon from Cyrene,y who was on his way in from the country, and put the cross on him and made him carry it behind Jesus.z

23:27
aLk 8:52

27A large number of people followed him, including women who mourned and wailed a for him. 28Jesus turned and said to them, "Daughters of Jerusalem, do not weep for me; weep for yourselves and for your children. 29For the time will come when you will say, 'Blessed are the barren women, the wombs that never bore and the breasts that never nursed!' b 30Then

23:29
bMt 24:19

> " 'they will say to the mountains, "Fall on us!"
>   and to the hills, "Cover us!" ' m c

23:30
cHos 10:8;
Isa 2:19;
Rev 6:16

23:31
dEze 20:47

31For if men do these things when the tree is green, what will happen when it is dry?" d

m *30* Hosea 10:8

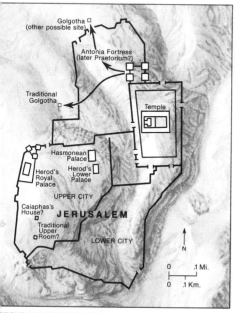

JESUS LED AWAY TO DIE As Jesus was led away through the streets of Jerusalem, he could no longer carry his cross, and Simon of Cyrene was given the burden. Jesus was crucified, along with common criminals, on a hill outside Jerusalem.

●**23:22** When Pilate said he would have Jesus "punished," he was referring to a punishment that could have killed Jesus. The usual procedure was to bare the upper half of the victim's body and tie his hands to a pillar before whipping him with a three-pronged whip. The number of lashes was determined by the severity of the crime; up to 40 were permitted under Jewish law. After being flogged, Jesus also endured other agonies as recorded in Matthew and Mark. He was slapped, struck with fists, and mocked. A crown of thorns was placed on his head, and he was beaten with a stick and stripped before being hung on the cross.

23:23, 24 Pilate did not want to give Jesus the death sentence. He thought the Jewish leaders were simply jealous men who wanted to get rid of a rival. When they threatened to report Pilate to Caesar (John 19:12), however, Pilate became frightened. Historical records indicate that Pilate had already been warned by Roman authorities about tensions in this region. The last thing he needed was a riot in Jerusalem at Passover time, when the city was crowded with Jews from all over the empire. So Pilate turned Jesus over to the mob to do with as they pleased.

23:27–29 Luke alone mentions the tears of the Jewish women while Jesus was being led through the streets to his execution. Jesus told them not to weep for him but for themselves. He knew that in only about 40 years, Jerusalem and the temple would be destroyed by the Romans.

23:31 This proverb is difficult to interpret. Some feel it means: if the innocent Jesus (green tree) suffered at the hands of the Romans, what would happen to the guilty Jews (dry tree)?

Jesus Is Placed on the Cross
(235/Matthew 27:35–44; Mark 15:25–32; John 19:18–27)

32Two other men, both criminals, were also led out with him to be executed.*e*
33When they came to the place called the Skull, there they crucified him, along
with the criminals — one on his right, the other on his left. 34Jesus said, "Father,
forgive them, for they do not know what they are doing."*n* And they divided up his
clothes by casting lots.*f*

35The people stood watching, and the rulers even sneered at him.*g* They
said, "He saved others; let him save himself if he is the Christ of God, the Chosen
One."

36The soldiers also came up and mocked him. They offered him wine vinegar*h*
37and said, "If you are the king of the Jews, save yourself."

38There was a written notice above him, which read: THIS IS THE KING OF THE
JEWS.

39One of the criminals who hung there hurled insults at him: "Aren't you the
Christ? Save yourself and us!"*i*

40But the other criminal rebuked him. "Don't you fear God," he said, "since you
are under the same sentence? 41We are punished justly, for we are getting what our
deeds deserve. But this man has done nothing wrong."

42Then he said, "Jesus, remember me when you come into your kingdom.*o*"

43Jesus answered him, "I tell you the truth, today you will be with me in paradise."*i*

23:32
*e*Mt 27:38

23:34
*f*Ps 22:18

23:35
*g*Ps 22:17

23:36
*h*Mt 27:48

23:39
*i*ver 35, 37

23:43
*j*2Co 12:3, 4;
Rev 2:7

Jesus Dies on the Cross
(236/Matthew 27:45–56; Mark 15:33–41; John 19:28–37)

44It was now about the sixth hour, and darkness came over the whole land until
the ninth hour, 45for the sun stopped shining. And the curtain of the temple was torn

n 34 Some early manuscripts do not have this sentence.   *o 42* Some manuscripts *come with your kingly power*

23:32, 33 The place called the Skull, or Golgotha, was probably
a hill outside Jerusalem along a main road. The Romans executed
people publicly as examples to the people.

23:32, 33 When James and John asked Jesus for the places of
honor next to him in his kingdom, he told them they didn't know
what they were asking (Mark 10:35–39). Here, as Jesus was preparing to inaugurate his kingdom through his death, the places on
his right and on his left were taken by dying men — criminals. As
Jesus explained to his two position-conscious disciples, a person
who wants to be close to Jesus must be prepared to suffer and
die. The way to the kingdom is the way of the cross.

23:34 Jesus asked God to forgive the people who were putting
him to death — Jewish leaders, Roman politicians and soldiers,
bystanders — and God answered that prayer by opening up the
way of salvation even to Jesus' murderers. The Roman centurion
and soldiers who witnessed the crucifixion said, "Surely he was the
Son of God" (Matthew 27:54). Soon many priests were converted
to the Christian faith (Acts 6:7). Because we are all sinners, we all
played a part in putting Jesus to death. The gospel — the Good
News — is that God is gracious. He will forgive us and give us new
life through his Son.

23:34 Roman soldiers customarily divided up the clothing of executed criminals among themselves. When they cast lots for Jesus'
clothes, they fulfilled the prophecy in Psalm 22:18.

23:38 This sign was meant to be ironic. A king, stripped and executed in public view, had obviously lost his kingdom forever. But
Jesus, who turns the world's wisdom upside down, was just coming into his kingdom. His death and resurrection would strike the

deathblow to Satan's rule and would establish Christ's eternal authority over the earth. Few people reading the sign that bleak afternoon understood its real meaning, but the sign was absolutely true.
All was not lost. Jesus is King of the Jews — and the Gentiles, and
the whole universe.

23:39–43 As this man was about to die, he turned to Christ for
forgiveness, and Christ accepted him. This shows that our deeds
don't save us — our faith in Christ does. It is never too late to turn to
God. Even in his misery, Jesus had mercy on this criminal who decided to believe in him. Our lives will be much more useful and fulfilling if we turn to God early, but even those who repent at the very
last moment will be with God in paradise.

23:42, 43 The dying criminal had more faith than the rest of Jesus' followers put together. Although the disciples continued to
love Jesus, their hopes for the kingdom were shattered. Most of
them had gone into hiding. As one of his followers sadly said two
days later, "We had hoped that he was the one who was going to
redeem Israel" (24:21). By contrast, the criminal looked at the man
who was dying next to him and said, "Jesus, remember me when
you come into your kingdom." By all appearances, the kingdom
was finished. How awe-inspiring is the faith of this man who alone
saw beyond the present shame to the coming glory!

23:44 Darkness covered the entire land for about three hours in
the middle of the day. All nature seemed to mourn over the stark
tragedy of the death of God's Son.

23:45 This significant event symbolized Christ's work on the
cross. The temple had three parts: the courts for all the people; the
Holy Place, where only priests could enter; and the Most Holy
Place, where the high priest alone could enter once a year to atone

23:46
k Mt 27:50
l Ps 31:5;
1 Pe 2:23
m Jn 19:30

in two. 46Jesus called out with a loud voice,k "Father, into your hands I commit my spirit."l When he had said this, he breathed his last.m

47The centurion, seeing what had happened, praised God and said, "Surely this was a righteous man." 48When all the people who had gathered to witness this sight saw what took place, they beat their breasts and went away. 49But all those who knew him, including the women who had followed him from Galilee,n stood at a distance,o watching these things.

23:49
n Lk 8:2
o Ps 38:11

Jesus Is Laid in the Tomb
(237/Matthew 27:57–61; Mark 15:42–47; John 19:38–42)

50Now there was a man named Joseph, a member of the Council, a good and upright man, 51who had not consented to their decision and action. He came from the Judean town of Arimathea and he was waiting for the kingdom of God.p 52Going to Pilate, he asked for Jesus' body. 53Then he took it down, wrapped it in linen cloth and placed it in a tomb cut in the rock, one in which no one had yet been laid. 54It was Preparation Day,q and the Sabbath was about to begin.

23:51
p Lk 2:25, 38

23:54
q Mt 27:62

55The women who had come with Jesus from Galilee followed Joseph and saw the tomb and how his body was laid in it. 56Then they went home and prepared spices and perfumes.r But they rested on the Sabbath in obedience to the commandment.s

23:56
r Mk 16:1
s Ex 20:10

Jesus Rises from the Dead
(239/Matthew 28:1–7; Mark 16:1–8; John 20:1–9)

24 On the first day of the week, very early in the morning, the women took the spices they had preparedt and went to the tomb. 2They found the stone rolled away from the tomb, 3but when they entered, they did not find the body of the Lord Jesus. 4While they were wondering about this, suddenly two men in clothes that gleamed like lightningu stood beside them. 5In their fright the women bowed down with their faces to the ground, but the men said to them, "Why do you

24:1
t Lk 23:56

24:4
u Jn 20:12

---

for the sins of the people. It was in the Most Holy Place that the ark of the covenant, and God's presence with it, rested. The curtain that was torn was the one that closed off the Most Holy Place from view. At Christ's death, the barrier between God and man was split in two. Now all people can approach God directly through Christ (Hebrews 9:1–14; 10:19–22).

23:50-52 Joseph of Arimathea was a wealthy and honored member of the Jewish Council. He was also a secret disciple of Jesus (John 19:38). The disciples who had publicly followed Jesus fled, but Joseph boldly took a stand that could cost him dearly. He cared enough about Jesus to ask for his body so he could give it a proper burial.

23:53 The tomb was likely a man-made cave cut out of one of the many limestone hills in the area around Jerusalem. Such a tomb was large enough to walk into. After burial, a large stone would have been rolled across the entrance (John 20:1).

23:55 The Galilean women followed Joseph to the tomb, so they knew exactly where to find Jesus' body when they returned after the Sabbath with their spices and perfumes. These women could not do "great" things for Jesus — they were not permitted to stand up before the Jewish council or the Roman governor and testify on his behalf — but they did what they could. They stayed at the cross when most of the disciples had fled, and they got ready to anoint their Lord's body. Because of their devotion, they were the first to know about the resurrection. As believers, we may feel we can't do much for Jesus. But we are called to take advantage of the opportunities given us, doing what we *can* do and not worrying about what we cannot do.

24:1 The women brought spices to the tomb as we would bring flowers — as a sign of love and respect. The women went home and kept Sabbath as the law required, from sundown Friday to sundown Saturday, before gathering up their spices and perfumes and returning to the tomb.

• **24:1-9** The two angels (appearing as "men in clothes that gleamed like lightning") asked the women why they were looking in a tomb for someone who was alive. Often we run into people who are looking for God among the dead. They study the Bible as a mere historical document and go to church as if going to a memorial service. But Jesus is not among the dead — he lives! He reigns in the hearts of Christians, and he is the head of his church. Do you look for Jesus among the living? Do you expect him to be active in the world and in the church? Look for signs of his power — they are all around you.

24:4 We learn from Matthew and John that these two men in gleaming clothes were angels. When angels appeared to people, they looked like humans.

look for the living among the dead? 6He is not here; he has risen! Remember how he told you, while he was still with you in Galilee:ᵛ 7'The Son of Man must be delivered into the hands of sinful men, be crucified and on the third day be raised again.' " 8Then they remembered his words.ʷ

9When they came back from the tomb, they told all these things to the Eleven and to all the others. 10It was Mary Magdalene, Joanna, Mary the mother of James, and the others with themˣ who told this to the apostles. 11But they did not believe the women, because their words seemed to them like nonsense. 12Peter, however, got up and ran to the tomb. Bending over, he saw the strips of linen lying by themselves,ʸ and he went away, wondering to himself what had happened.

24:6
ᵛMt 17:22, 23

24:8
ʷJn 2:22

24:10
ˣLk 8:1-3

24:12
ʸJn 20:3-7

Jesus Appears to Two Believers Traveling on the Road
(243/Mark 16:12, 13)

13Now that same day two of them were going to a village called Emmaus, about seven milesᵖ from Jerusalem.ᶻ 14They were talking with each other about everything that had happened. 15As they talked and discussed these things with each other, Jesus himself came up and walked along with them; 16but they were kept from recognizing him.ᵃ

17He asked them, "What are you discussing together as you walk along?"

They stood still, their faces downcast. 18One of them, named Cleopas,ᵇ asked him, "Are you only a visitor to Jerusalem and do not know the things that have happened there in these days?"

19"What things?" he asked.

"About Jesus of Nazareth," they replied. "He was a prophet,ᶜ powerful in word and deed before God and all the people. 20The chief priests and our rulers handed him over to be sentenced to death, and they crucified him; 21but we had hoped that

24:13
ᶻMk 16:12

24:16
ᵃJn 20:14; 21:4

24:18
ᵇJn 19:25

24:19
ᶜMt 21:11

p 13 Greek sixty stadia (about 11 kilometers)

• **24:6, 7** The angels reminded the women that Jesus had accurately predicted all that had happened to him (9:22, 44; 18:31–33).

• **24:6, 7** The resurrection of Jesus from the dead is the central fact of Christian history. On it, the church is built; without it, there would be no Christian church today. Jesus' resurrection is unique. Other religions have strong ethical systems, concepts about paradise and afterlife, and various holy Scriptures. Only Christianity has a God who became human, literally died for his people, and was raised again in power and glory to rule his church forever.

Why is the resurrection so important? (1) Because Christ was raised from the dead, we know that the kingdom of heaven has broken into earth's history. Our world is now headed for redemption, not disaster. God's mighty power is at work destroying sin, creating new lives, and preparing us for Jesus' second coming. (2) Because of the resurrection, we know that death has been conquered, and we too will be raised from the dead to live forever with Christ. (3) The resurrection gives authority to the church's witness in the world. Look at the early evangelistic sermons in the book of Acts: the apostles' most important message was the proclamation that Jesus Christ had been raised from the dead! (4) The resurrection gives meaning to the church's regular feast, the Lord's Supper. Like the disciples on the Emmaus Road, we break bread with our risen Lord, who comes in power to save us. (5) The resurrection helps us find meaning even in great tragedy. No matter what happens to us as we walk with the Lord, the resurrection gives us hope for the future. (6) The resurrection assures us that Christ is alive and ruling his kingdom. He is not legend; he is alive and real. (7) God's power that brought Jesus back from the dead is available to us so that we can live for him in an evil world.

Christians can look very different from one another, and they can hold widely varying beliefs about politics, life-style, and even theology. But one central belief unites and inspires all true Christians—Jesus Christ rose from the dead! (For more on the importance of the resurrection, see 1 Corinthians 15:12–58.)

• **24:11, 12** People who hear about the resurrection for the first time may need time before they can comprehend this amazing story. Like the disciples, they may pass through four stages of belief. (1) At first, they may think it is a fairy tale, impossible to believe. (2) Like Peter, they may check out the facts but still be puzzled about what happened. (3) Only when they encounter Jesus personally will they be able to accept the fact of the resurrection. (4) Then, as they commit themselves to Jesus and devote their lives to serving him, they will begin fully to understand the reality of his presence with them.

24:12 From John 20:3, 4, we learn that another disciple ran to the tomb with Peter. That other disciple was almost certainly John, the author of the fourth Gospel.

24:13ff The two disciples returning to Emmaus at first missed the significance of history's greatest event because they were too focused on their disappointments and problems. In fact, they didn't recognize Jesus when he was walking beside them. To compound the problem, they were walking in the wrong direction—away from the fellowship of believers in Jerusalem. We are likely to miss Jesus and withdraw from the strength found in other believers when we become preoccupied with our dashed hopes and frustrated plans. Only when we are looking for Jesus in our midst will we experience the power and help he can bring.

24:18 The news about Jesus' crucifixion had spread throughout Jerusalem. Because this was Passover week, Jewish pilgrims visiting the city from all over the Roman empire now knew about his death. This was not a small, insignificant event, affecting only the disciples—the whole nation was interested.

24:21 The disciples from Emmaus were counting on Jesus to redeem Israel—that is, to rescue the nation from its enemies. Most Jews believed that the Old Testament prophecies pointed to a military and political Messiah; they didn't realize that the Messiah had come to redeem people from slavery to sin. When Jesus died, therefore, they lost all hope. They didn't understand that Jesus' death offered the greatest hope possible.

24:21
*d*Lk 1:68

he was the one who was going to redeem Israel. *d* And what is more, it is the third day since all this took place. 22In addition, some of our women amazed us. They went to the tomb early this morning 23but didn't find his body. They came and told us that they had seen a vision of angels, who said he was alive. 24Then some of our companions went to the tomb and found it just as the women had said, but him they did not see."

25He said to them, "How foolish you are, and how slow of heart to believe all that the prophets have spoken! 26Did not the Christ*q* have to suffer these things and then enter his glory?"*e* 27And beginning with Moses*f* and all the Prophets,*g* he explained to them what was said in all the Scriptures concerning himself.

24:26
*e*1Pe 1:11
24:27
*f*Ge 3:15;
Nu 21:9;
Dt 18:15
*g*Isa 7:14; 9:6;
Eze 34:23

28As they approached the village to which they were going, Jesus acted as if he were going farther. 29But they urged him strongly, "Stay with us, for it is nearly evening; the day is almost over." So he went in to stay with them.

24:30
*h*Mt 14:19

30When he was at the table with them, he took bread, gave thanks, broke it*h* and began to give it to them. 31Then their eyes were opened and they recognized him, and he disappeared from their sight. 32They asked each other, "Were not our hearts burning within us while he talked with us on the road and opened the Scriptures to us?"

33They got up and returned at once to Jerusalem. There they found the Eleven and those with them, assembled together 34and saying, "It is true! The Lord has risen and has appeared to Simon."*i* 35Then the two told what had happened on the way, and how Jesus was recognized by them when he broke the bread.

24:34
*i*1Co 15:5

q 26 Or Messiah; also in verse 46

● **24:24** These disciples knew that the tomb was empty but didn't understand that Jesus had risen, and they were filled with sadness. Despite the women's witness, which was verified by other disciples, and despite the Biblical prophecies of this very event, they still didn't believe. Today the resurrection still catches people by surprise. In spite of 2,000 years of evidence and witness, many people refuse to believe. What more will it take? For these disciples it took the living, breathing Jesus in their midst. For many people today, it takes the presence of living, breathing Christians.

● **24:25** Why did Jesus call these disciples foolish? Even though they well knew the Biblical prophecies, they failed to understand that Christ's suffering was his path to glory. They could not understand why God did not intervene to save Jesus from the cross. They were so caught up in the world's admiration of political power and military might that they were unprepared for the reversal of values in God's kingdom — that the last will be first, and that life grows out of death. The world has not changed its values: a suffering servant is no more popular today than 2,000 years ago. But we have not only the witness of the Old Testament prophets, we have also the witness of the New Testament apostles and the history of the Christian church all pointing to Jesus' victory over death. Will we step outside the values of our culture and put our faith in Jesus? Or will we foolishly continue to be baffled by his Good News?

24:25–27 After the two disciples had explained their sadness and confusion, Jesus responded by going to Scripture and applying it to his ministry. When we are puzzled by questions or problems, we too can go to Scripture and find authoritative help. If we, like these two disciples, do not understand what the Bible means, we can turn to other believers who know the Bible and have the wisdom to apply it to our situation.

24:27 Beginning with the promised offspring in Genesis (Genesis 3:15) and going through the suffering servant in Isaiah (Isaiah 53), the pierced one in Zechariah (Zechariah 12:10), and the messenger of the covenant in Malachi (Malachi 3:1), Jesus reintroduced these disciples to the Old Testament. Christ is the thread woven through all the Scriptures, the central theme that binds them together. Following are several key passages Jesus may have men-

tioned on this walk to Emmaus: Genesis 3; 12; Psalms 22; 69; 110; Isaiah 53; Jeremiah 31; Zechariah 9; 13; Malachi 3.

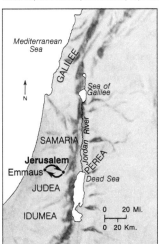

ON THE ROAD TO EMMAUS
After Jesus' death, two of his followers were walking from Jerusalem back toward Emmaus when a stranger joined them. After dinner in Emmaus, Jesus revealed himself to these men and then disappeared. They immediately returned to Jerusalem to tell the disciples the good news that Jesus was alive!

24:33, 34 Paul also mentions that Jesus appeared to Peter alone (1 Corinthians 15:5). This appearance is not further described in the Gospels. Jesus showed individual concern for Peter because Peter felt completely unworthy after disowning his Lord. But Peter repented, and Jesus approached him and forgave him. Soon God would use Peter in building Christ's church (see the first half of the book of Acts).

Jesus Appears to the Disciples Behind Locked Doors
(244/John 20:19–23)

36While they were still talking about this, Jesus himself stood among them and said to them, "Peace be with you."*j*

37They were startled and frightened, thinking they saw a ghost.*k* 38He said to them, "Why are you troubled, and why do doubts rise in your minds? 39Look at my hands and my feet. It is I myself! Touch me and see; a ghost does not have flesh and bones, as you see I have."

40When he had said this, he showed them his hands and feet. 41And while they still did not believe it because of joy and amazement, he asked them, "Do you have anything here to eat?" 42They gave him a piece of broiled fish, 43and he took it and ate it in their presence.*l*

Jesus Appears to the Disciples in Jerusalem
(249)

44He said to them, "This is what I told you while I was still with you: Everything must be fulfilled*m* that is written about me in the Law of Moses, the Prophets and the Psalms."

45Then he opened their minds so they could understand the Scriptures. 46He told them, "This is what is written: The Christ will suffer and rise from the dead on the third day, 47and repentance and forgiveness of sins will be preached in his name*n* to all nations,*o* beginning at Jerusalem. 48You are witnesses*p* of these things. 49I am going to send you what my Father has promised;*q* but stay in the city until you have been clothed with power from on high."

24:36 *j*Jn 20:19, 21, 26
24:37 *k*Mk 6:49
24:43 *l*Ac 10:41
24:44 *m*Mt 16:21; Lk 18:31-33
24:47 *n*Ac 5:31; 13:38 *o*Mt 28:19
24:48 *p*Ac 1:8
24:49 *q*Ac 1:4

● **24:36–43** Jesus' body wasn't just a figment of the imagination or the appearance of a ghost — the disciples touched him, and he ate food. On the other hand, his body wasn't merely a restored human body like Lazarus's (John 11) — he was able to appear and disappear. Jesus' resurrected body was immortal. This is the kind of body we will be given at the resurrection of the dead (see 1 Corinthians 15:42–50).

24:44 Many days may have elapsed between verses 43 and 44 because Jesus and his followers traveled to Galilee and back before he returned to heaven (Matthew 28:16; John 21). In his second book, Acts, Luke makes it clear that Jesus spent 40 days with his disciples between his resurrection and ascension.

24:44–46 The Law of Moses, the Prophets, and the Psalms is a way to describe the entire Old Testament. In other words, the entire Old Testament points to the Messiah. For example, his role as prophet was foretold in Deuteronomy 18:15–20; his sufferings were prophesied in Psalm 22 and Isaiah 53; his resurrection was predicted in Psalm 16:9–11 and Isaiah 53:10, 11.

24:45 Jesus opened these people's minds to understand the Scriptures. The Holy Spirit does this in our lives today when we study the Bible. Have you ever wondered how to understand a difficult Bible passage? Besides reading surrounding passages, asking other people, and consulting reference works, pray that the Holy Spirit will open your mind to understand, giving you the needed insight to put God's Word into action in your life.

24:47 Luke wrote to the Greek-speaking world. He wanted them to know that Christ's message of God's love and forgiveness should go to all the world. We must never ignore the worldwide scope of Christ's gospel. God wants all the world to hear the Good News of salvation.

● **24:50–53** As the disciples stood and watched, Jesus began rising into the air, and soon he disappeared into heaven. Seeing Jesus leave must have been frightening, but the disciples knew that Jesus would keep his promise to be with them through the Holy Spirit. This same Jesus, who lived with the disciples, who died and was buried, and who rose from the dead, loves us and promises to be with us always. We can get to know him better through studying the Scriptures, praying, and allowing the Holy Spirit to make us more like Jesus.

24:51 Jesus' physical presence left the disciples when he returned to heaven (Acts 1:9), but the Holy Spirit soon came to comfort them and empower them to spread the gospel of salvation (Acts 2:1–4). Today Jesus' work of salvation is completed, and he is sitting at God's right hand, where he has authority over heaven and earth.

24:53 Luke's Gospel portrays Jesus as the perfect example of a life lived according to God's plan — as a child living in obedience to his parents and yet amazing the religious leaders in the temple, as an adult serving God and others through preaching and healing, and finally as a condemned man suffering without complaint. This emphasis was well suited to Luke's Greek audience, who placed high value on being an example and improving oneself, and who often discussed the meaning of perfection. The Greeks, however, had a difficult time understanding the spiritual importance of the physical world. To them, the spiritual was always more important than the physical. To help them understand the God-man who united the spiritual and the physical, Luke emphasized

24:53
ʳAc 2:46

Jesus Ascends into Heaven
(250/Mark 16:19, 20)

⁵⁰When he had led them out to the vicinity of Bethany, he lifted up his hands and blessed them. ⁵¹While he was blessing them, he left them and was taken up into heaven. ⁵²Then they worshiped him and returned to Jerusalem with great joy. ⁵³And they stayed continually at the temple,ʳ praising God.

that Jesus was not a phantom human but a real human being who healed people and fed them because he was concerned with their physical health as well as the state of their souls.

As believers living according to God's plan, we too should obey our Lord in every detail as we seek to restore people's bodies and souls to the health and salvation God has in store for them. If we want to know how to live a perfect life, we can look to Jesus as our example.

STUDY QUESTIONS

Thirteen lessons for individual or group study

It's always exciting to get more than you expect. And that's what you'll find in this Bible study guide—much more than you expect. Our goal was to write thoughtful, practical, dependable, and application-oriented studies of God's Word.

This study guide contains the complete text of the selected Bible book. The commentary is accurate, complete, and loaded with unique charts, maps, and profiles of Bible people.

With the Bible text, extensive notes and helps, and questions to guide discussion, these Life Application study guides have everything you need in one place.

The lessons in this Bible study guide will work for large classes as well as small group studies. To get everyone involved in your discussions, encourage participants to answer the questions before each meeting.

Each lesson is divided into five easy-to-lead sections. The section called "Reflect" introduces you and the members of your group to a specific area of life touched by the lesson. "Read" shows which chapters to read and which notes and other features to use. Additional questions help you understand the passage. "Realize" brings into focus the biblical principle to be learned with questions, a special insight, or both. "Respond" helps you make connections with your own situation and personal needs. The questions are designed to help you find areas in your life where you can apply the biblical truths. "Resolve" helps you map out action plans for that day.

Begin and end each lesson with prayer, asking for the Holy Spirit's guidance, direction, and wisdom.

Recommended time allotments for each section of a lesson:

Segment	60 minutes	90 minutes
Reflect on your life	5 minutes	10 minutes
Read the passage	10 minutes	15 minutes
Realize the principle	15 minutes	20 minutes
Respond to the message	20 minutes	30 minutes
Resolve to take action	10 minutes	15 minutes

All five sections work together to help a person learn the lessons, live out the principles, and obey the commands taught in the Bible.

Also, at the end of each lesson, there is a section entitled "More for studying other themes in this section." These questions will help you lead the group in studying other parts of each section not covered in depth by the main lesson.

Do not merely listen to the word, and so deceive yourselves. Do what it says. Anyone who listens to the word but does not do what it says is like a man who looks at his face in a mirror and, after looking at himself, goes away and immediately forgets what he looks like. But the man who looks intently into the perfect law that gives freedom, and continues to do this, not forgetting what he has heard, but doing it—he will be blessed in what he does. (James 1:22-25, NIV)

REFLECT
on your life

1 What nonfiction book have you read lately? How do you know that what the author has written is true?

_____

_____

_____

_____

_____

2 Which of these sources of information do you trust the least: television news, radio news, newspaper, news magazine, tabloid magazine? Why?

_____

_____

_____

_____

3 Which of those news sources do you trust the most? Why?

_____

_____

_____

_____

Read the Introduction to Luke and the following notes:

☐1:1, 2   ☐1:1-4   ☐1:3   ☐1:3, 4

4 What reasons do you have for trusting the reliability of what Luke has written?

_____

_____

_____

5 What reasons did Luke give for writing his Gospel (1:1-4)?

_____

_____

_____

6 Who is Luke's audience—to whom did he write this book (1:3)?

_____

_____

_____

7 What is the significance of Luke's introductory words to his Gospel?

_____

_____

Luke wrote that he had "carefully investigated everything from the beginning" so that he could "write an orderly account" (1:3). Certainly Luke's investigation would have included interviews with eyewitnesses to Christ, checking and rechecking any written reports with the facts. As a Gentile, Luke could be objective in his research; as a doctor, he would be meticulous. As we read and study Luke's biography of Christ, we can be confident that it is an accurate account. Written to "Theophilus," the Gospel of Luke is for all those who love God.

8 Christians believe that Luke and the other Bible writers were inspired and guided by the Holy Spirit as they wrote, so all of the Bible is accurate. Why, then, is it important that Luke was a careful historian?

_____

_____

_____

9 In 1 John 1:1, 2, John wrote about being an eyewitness to the Word. What might have motivated Luke and John to begin their books with these strong claims of accuracy?

_____

_____

_____

_____

_____

10 Luke had to research and discover Jesus Christ for himself in order to share him effectively with others. Firsthand knowledge for Luke was essential to faith. Think back to when God became more than a word to you, when you discovered that he wanted a personal relationship with you. What first got your attention? How did you know it was true?

_____

_____

_____

_____

_____

RESPOND
to the message

11 Suppose you were to write a brief story of your personal experience with Christ—the "Gospel according to _____ (your name)." What would you say were your reasons for turning to Christ? How would you describe your life since then?

_____

_____

_____

_____

12 What specific people would you like to reach with your Gospel (for example, nonbelievers at work, in the neighborhood, at school, or in your family)?

_____

_____

_____

13 What questions about Christianity would they want answered?

_____

_____

_____

14 What would make you a credible, reliable witness to them?

_____

_____

_____

15 Name someone you know who would be encouraged to learn that Luke took pains to write accurate history?

_____

_____

16 Write a brief prayer of thanks for the reliability of the Bible.

_____

_____

_____

RESOLVE
to take action

A What qualifications did Luke have for writing a Gospel to a Gentile audience? What special qualifications do you have that God might use to tell others about Christ?

MORE
for studying
other themes
in this section

B Why was the theme of the "perfect man" especially appropriate for a Greek audience? What themes in Luke strike a responsive chord with you?

C In what ways is the Greek culture of the first century similar to ours today? Why is Luke's message especially appropriate for people in our world?

REFLECT
on your life

1 Describe some steps parents might take to prepare a child for first grade.

_____

_____

_____

2 How might a child respond to these preparations?

_____

_____

_____

READ
the passage

Read Luke 1:1—4:13, Zechariah's Profile, Mary's Profile, and the following notes:

❏1:13 ❏1:17 ❏1:18 ❏1:38 ❏2:8 ❏2:8-15 ❏2:49, 50 ❏2:52 ❏3:15

❏3:16 ❏3:23 ❏4:2

3 What was the angel's message to Zechariah (1:11-17)? How did he respond (1:18)?

_____

_____

_____

4 What was the angel's message to Mary (1:26-37)? How did she respond (1:38, 46-55)?

_____

_____

_____

5 What was the angel's message to the shepherds (2:8-14)? How did they respond (2:15-18)?

_____

_____

_____

6 What was John the Baptist's message (3:2, 3, 7-18)? How did the people respond? (3:10, 12, 14, 15)

_____

_____

_____

7 How did God prepare the world for Christ's coming?

_____

_____

REALIZE
the principle

_____

8 How did God prepare Jesus for his public ministry?

_____

_____

_____

God the Father did not spring his plan of salvation on the world. He prepared everyone involved at each step. He sent an angel to Zechariah and Mary. He sent John the Baptist to the people. And he allowed Jesus to experience temptation directly before ministering to others. God prepared each one for what was ahead, even if none of them knew exactly what it meant or what the future held. We may not know what God is doing in our life now, but we don't have to. Whatever God is doing, he is preparing us for what he *will* do. If we will trust him and be faithful to what he has given us to do now, we will be ready when his plans for our future unfold.

9 Why was it important for God to prepare the world for Christ's coming and ministry?

_____

_____

_____

10 How does God prepare people for his work today?

_____

_____

_____

11 How does God's work in our life invite us to trust him for the future?

_____

_____

_____

RESPOND
to the message

12 What past experiences has God used to prepare you for the work you do today? Try to recall one example.

_____

_____

_____

_____

13 What present experience requires you to trust God because you don't understand its purpose?

_____

_____

_____

14 How might your present experience be preparing you for the future?

_____

_____

_____

15 How can you show your trust in God through this time of preparation?

_____

_____

_____

16 In what area of your life can you be more trusting of God's unfolding plan?

_____

_____

_____

RESOLVE
to take action

17 How can you show your trust in God's plan for you over the next few days or weeks?

_____

_____

_____

A Why did being childless cause suffering for Zechariah and Elizabeth? How did God use their suffering to bring them joy? How is their experience like experiences you've had?

MORE
for studying
other themes
in this section

B Read Mary's song and Zechariah's song (1:46-55 and 1:68-79). What understanding of God's character and plan do their words reveal? How do you celebrate when you realize God has used you?

C The shepherds who visited Jesus on the night of his birth were at first terrified (2:10) but later returned to their fields, "glorifying and praising God for all the things they had heard and seen" (2:20). What marvelous works of God cause you to praise him?

D What enabled Simeon to die "in peace" (2:25-32)? In what ways is he an example of faithfulness? In what ways can we demonstrate the same kind of faithfulness?

E What do we learn about Jesus as an adolescent (2:41-52)? What does he show us about a balanced life? How might this affect our relationships?

F What was unusual about John the Baptist's ministry (3:1-20)? What basic message did he preach, and how did he get his point across? In what ways is your life like his?

G Why was Jesus baptized (3:21, 22)? What did he show us by way of example?

LESSON 3
WILL THE REAL JESUS PLEASE STAND UP?
LUKE 4:14—6:11

REFLECT
on your life

1 Describe a time when your reputation did not match who you really were.

_____

_____

_____

_____

2 How did that reputation cause people to react to you?

_____

_____

_____

READ
the passage

Read Luke 4:14—6:11 and the following notes:

❏4:24 ❏4:39 ❏4:40 ❏5:8 ❏5:11 ❏5:18, 19 ❏5:21 ❏5:28, 29

❏6:2

3 How did people respond to Jesus after each of the following events?

Teaching in the synagogue (4:14-30): _____

_____

Preaching in Capernaum (4:31, 32): _____

_____

Driving out the demon (4:33-37): _____

_____

Healing the sick (4:38-41): _____

_____

Providing the fish (5:1-11): _____

_____

Healing the man with leprosy (5:12-16): _____

_____

Forgiving the sins of the paralyzed man (5:17-26): _____

_____

Eating at Matthew's house (5:27-32): _____

_____

Picking grain and healing on the Sabbath (6:1-11): _____

_____

4 What might account for the differences in how people responded to Jesus?

_____

_____

_____

REALIZE
the principle

The people who met Jesus all met the same person, and he did something for
each of them. He taught them the truth, healed them, drove out demons, forgave
their sins. Yet they responded in different ways. Jesus' hometown friends said,
"You're no better than we are. We know your family." The Pharisees rejected him
because he didn't fit their system—he threatened their secure religious world.
Some in the crowds were curious. Some were amazed. Some left everything
and followed him. Jesus gets the same range of responses today, too. Some
people don't know who he is; others know who he is but aren't willing to follow
him for whatever reason. As Jesus confronts you today, how will you respond?

5 What ideas do people in your neighborhood or workplace have about Jesus today?

_____

_____

_____

_____

6 How do people react to Jesus today?

_____

_____

_____

_____

7 Who today opposes Christ with

outrage? _____

disinterest? _____

curiosity? _____

amazement? _____

RESPOND
to the message

8 What might it mean for you to leave everything and follow Christ?

_____

_____

_____

_____

9 What has it cost you to follow Christ?

_____

_____

_____

_____

10 What holds you back from responding to Christ with total commitment?

_____

_____

_____

_____

11 Take time now to write out a brief prayer of commitment to follow Christ.

_____

_____

_____

_____

RESOLVE
to take action

12 Whom can you enlist to hold you accountable for this commitment?

_____

_____

A What did Jesus show about his priorities by healing on the Sabbath? (See Luke 4:31-35, 38-41; 6:6-11.) With what did these priorities clash (6:11)? How does this affect your sense of what's most important?

B Why were tax collectors such as Levi despised by the Jews (5:27-32)? Who is despised for similar reasons in our society? How can Christians reach out to them?

C What was Levi risking and/or giving up when he followed Jesus (5:27-32)? What risks and/or sacrifices are involved for you in following Jesus?

MORE
for studying
other themes
in this section

REFLECT
on your life

1 If you were a detective checking out a person's values, where would you investigate? What would you collect as evidence?

_____

_____

_____

_____

2 According to the world's values, what brings happiness? What gives meaning to life?

_____

_____

_____

_____

READ
the passage

Read Luke 6:12—8:3 and the following notes:

❏6:20-23 ❏6:21 ❏6:24 ❏6:26 ❏6:27 ❏6:35 ❏6:37, 38 ❏6:45

❏7:11-15 ❏7:44ff ❏8:2, 3

3 Who is blessed or should be happy (6:20-23)?

_____

_____

_____

4 Who should be sad (6:24-26)?

_____

_____

_____

5 What actions did Christ tell his followers to take in loving others (6:27-42)?

_____

_____

_____

6 To what kind of people did Jesus minister (7:1—8:3)?

_____

_____

_____

7 Why would Jesus' words about happiness have been a surprise to the disciples?

_____

_____

_____

_____

REALIZE
the principle

8 In Luke 6 Jesus gave his disciples many specific instructions. How are these instructions different from how people usually act?

_____

_____

_____

_____

9 Why would it be unusual for someone to reach out to an enemy soldier, a widow, or a prostitute as Jesus did?

_____

_____

_____

_____

At this point in his life, Jesus "had it all." Crowds followed him. People shook their heads in amazement at his teaching. Everybody liked him. He was a genuine celebrity. According to all of the world's values, he had a bright future. But then Jesus surprised everyone with remarkable statements and deeds reflecting what is really important in life. Happiness comes to those who are poor, hungry, sad, and hated, he said—not to those who are rich, comfortable, well fed, and popular. He told his disciples that God wanted them to love their enemies and to do good to them. He told them not to judge but to forgive. Then he demonstrated these values by reaching out to an enemy soldier, a widow, a prostitute, and others with low status. Jesus seldom told people what they expected to hear; his values are the opposite of the world's. But God's values are right and true.

10 How do Jesus' values compare to our world's values today?

_____

_____

_____

_____

RESPOND
to the message

11 Describe a time when God has given you joy in difficult circumstances.

_____

_____

_____

12 What people in your life do you find it difficult to treat with kindness, compassion, generosity, etc. (6:27-42)?

_____

_____

_____

_____

13 What are ways you can reach out to people others have rejected, such as the Roman soldier, the widow, and the sinful woman?

_____

_____

_____

14 In what ways does Jesus challenge your values (your sense of what's important)?

_____

_____

_____

_____

15 Name someone to whom you can demonstrate Christ's love (someone who doesn't like you, a social misfit, someone who owes you something)?

_____

_____

_____

RESOLVE
to take action

A What qualifications did Jesus' disciples have (6:12-16)? What kind of men were they? How are you like them? What kind of people does Jesus use today?

MORE
for studying
other themes
in this section

B Who were the Jews' enemies at this time? Why was it difficult for the Jews of Jesus' day to show love to their enemies (6:27-36)? What difficulties do you have showing love to your enemies?

C How can we admit the truth about someone's sin without judging him/her (6:37-42)? How can you help someone without being judgmental or a gossip?

D What are some examples of good fruit (6:43-45)? Fruit grows and matures on trees. What should we be producing in our life? What kind of "fruit" are you producing?

E What kind of person builds his "house on the ground without a foundation" (6:46-49)? What is a solid foundation for our life? What can you do to build on it?

F Why was Jesus amazed at the centurion's faith (7:1-10)? Why did Jesus heal the soldier's servant? How does your faith compare?

G Why did John the Baptist have doubts about Jesus (7:18-23)? What did John do about those doubts? What can you do when you're confused or doubtful about God?

REFLECT
on your life

1 List several important people you have met. Over what or whom do these people have power or control?

_____
_____
_____
_____
_____

READ
the passage

Read Luke 8:4—9:50 and the following notes:

☐8:23 ☐8:25 ☐8:27, 28 ☐8:30 ☐8:33 ☐8:43-48 ☐8:45 ☐8:56
☐9:13, 14 ☐9:16, 17 ☐9:27 ☐9:29, 30

2 What evidence of Jesus' power do you see in each of the following events?

Calming the storm (8:22-25):

_____
_____

Healing the possessed man (8:26-39) and the boy with an evil spirit (9:37-43):

_____
_____

Healing the bleeding woman (8:43-48):

_____

_____

Raising Jairus's daughter (8:40-42, 49-56):

_____

_____

Feeding more than five thousand people (9:12-17):

_____

_____

Being transfigured (9:28-36):

_____

_____

3 What do you think the disciples learned about Jesus as they watched him perform these miracles?

_____

REALIZE
the principle

_____

_____

_____

Jesus' disciples and the crowds who followed him saw dramatic demonstra-
tions of power. Jesus cured diseases and disabilities with a word or touch; he
spoke to demons with authority and drove them out of their victims; he brought
dead people back to life; he revealed his power over nature itself. Jesus is
God—he has power over every aspect of your life. He also has power over all
the things you fear—natural disasters, Satan, hunger, death—everything. The
question is, Have you turned your fears over to him? You can turn over to God
everything you feel threatened by and know you are in good hands.

4 How would you answer Jesus' question, "Who do you say I am?" (9:20).

_____

_____

_____

5 What can a person do when he/she realizes that God has power over every-thing?

_____

_____

_____

6 How does knowing what Jesus is really like affect how you relate to him?

_____

_____

_____

RESPOND
to the message

7 Describe a time when you have seen Christ's power demonstrated in your life.

_____

_____

_____

_____

8 To what do you feel vulnerable (accidents, sickness, death, demons, some-thing else)?

_____

_____

_____

9 Which areas of your life (or what problems in your life) are you reluctant to give to God's control? Why?

_____

_____

_____

10 What could you tell someone who is afraid?

_____

_____

_____

11 What fear needs to be turned over to Christ's control?

_____

_____

_____

RESOLVE
to take action

12 How can the knowledge of Christ's power over your fears enhance your prayers this week?

_____

_____

_____

_____

A Why did Jesus speak to the crowds in parables (8:4ff)? What did he mean by, "He who has ears to hear, let him hear" (8:8)? What can you do to be more receptive to what Christ is telling you?

MORE
for studying
other themes
in this section

B Note the parable of the four soils (8:4-15). What kind of soil are you today? At what times in your life were you more like another type of soil? What does it take to be "good soil"?

C Who are Jesus' true brothers and sisters (8:19-21)? How can a person become part of his family?

D Why did Jesus tell the healed demon-possessed man to tell of his healing (8:38, 39) but asked Jairus and his wife not to tell anyone about his daughter coming back to life (8:56)? When is it best to tell of God's work in your life, and when is it best to let it speak for itself?

E What were Jesus' instructions to his disciples as he sent them out to preach (9:1-6)? What did he require of them that he also requires of you?

F How did the disciples respond to the hunger of the crowd (9:10-17)? What did they ask Jesus to do about it? What did Jesus do to stretch their faith in him? When have you seen God provide in unexpected ways?

G Who did the people think Jesus was (9:18-20)? Who do people today think he is? To whom can you reveal the truth about Christ? How can you do it?

H How are we to take up our cross daily (9:23)? . . . Lose our life for Christ's sake (9:24)? . . . Lose the world and gain our very selves (9:25)?

I How did Peter respond to what he saw on the mountain (9:28-36)? What is important about what God said from the cloud? What does this experience reveal to you about Jesus?

J Why did the disciples argue (9:46-48)? What does it take to be great in God's sight? What adjustments might this involve for you?

REFLECT
on your life

1 What is the most expensive purchase you have ever made?

_____

_____

2 Why did you want it?

_____

_____

_____

_____

3 How did you get the money to pay for it?

_____

_____

_____

READ
the passage

Read Luke 9:51—11:13, James's Profile, Martha's Profile, and the following notes:

❏9:51 ❏9:59 ❏9:62 ❏10:3 ❏10:23, 24 ❏10:27-37 ❏10:33 ❏10:38-42
❏11:4

4 Following Jesus is costly. What is the significance of the following costs Jesus asked his disciples to pay?

No place to lay his head (9:57, 58): _____

_____

Let the dead bury their own (9:59, 60): _____

_____

No one looks back (9:61, 62): _____

_____

Like lambs among wolves (10:3): _____

_____

Love with all your heart (10:26-28): _____

_____

A neighbor to the man who was beaten and robbed (10:29-37): _____

_____

Mary has chosen what is better (10:38-42): _____

_____

Forgive as we are forgiven (11:4): _____

_____

_____

5 What price did James pay for being dedicated to Jesus (see James's Profile)?

_____

_____

_____

_____

REALIZE
the principle

Jesus called many people to follow him. Some came right away; some started and then turned back; others refused entirely. To those who followed, Jesus made it clear that there would be a price to pay. Our commitment to Christ may affect our relationships, our position in a job, pay, and other areas. Following Christ costs us something. Even today in many places of the world, following Christ can mean rejection, imprisonment, or even death. We may not be called to die for our faith, but Jesus does ask us to pattern our life after his. Obeying him will always mean sacrifice of some kind.

6 What did following Christ (or doing what was right) cost

the disciples? _____

the 72 messengers? _____

the Good Samaritan? _____

Mary? _____

RESPOND
to the message

7 What makes faith in Christ something worth dying for?

_____

_____

_____

8 What might following Jesus (as described in Luke 9:51—11:13) cost a person in his/her

life-style? _____

decisions? _____

relationships? _____

goals? _____

finances? _____

9 Following Christ means doing what God has told us to do. What has God told you to do that you are hesitating over because of the cost?

_____

_____

10 What can you do this week to obey Christ in this area?

_____

_____

_____

RESOLVE
to take action

A Why did James and John want to "call fire down from heaven" on a Samaritan village (9:51-55)? When are you tempted to condemn people or retaliate?

MORE
for studying
other themes
in this section

B What instructions did Jesus give to the 72 messengers (10:3-11)? Why was their mission successful? In what ways was their mission like the one God has given you?

C In the parable of the Good Samaritan, two people passed by the injured man without helping him, while another stopped to help (10:25-37). What do each person's actions show about him? Who needs your help? To whom can you be a good Samaritan?

D How was Martha serving Jesus (10:38-42)? Why was she upset? When are you tempted to choose something good over what is best?

E Why did Jesus give this prayer to his disciples (11:1-4)? What is the significance of each phrase? How can your prayers reflect these priorities?

F Why did Jesus teach us to be persistent in prayer (11:5-13)? About what do you need to be persistent in prayer?

REFLECT
on your life

1 Finish these sentences:

A hypocritical peace activist is one who _____

_____

A hypocritical environmentalist is one who _____

_____

A hypocritical police officer is one who _____

_____

A hypocritical aerobics instructor is one who _____

_____

A hypocritical scientist is one who _____

_____

A hypocritical doctor is one who _____

_____

A hypocritical religious leader is one who _____

_____

Read Luke 11:14—13:17 and the following notes:

☐11:37-39 ☐11:41 ☐11:42-52 ☐11:44 ☐11:46 ☐11:52 ☐12:1, 2

☐12:8, 9 ☐13:10-17 ☐13:15, 16

READ
the passage

2 Who were the Pharisees?

_____

_____

3 List some ways the Pharisees demonstrated hypocrisy (11:37-52):

_____

_____

_____

4 What did Jesus say about hypocrisy? (See Luke 11:14—12:3; 13:10-17.)

_____

_____

Jesus had harsh words for the Pharisees and experts in the law. They accused him of being allied with Satan; he condemned them for their blatant hypocrisy. They took him to task for working on the Sabbath; he criticized them for caring more about their traditions than about obeying God. As a result, "the Pharisees and the teachers of the law began to oppose him fiercely" (11:53). The Pharisees and law experts were hypocrites because they claimed to be holy but were filled with sin; they went through religious motions but had no spiritual depth. They pretended to be devoted to God but were only concerned about themselves. In short, they focused on outward appearances and not on the inner condition of their heart. Jesus warned us to beware of hypocrites and hypocrisy in our own life.

REALIZE
the principle

5 What does it mean to focus on the inner condition of your heart?

_____

_____

_____

6 What is so bad about religious hypocrisy?

_____

_____

7 What are some examples of religious hypocrisy today?

_____

_____

8 What might a Christian hypocrite look like?

_____

_____

_____

RESPOND
to the message

9 Why is it easy to say one thing and live the opposite?

_____

_____

10 What might a Pharisee look like in your church?

_____

_____

_____

11 How can a Christian avoid being hypocritical?

_____

_____

_____

12 What are some of the hindrances to living what you profess to believe?

_____

_____

_____

13 How can you focus on the inner condition of your heart over outward appearances?

_____

_____

_____

14 What areas of your life do you need to make more consistent with your Christian faith?

_____

_____

_____

15 How will you know when you've made progress?

_____

_____

_____

A How did Jesus answer the charge that he was in league with Beelzebub (Satan) (11:14-23)?

B What is the danger for a person who makes a dramatic change of life-style (11:24-26)?

C How was Jonah a sign for the nation of Israel? What lessons can we learn from God's treatment of Nineveh and other nations in the past?

D How does what you see and focus on affect your thoughts and motives (11:33-36)? What do a person's eyes reveal about a person?

E How much does God know about you (12:6, 7)? How can God's love and care for you free you from fear?

F In what situations do you find it difficult to admit that you're a Christian (12:8-12)? What can you do to become more bold in your witness for Christ?

G How do people store up things for themselves (12:13-21)? What does God say about greed? What can you do to be "rich toward God"?

H What do people worry about most (12:22-34)? How does worry hurt us? What is God's antidote for worry?

I Why should believers be watchful and ready for Christ's return (12:35-48)? How should they live to be ready? What changes can you make so that you will be ready for Christ's return?

J How does (or can) faith in Christ bring division among people (12:49-53)? How should you respond when someone you love strongly opposes your faith?

K What kind of fruit is God looking for Christians to bear (13:1-9)? How can you be more productive for God?

LESSON 8
MOVIN' UP
LUKE 13:18—14:35

REFLECT
on your life

1 What are some signs of status?

_____

_____

_____

_____

2 Why is status important to some people?

_____

_____

_____

_____

READ
the passage

Read Luke 13:18—14:35 and the following notes:

❐13:30 ❐14:7-11 ❐14:7-14 ❐14:11 ❐14:16ff ❐14:28-30

3 Why did Jesus tell the parable of the wedding feast (14:7-14)?

_____

_____

_____

4 Why did Jesus tell the parable of the great banquet (14:15-24)?

_____

_____

_____

5 What do both parables have in common?

_____

_____

_____

6 What did Jesus say about those who seek honor and status for themselves (14:8, 9, 11)?

_____

_____

_____

_____

7 What's the problem with concern for status?

_____

REALIZE
the principle

_____

_____

The people of Jesus' time made distinctions among themselves on the basis of status. Pharisees and experts in the law had high status. Rich people and those with authority had high status. Healthy people had high status. Meanwhile, most everyone else—the poor, disabled, uneducated, and powerless—had low status. Jesus criticized the people for caring about these differences. He wanted his disciples to see things God's way, to realize that status doesn't matter to God—it matters only to the world. As a result, we should show concern for all people, especially those who have low, or no, status.

8 In your world, who are the "people to be seen with"?

_____

_____

_____

_____

9 Where are the "places to be"?

_____

_____

_____

10 What makes a person great in God's eyes?

_____

_____

_____

_____

RESPOND
to the message

11 Whom do you know who is great in God's eyes yet has low status in the world?

_____

_____

_____

12 What about your image have you tried to protect?

_____

_____

_____

13 Describe a time when you have tried to raise your own status.

_____

_____

_____

_____

14 Describe a time when you have avoided people because of their low status.

_____

_____

_____

15 What one status-seeking behavior are you contemplating avoiding (or stopping)?

RESOLVE
to take action

16 Who is one poor, disabled, uneducated, or otherwise low-status person to whom you can reach out?

A How is the kingdom of God like a mustard seed (13:18, 19)? How is the kingdom of God like yeast (13:20, 21)? How does this affect our expectations concerning how God works in the world?

B In what sense is the door to heaven narrow (13:22-30)? Why will some who associated with Jesus be unable to enter? Who might these people be today? What's the difference between associating with Jesus and knowing him? How can a person enter the narrow door?

C Why was Jesus determined to go to Jerusalem (13:31-35)? Why did God's people find it difficult to listen to God's prophets? Why did Jesus grieve over it? What can you do to reach those who oppose you?

D What excuses do people make today for not accepting Christ's invitation to salvation (i.e., his "great banquet") (14:15-24)? What can you do to "go out to the roads and country lanes and make them come in" (14:23)?

E What does Jesus mean when he says we must "hate" our families and even our life in order to be his disciples (14:26, 27)? How does this affect your relationships at home?

F Why must a person count the cost before following Jesus (14:28-33)? What will it cost you to be completely sold out to Christ?

MORE
for studying
other themes
in this section

REFLECT
on your life

1 What is the most valuable possession you've ever lost?

_____

_____

2 What did you do to try to find it?

_____

_____

_____

_____

_____

READ
the passage

Read Luke 15:1—17:37 and the following notes:

❒15:2 ❒15:3-6 ❒15:4, 5 ❒15:8-10 ❒15:20 ❒15:24 ❒15:25-31 ❒15:30

❒15:32

3 What did the shepherd do when one of his sheep wandered off (15:4)?

_____

_____

4 What did he do after he found it (15:5, 6)?

_____

_____

_____

5 What did the woman do when she lost a silver coin (15:8)?

_____

_____

_____

6 What did she do after she found it (15:9)?

_____

_____

_____

7 What did the father do when his son returned home (15:11-32)?

_____

_____

_____

8 What has God done to find sinners (16:27-31)?

_____

_____

9 At what point will God stop seeking sinners (17:22-37)?

_____

_____

10 Why do you think Jesus told the three parables in chapter 15?

_____

_____

_____

REALIZE
the principle

In their desire to remain pure and holy, the Pharisees wanted nothing to do with "sinners." They thought that godly people—those who observed all the Pharisees' traditions—could not associate with ungodly people—those who did not observe the traditions. What the Pharisees did not know, or did not care about, was that God seeks lost sinners. Through these three parables, Jesus pointed out that the Pharisees lacked a key element of God's heart—compassion for people who do not know God. God wants everyone to come to him; people who know God want the same thing.

11 How can a person become spiritually lost?

_____

_____

_____

12 What might cause a Christian to develop a callous attitude toward those who do not know God?

_____

_____

_____

13 What is God's attitude toward people who are lost?

_____

_____

_____

RESPOND
to the message

14 Who are the lost people you know?

_____

_____

_____

15 What can you do to help bring them to the Father?

_____

_____

_____

16 How can you avoid becoming exclusive about your relationship with God, like the older brother in the parable of the lost son?

_____

_____

_____

_____

17 Name the lost people for whom you can pray on a regular basis.

_____

_____

_____

RESOLVE
to take action

A How did the shrewd manager protect himself against his employer (16:1-8)? How does our use of money reflect our commitment to God?

MORE
for studying
other themes
in this section

B How can a Christian use money and possessions to help bring people to the Father (16:9)? What reward awaits the Christian who does this? How can you use your money and possessions to "gain friends"?

C Why is it important to be trustworthy in small matters (16:10-13)? What has God entrusted to you? How can you be faithful (or responsible) in these areas?

D How do some people try to serve "both God and Money" (16:10-13)? Why is it impossible? How can money come between a person and God?

E Why did the Pharisees ridicule what Jesus said about loving money (16:14-17)? In what areas are you tempted to rationalize your disobedience to God's law?

F Why would the story of the rich man and Lazarus upset the Pharisees (16:19-31)? Why did the rich man miss paradise?

G What's our responsibility toward other Christians (17:1-4)? Who looks to you as an example of the Christian life? Whom do you need to forgive?

H How did Jesus answer the disciples' request for greater faith (17:5-10)? What are you tempted to put off for "lack of faith"? What is your simple duty in that area?

I Why did the one leper return to thank Jesus (17:11-19)? What good things has God done for you? Why is it important to remember to thank God? What can you thank God for today?

J Why will many people not be ready for Christ's return (17:20-37)? How can a person get ready? What do you need to do now to get ready?

REFLECT
on your life

1 What does a single person give up when he/she gets married?

_____
_____
_____
_____

2 Why would a person willingly give all that up for marriage?

_____
_____
_____
_____

READ
the passage

Read Luke 18:1—19:27 and the following notes:

❐18:18ff ❐18:22, 23 ❐18:24-27 ❐19:8 ❐19:11ff ❐19:20-27

3 Why did the rich young ruler go away sad (18:18-23, 29, 30)?

_____
_____
_____

4 Why did Zacchaeus receive Christ's forgiveness (19:1-10)?

_____

_____

_____

5 Based on each man's past, which of them would seem to be the most likely to follow Christ (18:20, 21; 19:2, 7)? Why?

_____

_____

_____

6 What does God want us to do with money and other resources (19:11-27)?

_____

_____

_____

The rich young ruler came to Jesus confident of his religious credentials, but he went away sorrowful because he didn't love Christ as much as he loved his money. In contrast, Zacchaeus was willing to pay any price to follow Christ, even if it meant paying back four times the amount he had extorted. When confronted by Christ, each of these men had made a choice about money—one served it; the other used it to serve God. Money can either be our master or our servant, but it cannot be both. When we choose to serve God with our money and resources, we gain the proper perspective and free ourselves from the tyranny of greed.

REALIZE
the principle

7 Why is money so important to some people?

_____

_____

_____

8 In addition to money, what else can easily take God's place in people's lives today?

_____

_____

_____

_____

RESPOND
to the message

9 In what ways are you like the rich young ruler?

_____

_____

_____

_____

_____

10 In what ways are you like Zacchaeus?

_____

_____

_____

_____

_____

11 Name one thing that would be difficult for you to give up to follow Christ.

_____

_____

12 What resources do you have that can be "invested" for the kingdom?

_____

_____

_____

_____

_____

13 How can you invest them?

_____

_____

_____

_____

_____

14 How will you use money and possessions in service to God this week?

_____

_____

_____

_____   RESOLVE
                                                                    to take action

A Why is it important to persist in prayer (18:1-8)? How can you be more persis- MORE
tent in your prayer life?   for studying
                                                                                     other themes
B What's the difference between the prayer of the Pharisee and the prayer of   in this section
the tax collector (18:9-14)? Why was the tax collector justified? How can you
make your prayers more like his?

C Why did Jesus welcome the little children (18:15-17)? How can we come to
God as "little children"?

D How did Jesus answer the rich young man's question, "What must I do to
inherit eternal life?" (18:18-22). Why was this answer difficult for the man to
accept (18:24)? What barriers can stand in the way of your willingness to do
what God wants?

E What is one pitfall of wealth (18:24-25)? How can a person manage his/her
money to avoid this pitfall?

F What did Jesus predict would happen to him (18:31-34)? Why were the disciples surprised when Jesus rose from the dead (24:1ff)? What statement of
Jesus' have you recently "discovered"?

G What did the blind beggar ask for (18:41)? What did he receive (18:42-43)?
How did this affect the man (18:43)? What blessings has God given you that
inspire you to respond as this man did? How can you show that response this
week?

LESSON 11
OPPOSITION
LUKE 19:28—21:38

REFLECT
on your life

1 What are some motivational sports slogans you have heard?

_____

_____

_____

_____

2 What are some possible reactions to overwhelming opposition?

_____

_____

_____

_____

READ
the passage

Read Luke 19:28—21:38 and the following notes:

❒ 19:38 ❒ 19:47 ❒ 20:1-8 ❒ 20:9-16 ❒ 20:21 ❒ 20:27-38 ❒ 20:41-44

❒ 20:47 ❒ 21:7ff ❒ 21:12, 13 ❒ 21:14-19 ❒ 21:28 ❒ 21:36

3 What groups of people opposed Jesus (19:39, 47; 20:1, 19, 27, 46)?

_____

_____

_____

_____

_____

4 What tactics did the religious leaders use to try to trap Jesus (20:1-8, 19-33)?

_____

_____

_____

_____

_____

5 What kinds of persecution did Jesus tell his followers to expect (21:5-19)?

_____

_____

_____

6 Why did the religious leaders try to trap Jesus instead of admitting that he was the Christ?

_____

_____

_____

REALIZE
the principle

After Jesus' Triumphal Entry into Jerusalem, the opposition against him intensified. The Pharisees, teachers of the law, elders, Sadducees, and chief priests united against him and used a variety of tricks and traps to find some "legal" way to apprehend him. Jesus eluded their verbal traps while the crowds continued their fascination with him. But the opposition was real and would eventually lead to his arrest.

Jesus warned his followers to prepare themselves for similar treatment. Following him, he told them, would invite persecution from all sides, even from those closest to them. It would take a conscious effort for them to stand firm in their devotion to Christ. Following Christ today invites persecution just as surely as it did then. Knowing this is the first step in standing firm against opposition to our faith.

7 How did Jesus' warning in 21:17 come true for the disciples?

_____

_____

_____

8 Why was this persecution to be a positive sign?

_____

_____

_____

RESPOND
to the message

9 In what ways are true believers persecuted by religious leaders today?

_____

_____

_____

10 How might Christians be persecuted by the government? family? friends?

_____

_____

_____

_____

11 Where might you face opposition (and even persecution) for what you believe?

_____

_____

_____

12 Describe a time when you have been tempted to be silent or to compromise your faith because of opposition.

_____

_____

_____

_____

13 What truths will help you remain loyal to Christ when people oppose your faith?

_____

_____

_____

_____

_____

A What is the significance of the following events at Jesus' Triumphal Entry (19:28-46)?
☐ His entering the city on a colt
☐ The people joyfully praising God
☐ Jesus' telling the Pharisees that if the crowd was quiet, the stones would cry out
☐ His weeping over and words about Jerusalem
☐ His driving the money changers from the temple

How can you acknowledge Jesus' authority as King?

B How did the religious leaders react when Jesus said, "The stone the builders rejected has become the capstone" (20:17)? How should they have reacted? What can you do to avoid rejecting the right leaders and following the wrong ones?

C What lessons can we learn from the offering of the poor widow (21:1-4)? How does this challenge you to do things differently?

D What signs will signal the end of this age (21:20-31)? What can we do in the meantime (21:34-36)? What will you do to prepare for this time?

MORE
for studying
other themes
in this section

REFLECT
on your life

1 Check two or three experiences that you would consider to be the most painful:

❏ being betrayed by a close associate
❏ saying good-bye to close friends
❏ having a very close friend turn his/her back on you
❏ struggling with a difficult decision
❏ being deserted by friends and associates
❏ being falsely accused
❏ being mocked in public
❏ being convicted of a crime you didn't commit
❏ being tortured
❏ dying a slow death
❏ being executed publicly
❏ being totally alone

2 Why did you select these?

_____

_____

_____

_____

READ
the passage

Read Luke 22:1—23:56 and the following notes:

❏ 22:14-18 ❏ 22:19 ❏ 22:20 ❏ 22:41, 42 ❏ 22:44 ❏ 22:53 ❏ 22:54

❏ 22:70 ❏ 23:15 ❏ 23:22

3 Each of the following people or groups played a key role in the final hours of Jesus' life on earth. Briefly describe each person's part in the drama (22:1—23:25).

Judas: _____

_____

The 12 disciples: _____

_____

Peter: _____

_____

Religious leaders: _____

_____

Herod: _____

_____

Pilate: _____

_____

4 Why was Jesus in such agony when he went to pray (22:39-46)?

_____

_____

_____

In the final hours of his life on earth, Jesus suffered unimaginable pain, including desertion and betrayal by friends, public humiliation, and physical torture. But the greatest suffering he endured was bearing the sins of the world on a rugged, Roman cross. Suspended between heaven and earth, Jesus took our place, paying the penalty for our sins. He hung there totally alone, separated even from his Father. In dying for us, Jesus did more than we can comprehend. He not only took our sins away, but he also made it possible for us to have a living relationship with God.

REALIZE
the principle

5 Jesus was accused of many crimes during his trials (22:66—23:25). Of which accusations was he guilty?

_____

_____

_____

6 Why did Jesus have to die in order for God's plan to be accomplished?

_____

_____

_____

RESPOND
to the message

7 Why was Jesus' pain on the cross so excruciating?

_____

_____

_____

8 How would you explain the reason for Jesus' death to an unbeliever?

_____

_____

_____

_____

9 How have you responded to Jesus' sacrifice of his life for *your* sins?

_____

_____

_____

10 How can you celebrate or remember Christ's sacrifice for you?

_____

_____

_____

11 What can you do this week to express your gratitude to Christ for all he did for you?

RESOLVE
to take action

_____

_____

_____

_____

_____

A Why do you think Judas betrayed Jesus? Why did Peter disown him? When are you tempted to deny your association with Jesus?

B What is the significance of Jesus' words to his disciples regarding the bread and the cup during the Last Supper (22:14-20)? Why do Christians still celebrate this event? Why do you take Communion? What do you do to prepare yourself for Communion?

C When Jesus was arrested, where were the people who had cheered him a few days earlier? Where would you have been? Why?

D Why did the religious leaders have to take Jesus to Pilate, the Roman governor (23:1)? What were their accusations against Jesus then (23:2)? Why were these accusations different than the ones used before the Jewish council (22:66-71)? How did Jesus respond to these accusations? How do you respond when falsely accused?

E Why did Pilate give in to the religious leaders' demands to have Jesus crucified? What kinds of pressure do you face each day to do what is wrong? How can you resist that pressure?

F How did each of the crucified criminals respond to Jesus (23:39-43)? What does this teach us about salvation?

G Why did Jesus tell the women of Jerusalem, "Do not weep for me; weep for yourselves and for your children" (23:28)? For what do you weep?

H What was significant about the words exchanged between Jesus and the criminal on the cross (23:40-43)? In what ways do you identify with the criminal?

MORE
for studying
other themes
in this section

L E S S O N   1 3
ALIVE!
LUKE 24:1-53

REFLECT
on your life

1 What causes people in your age group to despair and lose hope?

_____

_____

_____

_____

_____

2 To what or whom do people look for hope?

_____

_____

_____

_____

_____

READ
the passage

Read Luke 24:1-53 and the following notes:

❐24:1-9 ❐24:6, 7 ❐24:11, 12 ❐24:24 ❐24:25 ❐24:36-43

❐24:50-53

3 Fill in the chart below:

What some expected from Jesus   What happened

(a) that Jesus would free Israel from
    Roman oppression and set up a   _____
    kingdom in Israel (24:21)
                                         _____

(b) that Jesus would save himself from   _____
    the cross (23:35)
                                         _____

(c) that crucifying Jesus would put an   _____
    end to this "troublemaker" (23:4, 5)
                                         _____

4 How did various people react to the news of Jesus' resurrection (24:1-53)?

_____

_____

_____

_____

_____

When Jesus died, the disciples despaired. Lost and leaderless, they huddled in fear behind closed doors. But when Jesus appeared to them, their lives changed forever. Why? Because all of a sudden they had hope. When they saw Jesus was alive, they knew that all he had taught them was true. They realized that he was the Christ who had brought salvation to the world and were assured of their own resurrection and place in heaven. Suddenly the future looked brighter than they had ever imagined. The resurrection of Christ continues to bring hope to those in despair today.

REALIZE
the principle

5 As Jesus explained to the disciples on the road to Emmaus, he fulfilled all of Scripture and accomplished all that God had planned. What difference does it make to the world that Jesus is who he said he is?

_____

_____

_____

_____

_____

_____

6 How did the resurrection give the disciples hope?

_____

_____

_____

_____

7 What difference does it make that Jesus is alive today?

_____

_____

_____

_____

RESPOND
to the message

8 If you had been one of Jesus' followers nearly two thousand years ago, how would you have reacted to his death on the cross?

_____

_____

_____

9 How would you have reacted to the amazing news of his resurrection?

_____

_____

_____

10 In what way does Jesus' resurrection give you hope?

_____

_____

_____

11 In what situations do you most need to remember the truth of the resurrection?

_____

_____

_____

12 What's one way you can keep the hope of the resurrection in your thoughts this week?

_____

_____

_____

_____

RESOLVE
to take action

A Why is the resurrection central to the Christian faith? How does this impact you?

MORE
for studying
other themes
in this section

B What did it take to convince the disciples that Jesus had indeed risen from the dead (24:36-40)? What assures you of the truth of his resurrection?

C How did Jesus spend his time with the disciples after the resurrection (24:45)? How did Jesus prepare the disciples to be his witnesses? In what ways have you been prepared to witness for Christ?

D How did the disciples respond to Christ's ascension (24:50-53)? What motivates you to worship and praise God?

"For God loved the world so much that he gave his only Son . . ."

If one verse changed your life . . . think of what 31,172 more could do.

THE LIFE APPLICATION BIBLE
Applying God's Word to real life

The Life Application Bible can give you real answers for real life. We can give you eight reasons why it has all the answers you've been looking for—right at your fingertips.

1. **Unique Life Application Notes** show you how to act on what you read, how to apply it to needs in your own life.
2. **Megathemes** tell you why the significant themes in each book are still important today.
3. **People Profiles** bring alive over fifty colorful and important Bible characters, their strengths and weaknesses.
4. **The Topical Index** gives you over 15,000 entries that tell you where to find real answers for real-life situations.
5. **Bible Timelines** give you dates, names, and places at a glance.
6. **Cross-references** direct you to scores of important passages.
7. **Outline Notes** give you an overview of content plus ideas for application.
8. **Harmony of the Gospels** uses a unique numbering system to harmonize all four Gospels into one chronological account.

Plus: Book Introductions, Vital Statistics, Maps, and Charts!

Available in *The Living Bible,* New International Version, King James Version, the New Revised Standard Version, and the New King James Version.

AT BOOKSTORES EVERYWHERE.

Life Application is a registered trademark of Tyndale House Publishers, Inc.